W9-AXZ-354

GLOBAL INVESTING
The Templeton Way

GLOBAL INVESTING
The Templeton Way

As told to
Norman Berryessa

and
Eric Kirzner

BUSINESS ONE IRWIN
Homewood, Illinois 60430

© Norman Berryessa and Eric Kirzner, 1993

All rights reserved. No part of this publication may be
reproduced, stored in a retrieval system, or transmitted,
in any form or by any means, electronic, mechanical,
photocopying, recording, or otherwise, without the prior
written permission of the copyright holder.

This publication is designed to provide accurate and
authoritative information in regard to the subject matter
covered. It is sold with the understanding that neither the
author nor the publisher is engaged in rendering legal, accounting,
or other professional service. If legal advice or other expert
assistance is required, the services of a competent
professional person should be sought.

*From a Declaration of Principles jointly adopted by a Committee
of the American Bar Association and a Committee of Publishers.*

Project editor: Gladys True
Production manager: Dennis S. Mendenhall
Jacket designer: Tim Kaage
Designer: Larry J. Cope
Compositor: Weimer Incorporated
Typeface: 11/13 Century Schoolbook
Printer: Arcata Graphics/Kingsport

Library of Congress Cataloging-in-Publication Data

Berryessa, Norman.
    Global investing : the Templeton way / as told to Norman Berryessa
and Eric Kirzner.
        p.   cm.
    Originally published: Homewood, Ill. : Dow Jones-Irwin, 1988.
    Includes index.
    ISBN 1-55623-873-8
    1. Investments, American. 2. Investments, Foreign.   3. Templeton,
John, date–   . I. Templeton, John. II. Kirzner, Eric.
III. Title.
HG4538.B458   1993   92–35239
332.6'092—dc20

Printed in the United States of America

1 2 3 4 5 6 7 8 9 0   K   9 8 7 6 5 4 3 2

To Helen, Jennifer, and Diana
Eric

*To my wife Shirley, my son
and daughters, and all my other
friends who kept this work alive*
Norman

FOREWORD

Simple common sense tells you that you will find more and sometimes better investment opportunities if you search everywhere in the world rather than limiting yourself to only one nation. Forty-seven years ago I opened an investment counseling firm in New York City for that purpose and the results have been gratifying. Templeton, Galbraith & Hansberger Ltd. now invests more than $21 billion worldwide and serves more than 800,000 investors from offices in five nations. Recently, more and more North American investors have begun to search worldwide. The purpose of this book is to be helpful in that search.

Professor Kirzner and Mr. Berryessa relate lucidly some of the ideas and experiences I shared with them in the course of many interviews. During my eighty years I have made my share of mistakes, but the authors thought it best to describe only those experiences and methods from which the reader may derive useful lessons.

Naturally this single book does not explain all the methods and information needed for investing in dozens of nations any more than a single book on medicine could possibly describe all that is known to medical research scientists. The authors have planned this book as a beginning survey so that investors may learn where and how to seek more information.

In addition, it may prove to be a useful resource for students who are planning careers as Chartered Financial Analysts. There are now more than 17,000 members of the Financial Analysts Federation worldwide. Many will benefit by expanding their horizons to the opportunities to be found in other nations.

One of the first principles of successful investing is to diversify—to be sure not to have all your eggs in the wrong basket at the wrong time. No rational investor would want to have all assets in one stock or in one industry, so why should all assets be invested in one nation? Bull and bear markets are a continuing fact of life for all nations, but often not at the same time. Therefore, the investor who has diversified across many nations may not suffer the shrinkage in market value that afflicts investors in a single nation.

Progress in all areas of life is accelerating, and the profession of international investing is no exception. In fact, the numbers of people investing beyond their own borders, the growing linkages between markets, and the greater availability of financial information are indicative of tremendous progress. This is good for everyone: good for investors, good for capital-starved developing economies, and good for the world's citizens. Adam Smith taught us long ago that where markets are free, an "invisible hand" moves scarce resources away from unproductive endeavors and into those that will do the greatest good. Progress in international investing helps further that process.

It is my hope that increasing investments across borders will lead not only to greater material prosperity, but to greater friendship and peace.

John M. Templeton
Lyford Cay, Bahamas

CONTENTS

GLOBAL INVESTING
The Templeton Way

CHAPTER 1

A PROFILE OF JOHN TEMPLETON

Light shines in the darkness for good men,
    for those who are kind, merciful, and just.
Happy is the man who is generous in his loans,
    who runs his business honestly.
A good man will never fail;
    he will never be forgotten.
He is not afraid of receiving bad news;
    his faith is strong, and he trusts in the Lord.
He is not worried or afraid;
    he is certain he will see his enemies defeated.
He gives generously to the needy, and his kindness
    is eternal; he will be powerful and respected.

—Psalm 112, Verse 4–9

There can be power behind a kindly face; there can be strength beneath a genuine humility; and if these special attributes are capped with a keen intellect and mixed with plain old common sense, you have the makings of a remarkable human being. Such a man is John Marks Templeton.

It would be difficult to find anyone in the ranks of professional investors who does not know of him. For them he is a market sage and "tribal elder" of considerable powers—what Babe Ruth is to baseball fans, except that Templeton is still here after half a century of investment counselling, still knocking them into the bleachers.

Over six hundred thousand people know him as the man who manages some portion of their assets through the Templeton Funds—one of the largest and most successful mutual funds groups in existence. Even the financial press treats him with uncharacteristic respect. In August 1982, when the Dow

Jones Industrials languished in the pitiful mid-700s they reported his assertion that the bear market was near a low ebb, and that common stocks—particularly in the U.S.—were grossly undervalued. His statement that we might see the Dow near 3,000 by 1990 was written up prominently, and undoubtedly comforted shell-shocked investors from Wall Street to Main Street.

For all his prominence among investors and his frequent media exposure, John Templeton remains an inscrutable character. This is something of a paradox. His extraordinary performance as an investment manager is a matter of public record; he travels from his home in the Bahamas to appear on "Wall $treet Week" at regular intervals and answers every query. He is the subject of frequent magazine articles and TV interviews, particularly on the occasion of the Templeton Prize, his annual award for progress in religion. Indeed, much has been written about his philanthropic pursuits. Still, the details of his work as a global investor have been treated, at best, superficially.

Anyone who attempts to learn the secrets of John Templeton's successful approach to stock investing will quickly discover the elements of his philosophy—the intuitively appealing part: look for the best stock bargains around the world, don't follow the crowd, use common sense. Templeton is given to general statements when asked general questions. Like a mature artist, he paints in broad, simple strokes. But instructive as these statements are, most of us need more detailed guidance. That is the purpose of this book.

This book is about global investing as practiced by John Templeton and the money management organization he founded, and is written with his cooperation. Much of the material is based on our visits with Templeton over the past three years—six times to his home in the Bahamas, in meetings which sometimes extended more than five days; at annual shareholders' meetings in both New York and Toronto; and in frequent telephone calls. We had access to all his writing, including unpublished letters from his old firm, Templeton, Dobbrow and Vance, Inc., and interviews with his closest friends and associates, present and past, as well as his wife Irene.

We came to this book from very different backgrounds as will, we suspect, many readers. Norman Berryessa, an advisor to high net worth investors, first became aware of Templeton's activities during the early 1960s while searching for some practical way to invest outside the U.S. This was largely unheard of at the time, and Templeton's fund was one of just a few bridges to other markets. A continuing interest in global investing, and articles he was then writing for *San Francisco Magazine* lead Berryessa to a meeting with Templeton in the Bahamas in 1984. He continued to follow the global thread by publishing *The Global Perspective* newsletter in San Francisco until a few years ago.

Eric Kirzner's background is academic. A toiler in the ivy towers, he has taught investments and written scores of financial articles and a reference book on foreign financial markets. As a regular contributor to *The Hume Moneyletter* on mutual funds and international investing, Kirzner was familiar with the Templeton organization and some of its professional staff. For him, the opportunity to probe the details of the Templeton way offered insights into how the theories of investment science were used—or ignored—by one of the world's most celebrated practitioners. And there was the attraction of working with someone who had consistently beaten the market, which according to the most sacred of investment theories, should not happen except by chance. Would he find a man who was extremely lucky, or someone who had made his own luck?

A PROFILE OF MR. T

Rural Appalachia is an unlikely starting point for a man who was to find his expression in the global investing field. Born in Franklin County, Tennessee—"next to Dogpatch" as he says—some 75 years ago, Templeton still speaks with the soft, distinct sounds of middle Tennessee. He reflects the personal calm that comes of growing up in a farming community where you never bothered to lock the door, and where graduation at the local high school was one of the year's biggest events.

His father was a self-taught country lawyer, but there was not enough legal business in the area to make ends meet.

Harvey Templeton, like other small town businessmen, practiced a number of trades, which collectively provided a comfortable income for his family. In addition to practicing law, he acted as an insurance agent, farmland speculator, and built and operated a small cotton gin. This enterprising spirit made an impression on young John who recalls that "my father used to say 'find a need and fill it.' So when I was in third grade I noticed there wasn't anyplace to buy fireworks around Winchester. So I sent off to the Brazil Novelty Company up in Cincinnati for some firecrackers and Roman candles. I'd take them to school and sell them at a considerable markup."

Probably more than anything, Templeton's greatest gift from his parents was a very long leash. They were quite willing to let him follow his own path and take responsibility for his actions. Given his fascination with mechanical and electric devices, his parents allowed him to pursue his interests to some point short of injuring himself or burning the house down.

> We loved to dabble in science . . . Mother saved enough to buy a set of volumes called *The Book of Knowledge* for my brother Harvey and me. With this and *Popular Mechanics* as guides, we carried out all sorts of experiments in our attic. Some were literally hair-raising. Using high-voltage, low-ampere electricity, we could make sparks come out of our fingers or cause a light bulb to glow simply by holding it aloft.[1]

For most born to this setting during the early decades of the century, this would remain the boundaries of their world; but not for John Templeton. He did well in school—never receiving a term grade below A in either grammar school or high school—and was admitted to Yale. This was in the early thirties, and times were tough. His father paid for his first year in college, but the Great Depression cut off any further financial support from this source.

John would have to make his own way for the remaining three years. This he did through a combination of part-time jobs, scholarships, a $200 loan from his uncle, and fairly systematic winnings at dormitory gambling sessions. "I made about 25 percent of what I needed for Yale from winning at poker," Templeton recalls. It was a game he had learned well from the older boys back in Winchester.

Although his father's trading on the New York and New Orleans cotton exchanges had been the subject of dinner table conversation years before, Templeton traces his interest in investing to his sophomore year when, as a student of economics, he was impressed by the great disparity in high and low prices for many shares of common stock. "It seemed to me that if you could find a way to determine the true value of a stock you would have made a great contribution." Templeton graduated second in his class as president of the Yale Chapter of Phi Beta Kappa, with a degree in economics and a Rhodes scholarship to Oxford. He had, by this time, set his mind on being an investment counselor, and since Oxford offered neither a course of study in investments or business, he earned a degree in law because it was closely related to his interests.

The mid-thirties was an interesting time to be in England. British life was in transition, struggling with both the vexations of a restive colonial system and changes within its own social order. In a sense, it was a proxy for the turmoils within the other leading European powers. And from England the tremors and the rumors of war could be more keenly felt. By his last year at Oxford, Hitler's Nazis were riding high in Germany and bullets were already flying in Spain and China. The world was changing fast.

Templeton's interests in global investing sprang from that sojourn in England. When he first arrived at Oxford, the 21-year-old American had $300 left from his jobs at Yale. He began buying stocks. His initial choices were U.S. shares, but as his understanding of non-U.S. markets and issues broadened, so too did his trading. These global interests were further nurtured by trips taken during university holidays and a seven-month tour of 27 countries following his Oxford studies. The latter trip took him, in company with an Oxford friend, through Europe, the Middle East, and the Far East. With one change of clothes each in their backpacks and 100 English pounds in their pockets, Templeton and James Inksetter fulfilled the fantasy of many young graduates: to explore the world, sample its sights and sounds, and learn from its many cultures.

Upon his return to America in 1937, Templeton took a research job at Fenner & Beane, later to become a part of Merrill, Lynch, Pierce, Fenner and Smith. "While still at Oxford I had written to 100 investment firms to see if they'd be interested in giving me a job," he recalls. "I only wrote to firms that had good reputations. Only twelve responded, and of these, three offered me a position." Fenner & Beane seemed like a good place to learn the trade: he would be only the third person hired for its new investment counsel division—not just a small cog in a large wheel.

Not long after, his friend and former Oxford classmate, geophysicist George C. McGhee, introduced him to the National Geophysical Company, where he became Vice President of Finance. The company prospered, as did Templeton. But he kept his mind set on the goal he had set for himself back at Yale. "I saved half my salary and when I had a chance in 1940 to buy an investment counseling business for $5,000 I had the cash." He had quite a bit more two years later when he sold his shares in National Geophysical for a $50,000 profit. He was in the investment counsel business at last, operating out of a small office in the RCA building in mid-town Manhattan.

Then as now, Wall Street was at the heart of American commerce. Its investment bankers found the financing for American industry, and traders provided the liquidity that attracted capital from both the heartland and distant shores. But by today's standards, the life of the financial industry was conducted at a slower pace. The number of professionals working in the business was relatively small, and many were men who had chosen their parents well and were there primarily to tend to the family fortune. "At that time [1940]," Templeton recalls, "a society of security analysts in New York had just recently formed, with only a few dozen members." Today there are 15,000 members of the various societies, not including the thousands of analysts in Europe and Asia.

From those early days in New York, beginning with only eight small clients, Templeton's enterprise grew steadily. But as anyone who has handled many private accounts will tell you, the telephone never stops ringing. Each account represents a unique set of objectives and sensitivities to taxes, timing, and risk. Each client quite rightfully makes claims on a money manager's time. And for Templeton, time has always been a thing to be treated as a gift. Templeton's close associate John W. Galbraith says that "by nature, he doesn't want to waste time—so you don't ever find yourself sitting around exchanging small talk. You always have a sense that he has more things to do than time to do it." We noted that our meetings with him would always begin within a few minutes of the designated time, and always ended on schedule. Just as he respects his own time, Templeton extends that respect to the time of others. John Hunter, one of his Canadian stock brokers, says that when he tells him he will call at 9:15 Canadian time, the call will invariably come through at precisely that time—from wherever Templeton is traveling in the world. In fact, to ensure that he is prompt, he has always set his watch 10 minutes fast.

His desire to use his time effectively and to help others through good money management found its logical expression in mutual funds—a means for "everyman" to stake a claim in the market. In a sense, he saw this field not only as a very good business, but as an opportunity to help families of many income levels save money and acquire wealth and security. A newspaper story covering a Templeton address to a Chicago financial group reported that among the stockbrokers and financial planners seeking his autograph was a young accountant who told Templeton "my daughter is two weeks old, and we just put $500 in your fund for her college education." Templeton shook his hand saying "we'll do our very best for you." He seemed genuinely concerned, and the man walked away with the satisfaction that his daughter's funds were in caring and capable hands.

From the time he began his investment counsel career in Manhattan in 1937, Templeton and his family began studying where they would really want to live after they accumulated enough wealth to have a choice. As a part of his usual long-range planning, he and his wife took holidays in dozens of places in many nations and always asked themselves, is this the place that has more advantages than anywhere else as a long-term base for our family and business? Every place had some advantages, but the Lyford Cay Club in the Bahamas had the most, and it was to this idyllic location that the Templetons moved in 1963 as a permanent home. Among other things, they were attracted by the deep religious spirit of the Bahamian people. Templeton also appreciated that life in the islands is still lived on a human scale, like the world of his childhood that he left over 50 years before.

Lyford Cay Club is a unique community. Located just 16 miles from Nassau, its 1,000 members represent 25 different nations and are among the world's movers and shakers. The availability of insightful financial information is in some ways better than in New York. Templeton credits the move with an improvement in his stock picking performance, noting that "if I want to know something about banking in Brazil, I talk with my neighbor, who is president of the largest bank in that country." Now, 24 years later, the investment results of the Templeton Mutual Funds have been even better from the Bahamas base than they were in the 23 years working from the New York area. One possible reason is that Templeton's distance from Wall Street makes it unlikely that he will be buying the same stocks as other professional analysts. "If you buy the same securities as other analysts," he notes, "you will have the same performance results."

The Templeton Growth Fund has been a "global" fund since its inception and its achievements as a medium of investment are well-known. But the success in promoting and distributing shares can be placed in the lap of John Galbraith, one of the major owners of Templeton, Galbraith and Hansberger, Ltd. For many years a Templeton enthusiast, Galbraith used his long experience in mutual fund distribution to build up a broker-dealer network to distribute the fund throughout the United States, in addition to the earlier network of distributors in Canada. He also convinced Templeton that they should offer investors a family of funds—a popular development in the past decade—as a means of better addressing the investment objectives of the public.

Templeton, Galbraith and Hansberger (popularly known as Templeton International) and its subsidiaries today manage a family of 12 mutual funds with $9 billion under management, 600,000 shareholders, and about 90 private accounts representing $3 billion in assets. The headquarters for this enterprise are in the Bahamas, but the subsidiaries in six nations have over 300 professional and support personnel working according to the plan of "Mr. T," as Templeton is affectionately known.

Any visitor to the offices of Templeton International is struck by the upbeat attitude of the personnel, perhaps the result of a Templeton admonition:

> As you wake up in the morning, direct your thoughts toward five things you're grateful for. That will set the pattern for your day. You can't be prey to negative emotions if your heart is full of joy and gratitude.

GIVING BACK

As in Dr. Seuss's story of "The 500 Hats of Bartholomew Cubbins," John Templeton finds that the more he gives away, the more he has.

Templeton established his first reputation and material fortune by being a skillful investor. His methods are the subject of this book. Yet like any extraordinary person, he has another side to him that must be addressed if we are to get a complete picture. Thomas Jefferson is celebrated as a man of many facets; indeed, his tombstone epithet reminds us that in addition to authoring the Declaration of Independence, he was founder of the University of Virginia—a fact of equal importance to him. John Templeton's other facet is in the realm of religion. "Nothing exists except God," he says, "all else are temporary appearances. God is not in the world like a raisin in a muffin but as the ocean is in a wave."

Having been raised in the Bible Belt, Templeton could not help but be affected by religious influences. His mother, Vella Templeton, a well-educated and active churchwoman, kept the Cumberland Presbyterian Congregation in Winchester alive by raising enough money to pay the salary for a part-time minister. Her son John was influenced by her charitable bent. In the late 1930s, he began the practice of giving 10 percent of his income to charity. But writing a check is often the easy part of charity. "I went through a period 20 years ago when religion was almost crowded out of my life," he says. "It was when I was trying to build a business and raise my children. I was working 80 hours a week or more and so the important things got squeezed out by the urgent things." This period was especially difficult for him, having lost his first wife in a Bermuda motor-bike accident and being faced with the challenge of raising three children. His youngest son, Christopher, played a part in his remarrying. Christopher, then six, had a friend on their street in Englewood, New Jersey. The friend's mother, Irene Butler, was trying to raise her own family. One day Christopher asked Mrs. Butler "if you ever think of getting married again, would you please consider my father?" She did.

As his business prospered, Templeton's philanthropic interests received more of his attention. These interests evolved into the Templeton Prize for Progress in Religion. Templeton felt that Alfred Nobel, who bequeathed the famous prizes for physics, medicine and literature had overlooked one of the most important areas of human endeavor—the spirit. His prize was to make up for this oversight.

The Templeton Prize now carries an unrestricted cash award of $400,000—more than the Nobel Prizes—and has been presented each year by Prince Phillip, followed by a lecture and ceremony in London's ancient Guildhall. The first recipient was Mother Teresa in 1973, seven years ahead of her winning the Nobel Peace Prize. Others have been Dame Cicely Saunders, founder of the Modern Hospice movement, Nikkyo Niwano, a Japanese Buddhist and recognized advocate of world peace, and Billy Graham, the American evangelist. Recipients are chosen by an international panel of nine famous leaders representing the five major world religions.

Closer to the field of investments, Templeton gave a $5 million gift at Oxford, England, in 1983 to develop the teaching of management science. He was interested in what could be done to advance management studies at the university, revitalize the British economy, and help people around the world to better manage their affairs and escape from poverty, famine, and disease. Today, Templeton College is a graduate school of that great institution, teaching British and foreign students and executives the latest methods of business management.

The Templeton organization has a unique way of opening its annual shareholders' meetings. They begin with prayer. As Templeton explains, "We don't pray that our stocks will go up. We pray for wisdom and to keep an open mind, because that allows us to think more clearly."

The following chapters explore the thinking of this pathfinder in global investing. We hope that readers will find the Templeton Way a useful and profitable guide. Chapters 2, 3, and 4 provide background information on the merits and pitfalls of global investing, modern developments in investment finance theory and applications, and the global investment market. Chapters 5 through 9 deal exclusively with John Templeton and his unique bargain-hunting approach.

ENDNOTE

1. John Templeton, *Guideposts*, September 1982, p. 18.

CHAPTER 2

THE GLOBAL INVESTOR

THE MERITS OF GLOBAL INVESTING

There are tens of thousands of securities or instruments traded on the world's stock, futures, and options exchanges and bond markets. These markets range from the jumbo New York and Tokyo Stock Exchanges to the tiny Cairo Stock Exchange. And from the modern, electronic Bermuda Futures Exchange to the antiquated Amsterdam Stock Exchange, with its "cubbyhole" trading process. Despite the vast array of investment opportunities, many investors, professional and otherwise, never look beyond the confines of their own country's borders.[1] They limit their analysis and selection to domestic instruments, missing the rich opportunities for portfolio diversification, superior returns, and risk reduction through international investment. And those investors who do venture into the international arena are often discouraged when they discover that their broker or advisor may know less than they do about foreign securities. However, as you will learn in this chapter, mastering the international investment process, although fraught with pitfalls, is by no means an impossible task. And the rewards make the effort worthwhile.

Let's first draw an important distinction. There are three approaches to international investing. The first we might call the *universal search for value,* in which we picture the active and well-informed international investor (such as Templeton International) searching among the global universe of available securities for the best bargains. This investor is hoping to reap superior or abnormal investment returns by discovering value among a wide range of opportunities. The second approach we designate as *international hedging,* which uses foreign securities, currency and option contracts, and other such instruments to reduce or offset inventory price, interest rate, and exchange rate business or portfolio risks. The third and most transparent approach can be called the *search for the world market portfolio,* analogous to those who construct domestic index funds to capture a domestic market. This investor (whether fund manager or private investor) builds a portfolio of securities, mutual funds, and foreign currency contracts in an attempt to replicate the performance of world capital markets. And to what end? Toward efficient diversification and/or an anticipated stronger portfolio performance than that available with strictly domestic securities.

Each of the three general types of international investor will pursue specific foreign opportunities toward his or her unique objectives. The global investor recognizes a number of motivating factors for international investing:

- An expanded investment opportunity set.
- Portfolio risk reduction through diversification.
- Foreign exchange risk reduction (or increased opportunity).
- Superior portfolio performance.

In the next section, we will review these four major reasons for international investment.

An Expanded Investment Opportunity Set

In 1991, the United States' share of this global marketplace, in terms of total market capitalization, was approximately 38%, representing a decline from 66% in 1970.[2] The United States' portion of the world bond market is an almost identical percentage. Thus, if you limit your security analysis to the domestic U.S. market you are neglecting some 62% of the existing investment opportunities.

These opportunities range from the specific, such as shares of companies in industries that are not indigenous to the United States; to the generic, such as specialized international mutual funds, gold or oil linked-bonds, and perpetual floaters. Furthermore, many foreign economies, economic/political structures, financial markets, and current public lifestyles and tastes are often radically different from those in the United States, resulting in market instruments that just aren't available locally. For example, some industries that are at the mature stage domestically are still at development or growth stages in Europe and the Far East, providing the U.S. investor with additional alternate investment possibilities. Investing in Japan and South Korea, for example, opens up opportunities in specialized automobile manufacturing that have passed their prime in North America.

Holding foreign securities broadens the investor's horizons and creates a much richer set of investment opportunities. There are many securities issued abroad that have different risk/return characteristics than domestic securities or that offer special features not otherwise available. Many of these complex yet useful instruments originate abroad, yet are readily available to the astute domestic investor. For example, the Swedish Export Credit Corporation has a bond issue outstanding for which the principal amount at maturity is linked to the closing level of the Tokyo Stock Exchange Nikkei-Dow Index.

Efficient Diversification

Among the most important advances in both theoretical and applied investment finance in the past 40 years have been the concurrent developments of portfolio theory, the capital asset pricing model (CAPM), and the efficient markets theory. From the early pioneering work of Harry Markowitz in 1948[3] and Tobin in 1957,[4] and the development of the CAPM by Sharpe, Lintner, and Mossin[5] and extensions by many others[6] it has been demonstrated both theoretically and empirically, that diversification reduces the risk of a portfolio, assuming that risk is measured by the variance about the returns on the component securities and the portfolio. Furthermore, the degree of risk reduction offered by each security added to the portfolio, reflects the security's covariance or co-movement with either the portfolio or an appropriate market index. Therefore, securities that have a low, and for maximum benefit, negative covariance with the portfolio of securities or a market index are valuable in reducing risk. In layman's terms, diversification means that you are selecting securities that do not always move together. Thus, on any given day, some of your investments may rise and some may fall; therefore the chances of major losses are substantially reduced.

Here is an illustration: Over the period 1981 to 1986, the annual compounded rate of return on a diversified portfolio of U.S. securities, as measured by the total return on the S&P 500 Composite Index, was 19.8%, with a standard deviation[7] of 18.2%. Over the same period, the rate of return on West German equities as measured by the return on the Commerzbank Index was 29.9% with a standard deviation of 21.5%. The degree of co-movement or correlation coefficient[8] between the two markets was 0.30. The investor who purchased the U.S. portfolio realized a healthy rate of return but also incurred substantial risk; an 18.2% standard deviation means that 19 times out of 20 the actual return could range between -16.6% and $+56.2\%$. However, the investor who created a portfolio combining the two market indexes not only earned (in this case) a higher return but also reduced the inherent risk of the portfolio. The rate of return on the portfolio equally weighted between the U.S. and West German markets was (.50)(19.8) + (.50)(29.9) = 24.85% while the standard deviation of the portfolio was 0.1603. Clearly this modestly diversified portfolio dominated the U.S. one, providing larger returns with a lower risk as measured by the standard deviation. In summary form:

	Annual Compounded Rate of Return	Standard Deviation
U.S. portfolio	19.8%	18.2%
West German portfolio	29.9	21.5
Combined U.S./West German portfolio	24.9	16.0

A number of scholars of investment finance[9] have clearly demonstrated that this principle of diversification applies quite powerfully to international portfolio diversification. Numerous studies indicate that the correlation between individual stock market indexes and the world stock market index is relatively low. A high degree of the variance in stock indexes is due to the unsystematic (or unique) risk of each country and can therefore be diversified away in an international portfolio of securities. Solnik[10] was the first to publish results on the value of global diversification. Using weekly price data for the period 1966 to 1971, he constructed securities portfolios of various sizes from the United States, the United Kingdom, France, West Germany, Italy, Belgium, the Netherlands, and Switzerland, as well as an international portfolio. He concluded that, "The gains from international diversification are substantial. In terms of variability of return an international well-diversified portfolio would be one-tenth as risky as a typical security and half as risky as a well-diversified portfolio of U.S. stocks (with the same number of holdings)."

As shown in Table 2–1, the U.S. equity market has relatively low correlations with most world markets. Three different studies covering different time frames have been cited. Note that the correlations do change over time, but there is some consistency, particularly between the *Financial Times* and Morgan Stanley results. Australia, Japan, and Germany are relatively large markets and thus ideal candidates for internationally diversified portfolios for U.S. investors, given their low correlations with U.S. markets.

As can be seen, the Canadian market with its consistently high correlation with the U.S. market is one of the least suitable candidates for the U.S. global diversifier.

Foreign Currency Risk Reduction (or Exposure)

International investment allows investors the opportunity to maintain some of their wealth in currencies other than their domestic currencies. The external value of the U.S. dollar has fluctuated widely throughout the 1980s and early 1990s. Investors who hold all of their wealth in U.S. dollars have discovered that as the U.S. dollar weakens, the cost of a trip to Paris or Tokyo correspondingly rises. The astute investor protects or

TABLE 2–1
Intercountry Correlations Studies—United States and Selected Markets—in U.S. dollars

	Correlation		
Country	(1)*	(2)	(3)
Australia	0.40	0.51	0.46
Canada	0.73	0.81	0.71
France	0.34	0.51	0.43
Germany	0.36	0.50	0.35
Hong Kong	0.33	0.69	0.29
Italy	0.26	0.35	0.25
Japan	0.29	0.28	0.28
Singapore	0.48	0.74	0.46
Switzerland	0.55	0.63	0.51
United Kingdom	0.57	0.69	0.51

Authors	Period Analyzed	Publication/Data Source
(1) Financial Times Actuaries	1981–1991	Ibbotson Associates' IDEAS Software Package
(2) Daiwa Securities America, Inc.	1988–1992	Tokyo Stock Market Quarterly Review, March 31, 1992
(3) Morgan Stanley Capital International	1970–1991	Ibbotson Associates' IDEAS Software Package

hedges against a decline in the dollar's value by holding some securities denominated in yen, mark, franc or other hard currencies. Hedging is of particular interest to firms that have foreign currency risk that can be reduced, if not eliminated, through proper risk-management techniques using foreign currency instruments such as foreign currency futures, foreign currency options, and other such devices.[11]

Superior Portfolio Performance

In 1986, the total return, not including transaction costs, on the New York Stock Exchange, as measured by the S&P 500 Composite Index was 18.6%. With a few exceptions, major equity markets elsewhere in the world recorded substantially larger gains over this same period. For example, the Australian equity market recorded a 47.6% gain, the Japanese market rose by 49.7%, and the French market was up 53.6%. And a particularly keen indicator, the Morgan Stanley Capital International World Index, representing a capitalization weighted portfolio of 25 equity markets, recorded a gain of 30.7%. Nor was this an isolated phenomenon. Over the 15-year period 1976 to 1991, the U.S. equity market, as shown in Table 2–2, has been outperformed by most major markets by a substantial margin.

These, of course, are crude measures of return as they neither identify the riskiness of the portfolios nor account for inflation. Nevertheless, in the past, internationally minded investors realized considerably higher rates of returns than those who confined their investments to strictly American vehicles.

TABLE 2–2
Rates of Returns—United States and Selected Markets, 1976–1991

Country	Annual Compounded Total Rates of Return (including dividends)	Cumulative Total Change
United Kingdom	19.4%	1337.6%
Sweden	19.2	1290.9
Netherlands	18.4	1157.6
France	17.8	1072.3
Hong Kong	17.5	1030.0
Japan	17.5	1022.0
Belgium	17.2	983.3
Italy	15.6	782.6
Denmark	15.5	771.4
Australia	14.7	684.6
Singapore/Malaysia	13.9	600.0
United States	13.8	597.3
Norway	13.5	564.7
Spain	12.8	507.2
Germany	12.7	504.8
Austria	12.5	485.3
Canada	12.5	484.9
Switzerland	11.3	400.8

SOURCE: *Morgan Stanley Capital International Perspective,* 1991.

THE PITFALLS OF INTERNATIONAL
INVESTMENT

There are a number of impediments to international investing, a few of which are insurmountable for the individual investor. These frictions or barriers, include:

- Lack of quality information.
- Different accounting and reporting standards.
- Variable transaction costs.
- Withholding and other taxes.
- Liquidity problems.
- Foreign currency risks.
- Political or sovereignty risk.
- Delivery and settlement delays.
- Foreign investor restrictions.

These frictions have paradoxical implications. On the one hand, they obviously result in increased search, analytic, and monitoring costs for the investor. On the other hand, they suggest the existence of market inefficiencies that can provide abnormal returns to the astute trader. Let's look at each of these impediments.

Availability and Quality of Information

There is an appalling lack of appropriate fundamental and technical information on particular companies and markets in many foreign countries. The variance in quality, quantity, and release of information results in disparate search costs for the international investor and analyst. However, the successful global investment managers are those who have successfully and consistently exploited these information weaknesses to earn excess returns. We will see in Chapter 6 that this search for, and exploitation of, information gaps lies at the very foundation of the Templeton Organization's bargain-hunting approach to global stock selection.

Different Accounting and Reporting Standards

Accounting standards vary across countries, making the task of comparative analysis on a consistent basis difficult. The substantial differences in reporting criteria and timing of releases by corporations add to the complexity of comparative investment analysis. For example, some Swiss corporations do not consolidate their financial statements. Long-term financial leases are not capitalized by most European companies. In France, there is no provision made for uncollectible accounts. In Germany, the emphasis in corporate financial reporting is on understating earnings, and unless major adjustments are made, the unwary investor is likely to significantly undervalue German stocks. Depreciation allowances are much more generous in Germany than in Canada or North America. In certain parts of Germany, up to 75% of the cost of buildings can be written off in the first year (in contrast to the typical 5% diminishing balance basis for tax reporting and the 20- or 30-year life assumption for financial reporting in Canada). A recent article in *Forbes* indicated that to approximate American-style earnings per share, analysts have to make some 70 adjustments to the typical German annual report.[12] Table 2–3 provides a broad sketch of differential accounting principles employed in ten countries.

Transaction Costs

Americans are used to paying brokerage commissions on stock trades in U.S. securities. However, the costs of trading in foreign securities may include not only the brokerage fees, but also stock turnover taxes, exchange taxes, transmittal fees, and other miscellaneous agency costs new to the typical American investor. These levies vary widely by type of investment and country. The issue is complicated by the fact that in some countries, commissions are negotiated and determined by the investor's own bargaining prowess. Costs are disparate. For example, combined brokerage commissions, turnover taxes, and other such levies on the purchase or sale of $10,000 of equities

TABLE 2-3
International Accounting Differences—Selected Accounting Principles

Accounting Principle	Country									
	Australia	Canada	France	Germany	Japan	Netherlands	Sweden	Switzerland	U.K.	U.S.
Goodwill amortized?	YES	YES	YES	NO	YES	MIXED	YES	NO*	NO*	YES
Provision for bad debts?	YES	YES	NO	YES	YES	YES	YES	YES	YES	YES
Discount/premium on long-term debt amortized?	YES	YES	NO	NO	YES	YES	NO	NO	NO	YES
Long-term financial leases capitalized?	NO	YES	NO	NO	NO	NO	NO	NO	NO	YES
Straight line depreciation adhered to?	YES	YES	MIXED	MIXED	MIXED	YES	YES	YES	YES	YES
Currency translation gains or losses reflected in current income?	MIXED	YES	MIXED	MIXED	MIXED	NO	MIXED	NO(1)	NO	NO
Financial statements reflect historical cost valuation (no price level adjustment)	NO	YES	NO	YES	YES	NO*	NO	NO	NO	YES
Supplementary inflation-adjusted financial statements provided?	NO*	NO*	NO	NO	NO	NO*	NO	NO*	YES	YES

KEY:
YES = The predominant accounting principle
NO = The accounting principle is not adhered to
* = Some exceptions
MIXED = Alternative practices followed with no majority
(1) = Translation gains or losses are deferred

Source: Frederick D.S. Chois and Vinod B. Bavishi, *Financial Executive*, August 1982.

Templeton on Accounting Practices

Accounting practices are different in almost every nation. In West Germany there are often hidden reserves, so that most everything that you earn can be hidden, except for what you wish to pay out as a dividend. Unless you know those things, you'll misjudge the value of some German stocks.

   Taxes vary. In some places, such as America, stocks are in competition with tax-exempt state and municipal bonds. In Canada the distinction is not recognized for tax purposes. So, in Canada it would be foolish to have somebody buy an American tax-exempt, say California bond, when they could do better buying a General Motors bond, which would have a higher yield. Both are taxed equally in Canada. Nation by nation you need to know the accounting differences, the tax differences, the political differences, the differences in attitude and the differences in savings plans.

---

averages .75% to 1.25% in France and Japan, but 2–3% in Canada, the Netherlands, and the United States. However, large scale transactions of hundreds of thousands of dollars will result in substantially lower commission.

Withholding and Other Taxes

Most countries levy withholding taxes on interest and dividend income earned by nonresidents on domestic investments, thus impairing the income stream on the investment. The existence of reciprocal tax conventions between the United States and many countries mitigates the impact. Also, investors who pay taxes will be eligible for a foreign tax credit for the taxes paid to foreign governments. The withholding tax on dividends in most countries is 15% (noticeable exceptions are Hong Kong and Singapore which impose no withholding taxes). Withholding taxes on dividends by shareholder domicile/company domicile are identified in Table 2–4.

TABLE 2–4
Dividend Taxation

Shareholder's domicile		Australia[8]	Austria	Belgium[1]	Canada	Denmark	Finland	France[3]	Germany[12]	Hong Kong	Italy[4]	Japan	Luxembourg[5]	Mexico[7]	Netherlands	New Zealand	Norway	Singapore[6]	Spain	Sweden	Switzerland	UK[11]	USA
Australia	I		15	15	15	15[15]	15	15[3]	15	0	15	15	15	0[7]	15	15	15	0	25	15	15	15[11]	15
	II		c	c	c	c	c	c	c	—	c	c	c	c	c	c	c	—	c	c	c	c	c
Austria	I	15[8]		15	15	10	10	15[3]	26.9	0	15	20	15	0[7]	15	30	15	0	15	10	5	15[11]	15
	II	c		c	c	c	c	c	c	—	c	c	D	c	D	c	—	c	c	c	c	c
Belgium[9]	I	15[8]	15		15	15	15	15[3]	15	0	15	15	15	0[7]	15	15	15	0	15	30	15	20[11]	15
	II	D[9]	D[9]		D[9]	D[9]	D[9]	D[9]	D[9]	—	D[9]	D[9]	D[9]	D	D[9]	D[9]	D[9]	—	D[9]	D[9]	D[9]	D[9]	D[9]
Canada	I	15[8]	15	15		15	15	15	15	0	15	15	15	0[7]	15	15	15	0	15	15	15	15[11]	15
	II	c	c	c		c	c	c	c	—	c	c	c	c	c	c	c	—	c	c	c	c	c
Denmark	I	15[8]	10	15	15		15	0	15	0	15	15	15	0[7]	15	15	15	0	15	15	0	15[11]	15
	II	c	c	c	c		c	—	c	—	c	c	c	c	c	c	c	—	c	c	c	c	c
Finland	I	15[8]	10	15	15	15		15[3]	15	0	15	15	15	0[7]	15	15	15	0	15	15	10	15[11]	15
	II	c	c	c	c	c		c	c	—	c	c	c	c	c	c	c	—	c	c	—	c	c
France	I	15[8]	15	15	15	0	0		15	0	15	15	15	0[7]	15	15	15	0	15	0	5	15[11]	15
	II	c	c	c	c	—	—		c	—	c	c	c	D	c	c	c	—	c	—	c	c	c
Germany	I	15[8]	25	15	15	15	15	0[3]		0	32.4	15	15	0[7]	15	15	15	0	15	15	15	0	15
	II	c	c	c	c	c	c	—		—	c	c	c	c	c	c	c	—	c	c	c	—	c
Hong Kong[10]	I	30[8]	25	25	25	30	25	25	26.9		32.4	20	15	0[7]	25	30	25	0	25	30	35	0	30
	II	—	—	—	—	—	—	—	—		—	—	—	—	—	—	—	—	—	—	—	—	—
Italy	I	15[8]	15	15	15	15	15	15	0	15		15	0	0[7]	15	15	15	0	15	15	15	15[11]	15
	II	c	c	c	c	c	c	c	c	—		c	c	c	c	c	c	—	c	c	c	c	c
Japan	I	15[8]	20	15	15	15	15	15[3]	15	0	15		15	0[7]	15	15	15	0	15	15	15	15[11]	15
	II	c	c	c	c	c	c	c	c	—	c		c	c	c	c	c	—	c	c	c	c	c
Luxembourg[2] Holding	I	30[8]	25	25	25	30	25	25	26.9	0	32.4	20		0[7]	25	30	25	0	25	30	35	0	30
	II	—	—	—	—	—	—	—	—	—	—	—		—	—	—	—	—	—	—	—	—	—
Mexico	I	30[8]	25	25	25	30	25	25	26.9	0	32.4	20	15		25	30	25	0	25	30	35	0	30
	II	c	c	c	c	c	c	c	c	—	c	c	c		c	c	c	—	c	c	c	—	c
Netherlands	I	15[8]	15	15	15	15	15	15[3]	15	0	32.4	15	15	0[7]		15	15	0	15	15	15	15[11]	15
	II	c	c	c	c	c	c	c	c	—	D	c	c	c		c	c	—	c	c	c	c	c
New Zealand	I	15[8]	25	15	15	15[15]	15	15[3]	15	0	15	15	15	0[7]	15		15	0	25	15	15	15[11]	15
	II	c	c	c	c	c	c	c	c	—	c	c	c	c	c		c	—	c	c	c	c	c
Norway	I	15[8]	15	15	15	15	15	15[3]	15	0	15	15	15	0[7]	15	15		0	15	15	15	15[11]	15
	II	c	c	c	c	c	c	c	c	—	c	c	c	c[16]	c	c		—	c	c	c	c	c
Singapore	I	15[8]	25	15	15	15	15	15[3]	15	0	15	15	15	0[7]	15	15	15		25	15	15	15[11]	30
	II	c	D	c	c	c	c	c	c	—	c	c	D	D	c	c	—		D	c	c	c	D
Spain	I	30[8]	15	15	15	15	15	15[3]	15	0	15	15	15	0[7]	15	30	15	0		15	15	15[11]	15
	II	c	c	c	c	c	c	c	c	—	c	c	c	c	c	c	c	—		c	c	c	c
Sweden	I	15[8]	10	25	15	15	15	15[3]	15	0	15	15	15	0[7]	15	15	15	0	15		5	15[11]	15
	II	c	c	c	c	c	c	c	c	—	c	c	c	c	c	c	c	—	c		c	c	c
Switzerland	I	15[8]	5	15	15	0	10	15[3]	15	0	15	15	15	0[7]	15	15	15	0	15	5		15[11]	15
	II	c	c	c	c	c	c	c	c	—	c	c	D	D	c	c	D	—	c	c		c	D
UK	I	15[8]	15	10	15	15[15]	5	15[3]	15	0	15[14]	15	15	0[7]	15	15	15	0	15	15	5		15
	II	c	c	c	c	c	c	c	c	—	c	c	c	c	c	c	c	—	c	c	c		c
USA	I	15[8]	12.5	15	15	15	15	15[3]	10	0	15	15	7.5	0[7]	15	15	15	0	15	15	15	15[11]	
	II	c	c	c	c	c	c	c	c[13]	—	c	c	c	c	c	c	c	—	c	c	c	c	

I. Indicates the effective rate of dividend withholding tax.

II. Describes the treatment of the foreign withholding tax in the shareholder's country of residence:

D = deduction for foreign tax paid; i.e., the shareholder's country of residence imposes its tax on net foreign dividends.

C = credit for foreign tax paid; i.e., the shareholder's country of residence imposes its tax on gross foreign dividends but the amount of this tax is reduced by the amount of the foreign dividend withholding tax.

(continued)

TABLE 2–4 *(continued)*

¹Prior to 1 January 1989, dividends of Belgian companies included the "crédit d'impôt," which was applicable exclusively to Belgian residents. This implied that until that date, the net dividends received by nonresident shareholders should be calculated by deducting 27% from these reported dividends before applying the withholding tax indicated in this column. The imputation system and the attached "crédit d'impôt" were abolished effective 1 January 1989, so that no adjustments are necessary for dividends payable after that date. Dividends on so-called A.F.V. shares issued by Belgian companies between 1977 and 1983 are deductible in computing the company's taxable profits, subject to conditions and limitations in time and amount. Such dividends may also qualify for preferential treatment in the hands of resident shareholders.

²The rates given apply only to shareholders who are holding companies.

³Dividends of French companies include the "avoir fiscal" which is applicable to residents of Australia, Austria, Belgium, Finland, France, Germany, Japan, Luxembourg, the Netherlands, New Zealand, Norway, Singapore, Spain, Sweden, Switzerland, the United Kingdom, and the United States. In the case of German shareholders, the "avoir fiscal" may be credited against German income tax. If a French company distributes a dividend to an Australian, Austrian, Belgian, Dutch, Finnish, Japanese, Luxembourg, New Zealand, Norwegian, Singapore, Spanish, Swedish, Swiss, United Kingdom, or United States resident, the "avoir fiscal" is paid directly by the French Government. To calculate the net dividend received by other shareholders, ⅓ or 33.3% should first be deducted from these reported dividends before applying the withholding tax indicated in this column.

⁴The Italian withholding tax (normally 30%, temporarily increased to 32.4%) may be reduced by the amount of foreign income tax imposed on the dividends in the shareholder's country of residence. However, the Italian withholding tax cannot be reduced below a minimum of 10.8%.

⁵Dividends distributed by Luxembourg holding companies are exempt from Luxembourg withholding tax. The rates indicated apply to non-holding companies only.

⁶Dividends payable by Singapore companies are not subject to dividend withholding tax. However, the companies may deduct for their own benefit the income tax due by them on their distributed profits.

⁷Effective 1 January 1989 a 10% withholding tax is imposed on dividends paid to nonresident individual shareholders, provided the dividends are paid out of distributable profits. This rate was reduced to nil as of 1 January 1990. A higher rate of 35% applies to dividends which are not paid out of distributable profits.

⁸Effective 1 July 1987, Australia introduced a system of full imputation regarding corporate profits distributed to resident shareholders, i.e., resident shareholders receiving qualifying dividends must include the dividend as grossed up by the credit (39/61 of the net dividend) in their income tax return and may then credit the amount of the imputation credit against their income tax liability. This system applies only to dividends paid out of profits which have been subject to corporate income tax at the full rate which currently is 39%. For nonresident shareholders, no imputation credit is available, but the dividend withholding tax (30% or 15%) will henceforth only be due with respect to dividends paid out of corporate profits which do not qualify for the imputation system.

⁹Net foreign-source dividends received through a paying agent in Belgium are subject to a Belgian withholding tax of 25%, which may be the final tax if the taxpayer so elects. Otherwise, the net foreign dividends are subject to income tax by assessment, at a maximum rate of 25% (plus municipal tax). As of the year of income 1989 there is no foreign tax credit available under Belgian national law. Since most treaties in their foreign tax credit provisions refer directly to Belgian national law, a foreign tax credit may likewise be unavailable under these treaties. Possible exceptions are the treaties with France, Italy, the United Kingdom and the United States. However, this matter is not resolved yet.

¹⁰Due to the territorial basis of the Hong Kong income tax, foreign dividends received are normally exempt from tax in Hong Kong.

TABLE 2–4 *(concluded)*

[11]The dividends of the U.K. companies include the special tax credit (25/75 of the dividend received) which is applicable to the resident shareholders which are entitled to credit it against their income tax liability on the dividend plus the credit. Upon renegotiations of treaties, this credit may also apply to nonresidents in the form of an additional payment, but in that case a 15% or 20% withholding tax will normally be imposed. This currently applies to residents of Australia, Austria, Belgium, Canada, Denmark, Finland, France, Italy, Japan, Luxembourg, Netherlands, New Zealand, Norway, Singapore, Spain, Sweden, Switzerland, and the United States. To calculate the net dividend received by other shareholders, 25% should first be deducted from these reported dividends before applying the withholding tax indicated in this column.

[12]Dividends of German companies include the "Steuerguthaben" which is applicable exclusively to German residents. To calculate the net dividend received by nonresident shareholders 36 percent should first be deducted from these reported dividends before applying the withholding tax indicated in this column.

[13]Due to a special treaty provision, U.S. shareholders of German companies must include 105.88% of gross dividend in taxable income and are entitled to a foreign tax credit of 15.88%, although the German tax actually withheld is 10% only.

[14]Shareholders of Italian companies who are domiciled in the U.K. are entitled to a payment equivalent to the Italian imputation credit equal to 9/16 of the dividend. Withholding tax is due on the aggregate of the dividend and the additional payment.

[15]Until 1991, a special 25% imputation credit was granted to resident shareholders of Danish companies, to be credited against the income due on the aggregate of the dividend and the credit. This special credit, extended by treaty to residents of Australia, New Zealand, and the United Kingdom has now been abolished.

[16]In the absence of a tax treaty between Norway and the country of source of the dividends the foreign tax on the dividends may be credited subject to approval by the Norwegian Ministry of Taxation.

[17]For shareholders domiciled in Switzerland, the foreign tax credit amounts to 15% of the gross dividend although the actual withholding tax is only 10%.

SOURCE: *Morgan Stanley Capital International Perspective*, December 1991, pp. 671–73.

Liquidity Problems

Liquidity, or the ability of an investor to dispose of his or her holdings quickly at market at a reasonable cost, can be a particular problem of investing abroad. Secondary markets in some countries are not particularly active and there can be particular problems involved in selling securities. Wide spreads between the bid/ask prices may exist. The Spanish, Danish, Italian, and French bourses are specific examples of notoriously thin markets. To overcome or at least mitigate the danger of buying too high or selling too low on an unfamiliar and illiquid foreign market, the investor should usually avoid market orders, using limit buy and sell orders only, where permitted.

Settlement and Delivery Problems

Settlement periods and processes vary widely. Trades made in the United States are normally settled in five business days from the date of the transaction, with theoretical delivery at that time. Trades made in the United Kingdom and France, however, can take weeks to settle, while those made on the Italian market can actually take over a year for eventual delivery! Trades by foreigners in Italian securities require actual physical delivery which is a cause of the now-famous delivery logjams in Milan. However, if the shares are held in custody by a U.S. broker, investors are not likely to be affected by delivery delays, as the brokerage firm will take responsibility for settlement or delivery problems.

Currency Risks

Foreign exchange fluctuations can have a serious impact, good or bad, on returns on foreign securities. Consider the following example.

Suppose you bought shares of a German company when they were priced at DM75 (75 deutschemarks). The exchange rate at the time was three deutschemarks for one dollar. Your stock, then, was selling at $25 a share in United States currency.

Now, suppose that a year or so later your shares on the German market have increased in price to DM100. You decide to sell and nail down that 33.33 percent profit. So far, you're doing great.

But when you convert your deutschemark gain into American dollars you find that the exchange rate has worked to your disadvantage. One dollar now equals four deutschemarks; the mark, in other words, has depreciated by one-third during the period in which you held your German shares. The net result? You've had a 33.33 percent gain, if you value your investment in marks. But you've gained nothing in terms of dollars. Considering the cost of in-and-out brokerage fees, you're a loser.

Looking to the positive side, a similar example could be constructed with the deutschemark gaining on the dollar and your investment gaining at an even greater rate when valued in dollars. But the fact remains that the disparity in currency values can be a source of confusion for the fledgling in global investing.

Foreign exchange aggravations can be reduced by holding foreign shares in bearer form, which allows the investor to receive dividends in U.S. dollars from the custodian intermediary. However, in some countries, nonresidents are only allowed to trade in registered shares, from which the dividends are received in the local currency. And, in a number of countries such as Italy, and the United Kingdom, bearer shares are either rare or nonexistent.

Political and Sovereignty Risk

Political risk is the danger of a government taking action that will reduce the value of an investor's assets, either held in that country or invested in that country's resources. The danger extends not only to the existing government, but also to a new one as a result of an election or revolution. The degree of political risk differs greatly across countries but must be viewed as a major concern when building an international portfolio. With careful portfolio selection, political risk can be sharply reduced through diversification.

Foreign Investor Restrictions

Some countries impose restrictions on foreign investing in their domestic markets. These restrictions include position limits that constrain the dollar, unit or percentage amount that a foreigner can invest in a particular security, commodity, or investment class; special taxes or levies placed on foreign investors; trading and delivery constraints[13] and outright prohibitions on trading by nonresidents.[14]

TRANSACTIONS IN FOREIGN SECURITIES

Is global investing, as the somewhat pretentious term implies, the province of only wealthy persons and mammoth corporate funds who can hire the best in portfolio managers? Not at all.

Global investing need not be substantially more difficult to the typical investor than is any other means of reaching for profits in securities. There are numerous vehicles available to carry you onto the global stage, many of which require the investment of only a few hundred dollars.

Investors who wish to diversify their portfolios internationally can either trade directly in interlisted securities on domestic markets and securities on foreign markets, or indirectly through American Depositary Receipts and global, international, and specific country mutual funds. These methods and vehicles are briefly described below.

Interlisted Foreign Securities

If you want to wet your toes in the worldwide ocean of investments, but aren't ready for the full-scale plunge, one option is to become familiar with foreign stocks by buying some of those listed on the New York and American exchanges or those traded on the American over-the-counter market.

Trading foreign stocks on your home soil gives you convenience and familiarity, significant advantages. They're quoted in United States dollars, adjusted daily for the fluctuations in currency exchange rates, and your broker can convert their dividends into American dollars. When the dividends are taxed by the country of origin, documentation is readily available to help American investors claim withholding tax credits on their 1040 Forms. You don't have to learn unfamiliar trading procedures or find new investment managers to take this route.

But there are some drawbacks. Chief among them is the limited range of stocks available through this channel; the broad panoply of world commerce is reduced to a fistful of corporate names. Furthermore, the foreign companies listed on U.S. exchanges are, as might be expected, among the best known and highest profile companies in their respective nations—Netherlands-based KLM Royal Dutch Airlines and Unilever, for example. And the prospects of finding bargains among such giants are small.

As a first exercise in getting to know foreign companies and preparing for possibly expanded efforts at global investing, however, the home-soil approach can be worthwhile. Furthermore, the opportunities for home trading in foreign securities will increase in the future. As a reflection of the recent trend toward deregulation and internationalization of world markets, a number of exchanges have introduced foreign trading sections, are listing foreign securities, or have developed direct trading links with exchanges of other countries. For example, the Montreal Exchange in 1985 introduced an international division in which the shares of foreign securities are listed, and for which trading is conducted by a certificateless, book-based computer system and in U.S. dollars. (Thus far, there has been a noticeable lack of interest by foreign companies for Montreal listings.) More promising are the three trading links between the Toronto Stock Exchange and the American Stock Exchange, the Toronto Stock Exchange and the Midwest Stock Exchange, and the Montreal Exchange and Boston Stock Exchange for which a selected number of interlisted stocks are eligible for two-way trading on the links. Investors who wish to buy or sell these shares (some examples are Coleco Industries, Sony, and McDonald's Corporation) can trade directly through U.S. brokers with foreign currency conversion taking place immediately at the time of the transaction. Although only a limited number of securities are currently available for linked trading (and confined at present to U.S. securities, the weakest candidate for international diversification purposes for Canadian investors), the development of these intermarket links appears to be accelerating with numerous discussions currently under way among the world's major exchanges. The day of the global marketplace in which investors will be able to trade securities located on virtually any nonrestricted bourse, directly by electronic means, is moving ever closer. Tables 2–5 and 2–6 provide examples of interlisted stocks traded on U.S. exchanges.

American Depository Receipts

A limited selection of foreign stocks can be purchased in the form of American Depository Receipts (ADRs). An ADR is not actually a stock certificate; rather, while it entitles the holder

TABLE 2–5
Non-U.S. Companies Traded on the NYSE (as of June 2, 1992)

Company	Symbol	American Depository Receipts (ADRs)
Africa		
ASA Limited	ASA	
Australia		
Broken Hill Proprietary Co. Ltd.	BHP	X
Coles Myer Ltd.	CM	X
FAI Insurance Limited	FAI	X
National Australia Bank Ltd.	NAB	X
News Corporation Ltd.	NWS	X
Orbital Engine Corp.	OE	X
Western Mining Corp. Ltd.	WMC	X
Westpac Banking Corp.	WBK	X
Bermuda		
ADT Limited	ADT	
Brazil		
Aracruz Celulose, S.A.	ARA	X
British West Indies		
Club Med, Inc.	CMI	
Canada		
Abitibi-Price Inc.	ABY	
Alcan Aluminum Ltd.	AL	
American Barrick Resources Corp.	ABX	
Avalon Corporation	AVL	
BCE Inc.	BCE	
Campbell Resources Inc.	CCH	
Canadian Pacific Ltd.	CP	
Cineplex Odeon Corp.	CPX	
Curragh Resources	CZP	
Domtar, Inc.	DTC	
Horsham Corp.	HSM	
Inco Ltd.	N	
InterTan Inc.	ITN	
LAC Minerals Ltd.	LAC	
Laidlaw Inc. (Class A & B)	LDW	
Mitel Corp.	MLT	
Moore Corporation	MCL	
NOVA Corporation	NVA	
Northern Telecom Ltd.	NT	
Northgate Exploration Ltd.	NGX	
Placer Dome Inc.	PDG	
Potash Corp.	POT	
Ranger Oil Ltd.	RGO	
Seagram Company	VO	

TABLE 2–5 *(continued)*

Company	Symbol	American Depository Receipts (ADRs)
TransCanada Pipeline	TRP	
United Dominion Industries Limited	UDI	
Westcoast Energy Inc.	WE	
Chile		
Compania de Telefonos de Chile	CTC	X
Denmark		
Novo-Nordisk A/S	NVO	X
France		
Alcatel Alsthom	ALA	X
Rhone-Poulenc S.A.	RPU	X
(two issues)	RPpr	X
Societe Nationale Elf Aquitaine	ELF	X
TOTAL	TOT	X
Hong Kong		
Hong Kong Telecommunications Ltd.	HKT	X
Universal Matchbox Group Ltd.	UMG	
Ireland		
Allied Irish Banks Pic	AIB	X
Israel		
Elscint Ltd.	ELT	
Italy		
Benetton Group S.p.A.	BNG	X
Fiat S.p.A.	FIA	X
Luxottica Group S.p.A.	LUX	X
Montedison S.p.A.	MNT	X
Japan		
Hitachi Ltd.	HIT	X
Honda Motor Co., Ltd.	HMC	X
Kubota Ltd.	KUB	X
Kyocera Corporation	KYO	X
Matsushita Electric Industrial Co.	MC	X
Mitsubishi Bank, Ltd.	MBK	X
Pioneer Electronic Corp.	PIO	X
Sony Corporation	SNE	X
TDK Corporation	TDK	X
Mexico		
Telefonos de Mexico S.A.	TMX	X
Vitro, Sociedad Anonima	VTO	X
Empresas ICA Sociedad	ICA	X
Controladora, S.A. de C.V.		
Netherlands		
AEGON N.V.	AEG	X**

(continued)

TABLE 2–5 *(continued)*

Company	Symbol	American Depository Receipts (ADRs)
KLM Royal Dutch Airlines	KLM	X*
Philips N.V.	PHG	X**
Polygram N.V.	PLG	X**
Royal Dutch Petroleum Co.	RD	X*
Unilever N.V.	UN	X**
Netherlands Antilles		
Schlumberger, Ltd.	SLB	
Singer Company N.V. (The)	SEW	
New Zealand		
Telecom Corp. of New Zealand Ltd.	NZT	X
Norway		
Norsk Hydro a.s.	NHY	X
Philippines		
Benguet Corporation	BE	
Spain		
Banco Bilbao Vizcaya S.A.	BBV	X
Banco Central, S.A.	BCM	X
Banco de Santander	STD	X
Empresa Nacional de Electricidad, S.A.	ELE	X
Repsol, S.A.	REP	X
Telefonica de Espana, S.A.	TEF	X
United Kingdom		
Attwoods plc	A	X
Barclays PLC	BCS	X
Bass PLC	BAS	X
BET PLC	BEP	X
British Airways Plc	BAB	X
British Gas PLC	BRG	X
British Petroleum p.l.c.	BP	X
British Steel PLC	BST	X
British Telecommunications PLC	BTY	X
Cable and Wireless plc	CWP	X
ECC Group	ENC	X
Glaxo Holdings p.l.c.	GLX	X
Grand Metropolitan PLC	GRM	X
Hanson PLC	HAN	X
Huntingdon International Holdings	HTD	X
Imperial Chemical Industries PLC	ICI	X
National Westminster PLC	NW	X
Royal Bank of Scotland Group plc	RBS	X
RTZ Corporation PLC	RTZ	X
Saatchi & Saatchi Co. PLC	SAA	X

TABLE 2–5 *(concluded)*

Company	Symbol	American Depository Receipts (ADRs)
"Shell" Transport and Trading Co. Ltd.	SC	X
Smithkline Beecham Plc	SBE	X**
(two issues)	SBH	X
Tiphook plc	TPH	X
Unilever PLC	UL	X
Vodafone Group plc	VOD	X
Waste Management Plc	WME	X
Willis Corroon plc	XCG	X

X* Guilder shares.
X** New York shares.

to any dividends and capital gains accruing to the share and can be traded just as the underlying shares are, it is a stock certificate stand-in. It is a negotiable receipt issued by an American bank, such as Citibank or Morgan Guaranty, for foreign shares held in safekeeping abroad. However, the ADR holder has the right to convert it into the specified number of underlying common shares by due notification to the depository bank. A small fee, normally in the order of $.05 per instrument, is charged in this event. ADRs are listed on domestic exchanges with the majority of issues traded on the New York and American Stock Exchanges. Hence, an interested investor can buy directly through his U.S. broker without having to deal through foreign brokers or banks.

An ADR represents anywhere from a fractional share to a substantial multiple of the underlying stock. The ADR ratio refers to the number of common shares underlying an ADR. A ratio of 100, for example, means that 100 shares of the company are represented by the receipt.

ADRs have been issued in the United States since the turn of the century, with about 10 major banks handling the majority. Morgan Guaranty, an ADR pioneer, has led in the practice. It had more than 225 issues trading in 1986. Because the concept was developed in Europe, most ADRs—like most

TABLE 2–6 Foreign Equities (other than Canadian) Listed on the American Stock Exchange (June 1992)

Listing Date	Stocks	Ticker Symbol	Country
04/26/90	A/S Eksportfinans (Put Wts.)	EXW.WS	Norway
02/21/92	A/S Eksportfinans (Curr. Wts.)	DPW.WS	Norway
08/26/59	American Israeli Paper Mills Ltd. (Ord.)	AIP	Israel
05/09/56	Atlas Consolidated Mining & Development Corp. (Cl.B Cap.)	ACM.B	Philippines
03/30/28	*B.A.T. Industries Ltd. (ADRs Ord.)	BTI	Great Britain
08/17/88	B+H Ocean Carriers Ltd. (Com.)	BHO	Liberia
02/03/89	B+H Maritime Carriers Ltd. (Com.)	BHM	Bermuda
10/22/86	Carmel Container Systems Ltd. (Ord.)	KML	Israel
05/01/28	*Courtaulds PLC. (ADRs Ord. Reg.)	COU	Great Britain
11/15/90	*Drug Research Corporation, Plc. (Elan) (ADR Units)	ELN.U	England
09/13/72	Etz Lavud Ltd. (Com. & Cl.A Com.)	ETZ, ETZ.A	Israel
01/03/90	*Elan Corporation (ADRs)	ELN	Ireland
12/28/89	Electrochemical Industries (Frutarom) Ltd. (Ord.)	EIF	Israel
12/16/88	Global Ocean Carriers Limited (Com.)	GLO	Greece
12/05/91	Hanson Plc (Cl.B Wts.)	HAN.WS.B	England
01/12/90	Kingdom of Denmark (Put Wts.)	DXA.WS	Denmark
02/03/82	Laser Industries Ltd. (Ord.)	LAS	Israel
05/23/89	MC Shipping Inc. (Com.)	MCX	Bermuda
09/30/91	*MEDEVA PLC (ADRs Ord.)	MDV	England
04/06/90	*NFC, Plc (ADRs)	NFC	England
02/03/87	Norex America Inc. (Com.)	NXA	Cayman Islands
10/31/46	*O'Okiep Copper Company Limited (ADRs)	OKP	South Africa
06/19/92	Oriental Federal Savings Bank (Com.)	OFB	Puerto Rico
06/27/55	Philippine Long Distance Telephone Company (Com.)	PHI	Philippines
07/09/90	Rhone-Poulenc S.A. (CVRs)	RCV	France
03/05/58	San Carlos Milling Co., Inc. (Com.)	SAN	Philippines
02/22/89	Scandinavia Company, Inc. (The) (Com.)	SCF	Cayman Islands
11/05/90	Societe Generale Warrants Limited N.V. (Put Wts.)	SGG.WS	Netherlands Antilles
06/29/67	*Tubos de Acero de Mexico, S.A. (ADRs)	TAM	Mexico

*ADRs

34

European stocks—are issued in bearer form. The person holding the ADR is presumed to be the owner.

ADR holders receive their dividends denominated in U.S. dollars minus the depository's fee (typically U.S. $.01 per share). ADRs are sometimes cheaper to buy than the stocks themselves. For example, the transaction costs associated with the direct purchase of Australian stocks can at times be more expensive than those associated with an Australian company ADR purchased on the New York Stock Exchange.

Morgan Guaranty Trust also issues International Depositary Receipts (IDRs), which are similar to ADRs but designed for foreign investors who wish to hold U.S. securities. IDRs, for example, are available in Europe for U.S. equities.

ADRs can serve to bring the small investor a step closer to global markets. They let him rely upon domestic banking institutions whose practices are familiar to him while at the same time providing a foothold in the field of international finance. Unfortunately, at this time only a small fraction of international issues are available in ADR form.

Direct Dealings Overseas

The more adventurous investor might consider jumping past the ADR to deal directly with a foreign brokerage house or bank. Alternatively, he or she might use an American broker as a go-between in setting up a trading arrangement with a foreign investment firm.

Either route leads to a much wider universe of overseas investment opportunities. By dealing directly with a domestic or foreign broker, the investor has access to securities traded on most world markets.

Significant drawbacks come with this potential, however. First is the element of risk. When dealing with a domestic exchange or an ADR, the investor at least enjoys a modicum of screening by a familiar organization—the exchange or the sponsoring bank. He or she is likely to be buying a relatively stable security, or at least one whose price fluctuations and earnings progress are often reported in the American press. And, if problems with the investment should crop up, the investor has a familiar corporate partner to stand by while those problems are resolved.

Not so, of course, when investors try to go global on their own. Then the investors become exposed possibly to more cost and very likely to more risk. The investors must make a major investment in time as well: it becomes their responsibility to study the economy, the tax picture, the investment opportunities, the customs, the trading rules, and the attitudes that prevail in the countries that interest them. They also must investigate possible overseas agents. They must, in short, develop a high level of expertise in the markets of their chosen investment realm. In general, however, this is a cumbersome method of trading in foreign securities, as it will require the search for a reputable firm, making appropriate custody arrangements, foreign currency conversions, and other such annoyances.

Domestic Branches of Foreign Banks

The domestic branches of foreign banks will normally handle foreign security transactions for clients, including initial foreign currency conversions, delivery and custody arrangements, and currency conversion at time of sale. Typically, however, the banks set minimum transaction amounts at $100,000. There are a number of sources and methods by which Americans can buy or sell foreign securities directly. These include the following.

American Brokerage Firms
Full-service American brokerage firms will place buy and sell orders for clients for foreign securities, typically for a relatively large commission that will reflect the commission schedule on the foreign stock market plus an increment for the U.S. broker. Investors should expect some time delay as the broker may have to wire abroad for a quote on the security. One and two day lags between the time the order is placed and a confirmation from the broker are not at all uncommon for foreign security transactions.

U.S. brokerage firms can buy or sell American Depository Receipts for clients as well. Investors who buy shares directly may be faced with the problem of custody since the securities in many foreign countries cannot leave the country, and must be held by a custodian bank or other financial institution. However, by dealing with a large U.S. brokerage firm that has established overseas global custody accounts and leaving the shares in "street form" with the broker, the investor can avoid the problems of opening numerous custody accounts abroad with foreign banks.

Foreign Banks and Brokerage Firms

The more adventurous global investor can open accounts with overseas banks or brokerage firms. And some firms, such as Nomura Securities of Japan, will allow nonresident clients to trade securities listed on Japanese, Hong Kong, Australian and certain European bourses. Investors who wish to trade directly should contact local branches of foreign banks or trade embassies for the names of reputable banks or brokerage firms.

Indirect Transactions

Investors wishing to reduce or minimize search costs, trading frictions, and other aggravations associated with foreign investment can trade in global and international mutual funds and specialty country funds.

Global and International Mutual Funds

Because most other forms of overseas investing come with built-in handicaps, the vast majority of small investors with global interests have turned to mutual funds with overseas assets. The reasons are basic, and they relate to the popularity of mutual funds in general:

Mutual funds, which began in the United States in 1921, allow an investor of modest means to participate in the investments of a professional money manager and to take advantage of the resources of a major investment company. The relatively small assets of hundreds—often hundreds of thousands—of individual investors, when pooled together in a mutual fund, are large enough to attract some of the world's best investment talent. As a result, each of those individuals enjoys the same potential for gain. Regardless of how modest the individual investor's assets might be—or how sophisticated he or she might be in investment matters, the investor stands to achieve the same percentage of gain (or loss) that accrues to the experienced professional.

Applying that same reasoning in a global context, mutual funds provide still another plus. They allow individual investors to buy into international expertise and research that they could not afford on their own. They expand the investor's horizons and lessen the risks by applying a specialist's knowledge of the markets and economic conditions abroad.

Mutual funds specializing in overseas investment are classified by the American financial community as either international or global. The seeming nit-pick in terminology can, in real terms, be quite meaningful. To U.S. investors, international funds are those that limit their investments to markets *outside* the United States. They might even restrict their investment activities to a specific region, country, or continent. Global funds, in contrast, know no geographic bounds; they invest anywhere that their management believes a bargain can be found—including the United States.

An international fund does not really free the investor from the burden of attaining knowledge. The investor still must determine such questions as whether an Australia-oriented fund is a better value at a given time than a Korea-oriented one or whether prospects are better in Europe than in Asia. This calls for some of the research and understanding of world finance that participation in a mutual fund should alleviate. In a sense, international funds still require the individual investor to become something of an investment manager.

As in all investments, there is a positive side as well. International funds, because they seek out localized advantages, sometimes can maximize their exposure to temporary swings in a given economy to produce outstanding investment results. There is always the danger inherent in too little diversification, however. Unless the investor is well keyed into the factors underlying such positive spikes, he could have his money in the wrong fund when the spike peaks out.

Global funds, it can be argued, exhibit superiority in that they free the investor almost entirely from any need to become an expert. The investor can rely upon the professional securities analysts and portfolio managers of the funds to determine where in all the world the best investment values are likely to be found. He is assured that when the best bargains reside in American markets, his money will be invested there; when the bargains lie elsewhere, so will his money. The flexibility of global funds is the key to their unique value as investment opportunities.

To be fair, however, it must be said that global funds are less likely than the internationals to produce blazing short-term returns, since they are apt to be diversified around the globe. If Korea booms in a given year, the Korea funds can be expected to outperform others, including the more diversified global funds. On the other hand, if Korea's investment climate subsequently clouds, those funds concentrated in Korea stocks are very likely to experience much greater decline than the geographically diverse globals.

Investors considering international or global funds have other decisions to make. International and global investment companies include open-ended and closed-ended funds. The open-ended variety are more familiar and are commonly called mutual funds. They are called open-ended because the fund can sell additional shares to the public at virtually any time with little or no restriction. The proceeds from the sale of shares are then used to buy additional securities for the portfolio. The shares or units of open-ended funds are bought from and sold to the mutual fund corporation itself; there is no secondary market for the shares. The owner can redeem shares at any time at the net asset value that day.

Closed-end funds, on the other hand, have a fixed capital structure in that shares are initially sold to the public and the proceeds invested in a portfolio of securities according to a set of objectives. As in the open-ended fund, the management of the closed-ended fund is paid a fee to manage the portfolio which may be subject to constant revisions. However, unlike the open-ended fund, new shares in the closed-ended fund are only issued in specific cases (such as a new investment opportunity or a takeover) and then only with the approval of the appropriate regulatory bodies. The shares of closed-end funds

are traded on stock exchanges in the same manner as shares
of public companies.

Specialized International Investment Funds

The single country closed-end specialized mutual funds have
proliferated in recent years. Their introduction and continued
popularity mirrors three distinct developments in world capital
markets:

1. The increased interest of investors in global or foreign
   equity markets.
2. The strong performance of some of the smaller markets
   relative to the giants (U.S., Japan, U.K.) even after foreign currency adjustments to the investor's currency
   denomination.
3. The trend to innovative products and packaging, primarily by major North American and European brokerage firms.

These closed-end funds have a curious and erratic history. The first was the Mexico Fund introduced in 1981, at
U.S. $12.00 a share. However, the fall in oil prices exacted its
toll and the shares were trading in 1986 as low as U.S.$3.00,
or 75% *below* the initial issue price. In 1987, however, the
shares rocketed in value to over U.S.$14.00 in late summer be-
fore falling back in the October market crash. The Scandinavia
Fund issued in 1986 at U.S.$10.00 fell steadily after issue to
U.S.$6.75, before recovering in early 1987. The India Fund is-
sued in the Fall of 1986 on a restricted basis at BP1.05 was
also trading below issue price by year-end. Others have fared
better; the Korea Fund issued in 1984 at U.S.$12.00 was trad-
ing as high as U.S.$87.00 in 1987. And most spectacularly, the
Taiwan Fund issued in late 1986 at U.S.$12.00 with Merrill
Lynch Capital Markets as lead manager, was heavily oversub-
scribed and began trading almost immediately at $18.00 per
share, and was trading in the $54.00 range in late 1987.

The majority of the closed-end funds trade at discounts to
their net asset values. The specialty country funds that invest
in the smaller countries whose markets are blocked or restricted to nonresidents are particularly interesting in that

TABLE 2-7
Closed-End Single Country and Specialty Funds

Fund Name	Exchange Traded	Price July 1992	Net Asset Value	Premium (discount) to Net Asset Value
Argentina Fund	NYSE*	$12.50	$11.85	5.49%
Asia Pacific Fund	NYSE	16.63	15.09	10.17
Austria Fund	NYSE	8.38	9.72	−13.84
Brazil Fund	NYSE	16.00	14.32	11.73
Brazilian Equity Fund	NYSE	11.13	9.59	16.01
Chile Fund	NYSE	37.38	40.08	− 6.75
Emerging Germany	NYSE	8.00	9.52	−15.97
Emerging Mexico	NYSE	18.13	20.66	−12.27
First Australia Fund	AMEX†	9.13	10.54	−13.43
First Iberian Fund	AMEX	7.75	9.15	−15.30
First Philippine Fund	NYSE	12.00	14.30	−16.08
France Growth Fund	NYSE	9.63	11.95	−19.46
Future Germany Fund	NYSE	13.25	16.15	−17.96
Germany Fund	NYSE	11.38	12.21	− 6.84
Growth Fund Spain	NYSE	9.63	10.95	−12.10
GT Greater Europe Fund	NYSE	9.50	11.49	−17.32
India Growth Fund	NYSE	15.88	20.01	−20.66
Indonesia Fund	NYSE	10.13	9.04	12.00
Irish Investment Fund	NYSE	7.88	9.48	−16.93
Italy Fund	NYSE	9.00	9.49	− 5.16
Jakarta Growth Fund	NYSE	8.00	7.24	10.50
Japan OTC Equity Fund	NYSE	10.13	8.06	25.62
Korea Fund	NYSE	11.38	10.71	6.21

(continued)

TABLE 2–7 *(concluded)*

Fund Name	Exchange Traded	Price July 1992	Net Asset Value	Premium (discount) to Net Asset Value
Latin America Equity Fund	NYSE	16.63	17.03	– 2.38
Latin America Investment Fund	NYSE	27.38	29.69	– 7.80
Malaysia Fund	NYSE	13.13	15.29	–14.16
Mexico Fund	NYSE	22.63	28.23	–19.85
Mexico Equity Fund	NYSE	14.50	16.53	–12.28
New Germany Fund	NYSE	11.50	13.91	–17.33
Pacific Eur Growth Fund	NYSE	10.38	10.83	– 4.20
Portugal Fund	NYSE	10.63	11.76	– 9.65
ROC New Taiwan Fund	NYSE	9.00	9.54	– 5.66
Scudder New Asia Fund	NYSE	15.50	15.61	– 0.70
Scudder New Europe	NYSE	9.13	10.55	–13.51
Singapore Fund	NYSE	11.50	12.12	– 5.12
Spain Fund	NYSE	10.50	11.61	– 9.56
Swiss Helvetia Fund	NYSE	13.63	15.22	–10.48
Taiwan Fund	NYSE	19.88	21.43	– 7.26
Templeton Emerging Markets	AMEX	22.00	19.46	13.05
Thai Capital Fund	NYSE	9.13	9.45	– 3.44
Thai Fund	NYSE	15.88	15.96	– 0.53
Turkish Investment Fund	NYSE	6.88	5.93	15.94
United Kingdom Fund	NYSE	9.75	11.07	–11.92

*NYSE = New York Stock Exchange.
†AMEX = American Stock Exchange.

they offer both unusual investment opportunities for globally minded investors and "market completion" devices for professional investment managers. Table 2–7 identifies some of the specialty country funds issued since 1981.

Now that you are familiar with the characteristics and methods of global investing, you can learn in the next chapter about some of the important developments that have taken place in investment finance in recent years, events that have shaped the modern and sophisticated global marketplace. This is the domain of Templeton and his team of global bargain-hunters.

ENDNOTES

1. Of course, there are certain domestic institutions that have restricted ability to invest abroad. For example, in many countries pension funds are limited to investing no more than 10 to 15 percent in foreign securities, and financial institutions such as savings and loan and insurance companies are severely constrained in their international investing activities.
2. From Capital International Perspective S.A., Geneva, 1979; Morgan Stanley Capital International Perspective, S.A., Geneva, 1986, 1987.
3. Harry Markowitz, "Portfolio Selection," *Journal of Finance,* March 1952, pp. 77–91. This is probably the best exposition of Markowitz's work.
4. James Tobin, "Liquidity Preference as Behaviour Toward Risk," *Review of Economic Studies,* 26, no. 1 (February 1958), pp. 65–86.
5. William F. Sharpe, "A Simplified Model for Portfolio Analysis," *Management Science,* January 1963, pp. 273–293; Jan Mossin, "Equilibrium in a Capital Asset Market," *Econometrica,* October 1966, pp. 768–783.
6. See, for example, Eugene Fama, "Risk, Return, and Equilibrium: Some Clarifying Comments," *Journal of Finance,* March 1968, pp. 32–33. Recently, a more general asset pricing model called the Arbitrage Pricing Model has been developed. See S.A. Ross, "The Arbitrage Pricing Theory of Capital Asset Pricing," *Journal of Economic Theory,* December 1976, pp. 344–360.
7. The *standard deviation* is a statistical measure of the variability of a security or index. A security with a high (low) standard

deviation tends to fluctuate within a wide (narrow) range. The standard deviation of a portfolio of two risky assets is calculated by the formula:

$$[X_1^2\partial_1^2 + X_2^2\partial_2^2 + 2X_1X_2\partial_1\partial_2\partial_{12}]^{1/2}$$

where

X_1 = weight of security 1 in portfolio
X_2 = weight of security 2 in portfolio
∂_1^2 = variance of security 1
∂_2^2 = variance of security 2
∂_1 = standard deviation of security 1
∂_2 = standard deviation of security 2
∂_{12} = correlation coefficient between securities 1 and 2

In the example in the text, the standard deviation is

$$[(.50)^2(.182)^2 + (.50)^2(.215)^2 + 2(.5)(.5)(.30)(.182)(.215)]^{1/2} = .1603$$

8. The correlation coefficient of returns between two securities measures the degree to which the two fluctuate together. The range is $+1$ (perfect positive correlation) to -1 (perfect negative correlation). Two securities with a correlation coefficient of $+1$ move in perfect lock-step. Securities with a low correlation of 0.30 tend to move together only about 30% of the time.
9. Bruno H. Solnik, "Why Not Diversify Internationally?" *Financial Analysts Journal,* July–August 1974, pp. 48–54; D.R. Lessard, "World, Country and Industry Relationships in Equity Returns; Implications for Risk Reduction Through Diversification," *Financial Analysts Journal* 32, no. 1 (January–February 1976), pp. 2–8; Haim Levy and Marshall Sarnat, "International Diversification of International Portfolios," *American Economic Review,* September 1970, pp. 668–675.
10. Bruno H. Solnik, "Why Not Diversify Internationally?" *Financial Analysts Journal,* July–August 1974, p. 51.
11. See Margaret Piton, "Go Global," *Your Money,* January 1987, pp. 68–70, for a detailed discussion of foreign exchange trading methods.
12. See Richard Moranis, "Invisible Ink," *Forbes,* December 15, 1986, p. 44.
13. In Italy, for example, all trades by foreigners must take place through a bank.
14. For example, Nigeria, South Korea, and Brazil prohibit direct investment by foreigners. The India and Pakistan equity markets are open only to nonresident Indians and Pakistanis.

CHAPTER 3

THE GLOBAL MARKETPLACE

John Templeton began his career in 1940 when the structures of the modern financial world were being subjected to one of history's most wrenching experiences. In more than four decades of investment counselling since then, he has had a unique opportunity to witness and learn from an extraordinary mosaic of recessions, expansions, revolutions, and the birth of new nations. From this experience he has developed and tested a unique group of methods for both thinking and investing. The Templeton style being followed so widely today by younger investment counsellors has been shaped by that long look at the verities of fiscal reality. If John Templeton has been more successful than most other investment managers, it is in large part because of timing. His investment senses were awakened at essentially the same time that world affairs were spawning an entirely new brand of economy. That fortuitous timing has provided him with better yardsticks for measuring economic variables than today's money managers have had available.

The word that characterizes the Templeton approach most precisely is adaptability. The Templeton organization over the past four decades has flourished, earning consistently above average returns in a constantly changing economic and financial market background portmanteau.

The flagship fund of the Templeton organization, the Templeton Growth Fund, was launched in November 1954. As illustrated in Table 3–1, the value of $10,000 invested in the Fund at inception and after paying initial commissions would today be worth $1,531,487 (on December 31, 1991)! In only 9 of the 37 years have returns been negative (and these coincided,

TABLE 3–1
Performance of the Templeton Growth Fund, 1954–1991

Year Ended Dec. 31	Value of $10,000 Investment— Templeton Growth Fund	Annual Rate of Return— Templeton Growth Fund	Cumulative Total Rate of Return— Templeton Growth Fund	Annual Compounded Rate of Return Nov. 1954 Base— Templeton Growth Fund
1954	$ 9,296			
1955	9,950	− 7.04%	− 0.50%	−0.50%
1956	10,412	4.64	4.12	2.04
1957	8,651	−16.91	−13.49	−4.72
1958	12,873	48.80	28.73	6.52
1959	14,675	14.00	46.75	7.97
1960	16,706	13.84	67.06	8.93
1961	19,762	18.29	97.62	10.22
1962	17,091	−13.52	70.91	6.93
1963	17,969	5.14	79.69	6.73
1964	23,105	28.58	131.05	8.74
1965	28,222	22.15	182.22	9.89
1966	26,726	− 5.30	167.26	8.54
1967	30,398	13.74	203.98	8.93
1968	41,875	37.76	318.75	10.77
1969	50,111	19.67	401.11	11.34
1970	46,884	− 6.44	368.84	10.14
1971	57,164	21.93	471.64	10.80
1972	96,354	68.56	863.54	13.41
1973	86,793	− 9.92	767.93	12.05
1974	76,318	−12.07	663.18	10.70
1975	105,004	37.59	950.04	11.85
1976	154,083	46.74	1440.83	13.24
1977	185,478	20.38	1754.78	13.54
1978	221,105	19.21	2111.05	13.77
1979	280,448	26.84	2704.48	14.27
1980	353,049	25.89	3430.49	14.69
1981	352,201	− 0.24	3422.01	14.10
1982	390,265	10.81	3802.65	13.98
1983	518,687	32.91	5086.87	14.59
1984	529,935	2.17	5199.35	14.15
1985	677,177	27.78	6671.77	14.57
1986	820,982	21.24	8109.82	14.77
1987	846,478	3.11	8364.78	14.40
1988	1,046,219	23.60	10362.19	14.66
1989	1,282,250	22.56	12722.50	14.88
1990	1,166,142	− 9.06	11561.42	14.13
1991	1,531,487	31.33	15214.87	14.57

as you would expect, with down years in worldwide equity markets). From November 1954 to December 1991 the fund has achieved an annual compounded rate of return of 14.57%. Table 3–2 compares the performance of the Templeton Growth Fund to that of a large portfolio of U.S. equities.

TABLE 3–2
Comparison of a $10,000 Investment in the Templeton Growth Fund to a Large Portfolio of U.S. Equities, 1954–1991

Year Ended Dec. 31	Value of $10,000 Investment— Templeton Growth Fund	Value of $10,000 Investment— U.S. Equities
1954	$ 9,296	$ 9,700
1955	9,950	12,765
1956	10,412	13,607
1957	8,651	12,138
1958	12,873	17,405
1959	14,675	19,494
1960	16,706	19,592
1961	19,762	24,862
1962	17,091	22,699
1963	17,969	27,874
1964	23,105	32,474
1965	28,222	36,533
1966	26,726	32,843
1967	30,398	40,726
1968	41,875	45,246
1969	50,111	41,400
1970	46,884	43,056
1971	57,164	49,213
1972	96,354	58,564
1973	86,793	49,955
1974	76,318	36,717
1975	105,004	50,376
1976	154,083	62,365
1977	185,478	57,875
1978	221,105	61,695
1979	280,448	73,047
1980	353,049	96,714
1981	352,201	91,975
1982	390,265	111,658
1983	518,687	136,781

(continued)

TABLE 3–2 *(concluded)*

Year Ended Dec. 31	Value of $10,000 Investment— Templeton Growth Fund	Value of $10,000 Investment— U.S. Equities
1984	529,935	145,398
1985	677,177	192,216
1986	820,982	227,776
1987	846,478	239,689
1988	1,046,219	279,980
1989	1,282,250	368,146
1990	1,166,142	356,476
1991	1,531,487	465,379

SOURCES:
Securities Fund Investors, Inc., internal documents and brochures, undated.

R. G. Ibbotson and R. A. Sinquefield, *Stocks, Bills, Bonds and Inflation,* Financial Analysts Research Foundation, Charlottesville, Va., 1982, pp. 88–89.

R. G. Ibbotson, L. B. Siegel, and K. S. Love, "World Wealth, Market Values and Returns," *Journal of Portfolio Management,* Fall 1985, pp. 4–23.

Wood Mackenzie & Co. Ltd. "International Market Returns," various issues.

Let's examine the major events that have shaped the financial environment over the "Templeton Era." John Templeton's insight and reaction to these developments will be highlighted.

MODERN INVESTMENT THEORIES AND DEVELOPMENTS

Investment finance has gone through a revolutionary metamorphosis over the past 40 years. New theories of investment and investor behavior have emerged, coupled with the introduction of new direct and derivative investment vehicles and portfolio strategies designed to activate these theoretical developments. In some cases, the actual investment applications arrived close on the heels of the publication of these theories, attesting to the close relationship between researchers and investment bankers and brokerage firms.[1] These new developments constitute an eclectic bag of theories and innovations, including Modern Portfolio Theory and the Capital Asset Pricing Model, Efficient Markets Theory (and some anomolous findings), the Black-Scholes Option Pricing Model, the introduction of innovative and complex securities, derivative products, and new futures markets, market index futures and options contracts, and new mutual fund products, the internationalization of world equity markets (including open-door policies and market links), and the persistence of inflation. The remainder of this chapter is devoted to these important developments.

Modern Portfolio Theory

The landmark theoretical development in investment finance was that of Harry Markowitz's Portfolio Theory in 1948.[2] Markowitz argued that investors should be concerned with only two elements of their portfolio; *expected return* as measured by the mean rate of return and *risk* as measured by the standard deviation or variance about the return. Given some specific assumptions (always necessary for the development of a model), Markowitz showed that investors should hold diversified portfolios containing financial assets that are less than positively correlated with each other. In other words, if you are going to invest in stocks, buy a bunch of different issues and be sure that they are not stocks that rise and fall in unison. Called efficient portfolios, these combinations of financial assets offer, on an ex-ante basis, greater return for the same level of risk, or less risk for the same level of return, than naively diversified ones.

Markowitz's work was extended by William Sharpe (his doctoral student), John Lintner, and Jan Mossin[3] into a theory, called the Capital Asset Pricing Model (CAPM), of how risky assets are priced. The CAPM provides a theory of the relationship between security and portfolio rates of returns, and those of a representative market index which is a proxy for the overall stock market.[4] A resulting single measure called *beta* estimates the asset's or portfolio's volatility relative to the volatility on a market index. A security or portfolio that moves proportionately and in lock-step with the market has a beta of one. High beta securities and portfolios (betas greater than one) are more volatile than the market and provide greater rates of returns than the market when the market rises and take a greater beating than the market during general declines. These are deemed aggressive securities or portfolios. Low beta securities and portfolios (betas less than one) are less volatile than the market and provide smaller rates of returns than the market when the market rises. And naturally they suffer less than the market during periods of general market decline. These are defensive securities. Figure 3–1 illustrates aggressive, neutral, and defensive betas.

Betas are calculated using past security and portfolio data and hence are simply estimates of future relationships. In fact, betas for individual securities are quite unstable, although over long time periods, portfolio betas do display reasonable consistency.

The CAPM caught on quickly with the investment community, and by the early 1970s, most major brokerage firms, and money managers were using beta estimates in their stock selection techniques. Now beta is literally a household word in the investment world. However, a recent theoretical development threatens to replace the CAPM. The Arbitrage Pricing Theory, originally developed by Stephen Ross of Yale University,[5] is a more general asset pricing model, which states that security returns are related to a number of factors such as expected GNP levels, expected real interest rates, expected inflation levels, and expected gold prices. Although elegant in form, the new model is not as readily adaptable to security analysis as the CAPM, as the factors relevant for each individual security must be empirically identified.

As Templeton's career started well before the development of the CAPM, he had no opportunity to benefit from it during his earlier years. Yet like other savvy operators, a dearth of theory never got in the way of making money. Today, Templeton recognizes the theory underlying beta determination but is sceptical about its universal application. "We find that betas are unstable and therefore not a totally reli-

FIGURE 3–1
Illustrative Betas

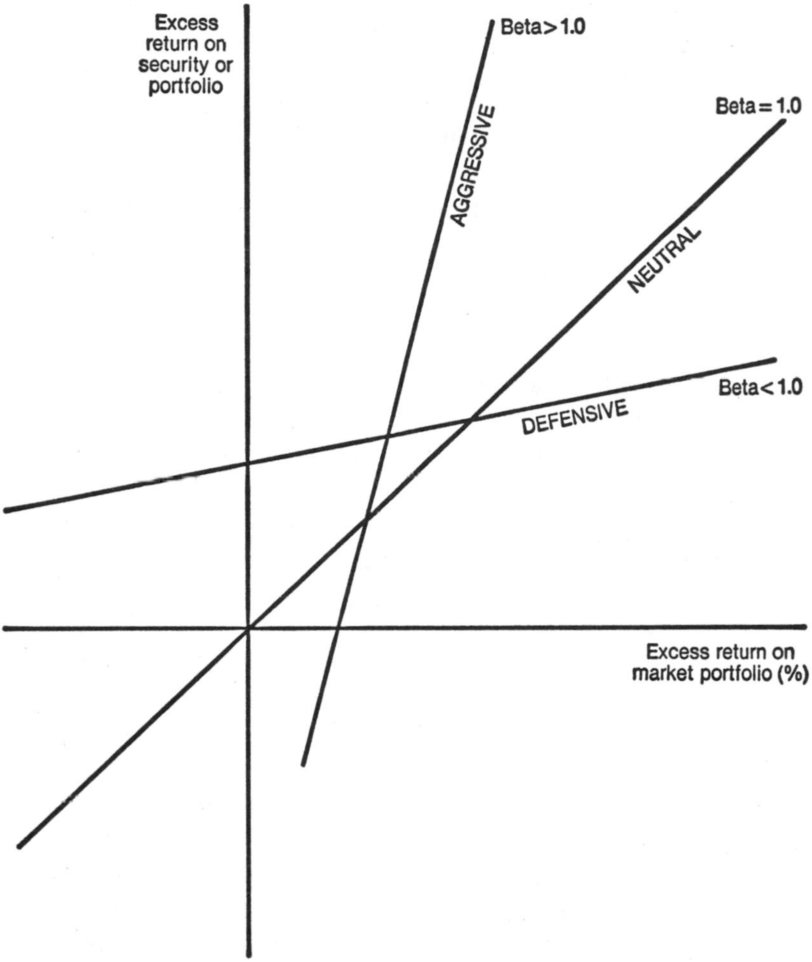

Excess return on security or portfolio

Beta > 1.0

Beta = 1.0

AGGRESSIVE

NEUTRAL

Beta < 1.0

DEFENSIVE

Excess return on market portfolio (%)

able investment indicator. We prefer to use our fundamentally based approaches, but will however calculate betas on our portfolios, making revisions if necessary to reflect our objectives. In our opinion, beta is overemphasized. We do use betas later on as a check on our portfolio manager, to see what the beta of specific fund portfolios is and to make sure that no one portfolio has taken on too much risk. But we don't use it at the initial stages. Instead we look for what we call yardsticks of value which are fundamentally based measures, such as share price relative to sustainable future earnings or cash-flow per share. Everyone should read about modern portfolio theory but honestly, they are not going to make much money with it. I've never seen anybody that came up with a really superior long-term record using only modern portfolio management."

Templeton points out as well that beta is highly sensitive to the market index selected, which poses a challenging problem for global portfolios with (changing) country mixes.

Efficient Markets Theory

Remember the observation of the movement of particles under a microscope from high school chemistry? How they wandered in seemingly random manner? The movement is known as the Law of Brownian Motion and represents one important theory of security price movements. The theory which at least until recently was embraced by academics almost as holy writ, is called the Efficient Markets Hypothesis and it has major implications for security valuation, the value of information, and bargain hunting for stocks.

Although there were earlier published studies on the subject,[6] the major impetus in the late 1950s and early 1960s came from the work of university researchers.[7] The initial studies focused on stock price movements themselves. They reported that security prices seemed to behave in a manner similar to a (fair) roulette wheel, i.e., that the past had no influence on the future and could not be used to predict the future. If a roulette wheel is fair, then knowledge of recent outcomes (despite the outcries of the system players) will not be of any value in predicting the results of the next spin of the wheel. Similarly, these researchers found through a series of studies, ranging from simple filter tests[8] to more complex statistical studies,[9] that past price changes in securities provided *no clues* as to future movements; that the size and direction of future stock price changes could not be predicted from the size and direction of past movements. Despite obvious scepticism from the brokerage industry, the theory, then called the Random Walk Theory, began to gain some acceptance. In the late 1960s the theory was extended into the Efficient Markets Hypothesis, which has three forms. The weak form (a slightly modified version of the random walk) states that security prices fully reflect all past information. Or, stated another way, that analysis of the past cannot provide a profitable trading strategy. This form of the theory wasn't and still isn't particularly popular with technical analysts! The semi-strong form holds that security prices fully reflect all available public information, including that found in published financial reports. (Nasty implications for fundamental analysis). The strong form states that prices fully reflect *all* available information including both insider and monopolistically controlled information.

Tests of the efficient markets theory have supported the weak and semi-strong form, as well as the strong form with respect to mutual fund managers, although not with respect to insiders. Recently, however, a number of anomalies have surfaced, providing both some negative implications for the theory and positive encouragement for investor trading opportunities. One of the most important of these anomalies is the low P/E Multiple Effect,[10] a finding that securities with low Price/Earnings multiples have tended to yield higher returns than predicted. A similar finding is the Small Firm Effect,[11] that securities of smaller companies have higher returns than those of their larger counterparts. The Day of the Week Effect, a third anomaly, indicates that stock returns and prices on average are lowest on Mondays and highest on Fridays.[12] Finally, researchers have uncovered an End of the Year Effect, an apparent tendency for securities, particularly those of small firms, to on average, yield lower returns in December, and higher returns in January.[13] These seeming anomalies provide grist for the view that superior investment analysis and investigation will yield positive returns. However, readers should be cautioned that although these peculiarities are well supported, the associated abnormal returns do not typically provide a profitable trading strategy for the retail investor, after commissions and other trading costs.

> **Templeton on the Low Price Earnings Effect**
>
> A number of fund managers have adopted the low price/earnings
> multiple approach. Several books have been written about how you
> can do well selecting on this basis. And there is something to it. In
> a way it is consistent with our fundamentally based analytic selec-
> tion criteria in that we are constantly searching for undervalued
> securities, and a low price/earnings multiple is *one* yardstick of a
> bargain. But it's too restrictive for our organization. It's only one
> method of the dozens of approaches.

Black-Scholes Option Pricing Model

In 1967 Kassouf and Thorpe published a book entitled *Beat the
Market*.[14] However, unlike the other investments books of the
Dancing Your Way to Millions and *How to Get Rich on Wall
Street* ilk, this one was not only respectable, it was down-right
pathbreaking. Kassouf and Thorpe set out the principles of
warrant hedges, how to create profitable trading positions by
combining short positions in warrants with long positions in
common stocks using a specific set of rules. The warrant hedge
indeed became the forerunner of the Option Pricing Model as
developed and published by Black and Scholes in 1972.[15] The
Black-Scholes Option Pricing Model, an application of the heat
exchange equation from physics, provides a valuation equation
for an exchange traded European-style (exerciseable at maturity only) option contract. Only minor modifications are necessary to adapt the equation to the valuation of American-style
(exerciseable at any time up to maturity) options on dividend
paying stocks. Commensurate with the development of the
Black-Scholes Option Pricing Model, now used by almost all
brokerage firms for estimating option values, was the introduction in the 1970s and 1980s of a host of new and exciting option
contracts on numerous U.S. and other exchanges, including
stock options (1974), commodity options (1982), financial instrument options (1982), precious metals options (1982), currency options (1982) and index options (1983). These derivative
products, besides providing the obvious speculative applica-

tions, are useful, when properly applied, in allowing both investors and business concerns to reduce risks associated with adverse security, currency, interest rate, and commodity price movements.

Templeton on Options

The Templeton Organization's philosophy has always been that investment is a long-term proposition. We are not as concerned with the short-term fluctuations in the market, as we are confident that our bargain-hunting selection criteria and global approach will provide high annual returns for our shareholders over a ten, fifteen, or twenty year period. So we haven't been willing to sacrifice our long-term results by paying for option premiums for what we consider to be, for us, unnecessary portfolio insurance. However, we are staying current on these developments. The day may come when we want to hedge our positions if we anticipate a major market correction, or we wish to bolster the returns on our fixed-income funds.

The Introduction of Innovative and Complex Instruments

In recent years new and innovative, and complex, investment vehicles have been introduced in world markets at a remarkable pace. Many of these instruments contain put or call options, combinations of options, or have option characteristics. These new developments have ranged from simple zero coupon bonds to complex creations like flip-flop perpetual floaters. And from the highly successful dutch auction preferreds to the failures such as gold-denominated bonds.

Some of these instruments have genuine economic value, and have served to expand the investment and hedging opportunities in the marketplace. For example, the oil-linked bonds introduced by Standard Oil in 1986 were designed to allow firms to hedge against rising oil prices. Salomon Brothers' 1986 U.S. $100,000,000 issue of U.S. $1,000 zero coupon bonds include what constitutes a four-year-call option on the S&P 500 Composite Index, a useful and heretofore unavailable long-term market hedging device. The 1985 Salomon Brothers Range Forward Contract is a foreign currency foreign exchange contract that combines features of forward contracts with option contracts, and provides a valuable hedging tool for the firm faced with substantial foreign currency risk.

In other cases the motivation for the introduction of specific complex instruments was and is less transparent. And indeed, even some officials at futures and options exchanges have admitted that they are willing to introduce new contracts to see what happens. The purpose of specific innovations may have been strictly an anticipated premium accruing to the issue in the after-market for innovative packaging for the benefit of the underwriters and insiders of the issuer. That seems to be the case with, for example, piggyback warrants (as described in Table 3–3) which have no apparent benefit other

TABLE 3–3
Complex and Innovative Security Issues—Recent Examples

A. Commodity Linked

COMMODITY LINKED BONDS AND PREFERRED SHARES such as International Nickel Commodity Indexed 8%, $25 par value preferred share that is convertible into the cash equivalent of 23.91 pounds of copper or 6.6 pounds of nickel. The shares are traded on the Toronto Stock Exchange.

COMMODITY PURCHASE WARRANTS the Echo Bay gold purchase warrants that allow the holder the right to buy .01765 oz. of gold at a price of U.S. $297.50 at a specific date. The warrants are traded on the Toronto Stock Exchange.

B. Currency Linked

CURRENCY INDEXED BONDS such as the AMEX Credit Corporation, Japanese yen denominated bond for which the redemption proceeds are an inverse function of the external value of the yen, vis-a-vis the U.S. dollar.

DUAL (MULTI) CURRENCY DENOMINATED BONDS AND PREFERRED SHARES such as the Canada Development Corporation $25 par value preferred share that provides the holder with the option of receiving as quarterly dividends the greater of: C$2.35 and U.S. $1.92. The preferred shares are traded on the Toronto Stock Exchange.

CURRENCY PURCHASE WARRANTS such as the Canada Development Corporation nontransferable warrant attached to the $25 par value dual

TABLE 3–3 *(concluded)*

currency preferred share. The warrant allows the holder the right to buy U.S. $20.39 for C$25 on June 1, 1990.

COMPLEX CURRENCY INSTRUMENTS such as the Salomon Brothers Range Forward Contracts that through a quasi-auction process sets upper and lower limits for the purchase and sale of specific foreign currencies in U.S. dollar numeraries.

C. Interest Rate Linked

BOND PURCHASE WARRANTS such as the Texaco bond purchase warrants that allow the holder the right to buy an 8-year bond with a 12 7/8% coupon rate at any time over a three year period.

PERPETUAL FLOATERS such as the Barclay's Bank (U.K.) perpetual floating rate note.

"BUNNY" BONDS such as the Chrysler 10 3/4% 1996 bond that allows the holder the right to receive interest in cash or in 10 3/4% bonds maturing in 1991.

"FLIP-FLOP" BONDS such as the World Bank perpetual bond that can be flipped into a three-month note and subsequently flopped back into the perpetual or sold back (put) to the World Bank.

DUTCH AUCTION PREFERREDS such as the Northern Telecom issue in which the dividend rate is set each month by auction subject to a maximum dividend rate of the 30-day bankers' acceptance rate plus 40 basis points.

D. Market Index Linked

STOCK INDEXED BONDS such as the Swedish Export Credit five-year bonds whose redemption proceeds at maturity are tied to the level of the Nikkei Dow Index of the Tokyo Stock Exchange. The redemption proceeds are an increasing function of the level of the index for the bull version of the bond and a decreasing function for the bear version.

E. Common Stock Linked

PERFORMANCE WARRANTS such as the Medcomp (U.S.) warrant for which the exercise terms are adjusted in accordance with the net income of the company. The lower Medcomp's net income; the greater the number of common shares received by the warrant holder on exercise.

PIGGYBACK WARRANTS such as the Goldcorp (Canadian) Series 1 warrant that allowed the holder the right to obtain a class A share and if exercised before a specific date, an additional warrant exerciseable into an additional class A share.

DUAL SECURITY WARRANTS such as Nova Corporation (Canada) warrants that are exerciseable into three common shares or 1 $25 par value preferred share.

than to obfuscate the market valuation of the underlying common stock, and the warrants themselves.

The valuation of these complex securities poses a challenging problem to investors, both domestic and global. Financial economists have developed valuation models, in some cases prior to the arrival of the actual instrument, in other cases after the fact, and in yet other cases not at all. The Black-Scholes model and its extensions are now widely used in the financial community to value option contracts in which the holder can acquire an underlying asset by exercising it against an (unidentified) writer. Since many of the above instruments can be viewed as options or combination of options, it is natural to use a Black-Scholes Option Pricing approach to valuing them. However, many of these instruments have features so complex that they require either major modifications to Black-Scholes, or indeed such robust extensions that the technology does not yet exist to provide for a solution to the valuation problem![16]

In Table 3–3 we provide a classification scheme for some of these new and intriguing instruments.

Templeton on New and Innovative Securities

We find these fascinating. Up to now we haven't bought many in our funds but that's because we are still learning how to value them. Remember, we are bargain hunters and we only buy if we calculate that something is undervalued. We have to know how to value them in order to determine whether they are bargains. I suspect that Templeton International will be adding others of the new instruments to our portfolios in the future. Some of these complex securities may lose their popularity and become available at real bargain prices in the next bear markets, as happened to the older convertibles and gold-linked debentures in past years.

The Debut and Growth of Derivative Products

The introduction of exchange traded stock options by the Chicago Board Options Exchange (an adjunct of the huge Chicago

Board of Trade) in 1974 provided a new dimension to securities trading. Options contracts represent the right to buy (call option) or to sell (put option) a specified quantity of an underlying asset at a specified price within a specified time period. An option contract that can be exercised over a time period is called an *American* option; one exerciseable at a single future date only is a *European* option.

Some well-meaning but misinformed critics argued that options trading was no more than legalized gambling, failing to recognize that although speculators (or indeed gamblers) do indulge their gambling instincts with these highly leveraged instruments, these derivative markets provide a useful and powerful method of hedging investment portfolios, a valuable economic benefit to prudent participants.[17]

Options became very popular right from the start and exchange trading in options quickly spread to other U.S. and foreign exchanges. Subsequently, option contracts for underlying assets including currencies, commodities, market indexes, and financial instruments were introduced on U.S., Canadian, Dutch, U.K., and Australian markets. Table 3–4 sets out the markets and options contracts traded around the world.

TABLE 3–4
Option Contracts and Markets by Country

Country	Number of Option Markets	Options Traded
Australia	(2) Sydney Futures Exchange Australia Financial Futures Market	Puts, calls on common shares, common share futures, gold, silver, platinum, All Ordinaries Share Price Index, foreign currencies, bank bill futures, Australian dollar futures, U.S. dollar futures, 10-year Treasury note futures

(continued)

TABLE 3–4 (*continued*)

Country	Number of Option Markets	Options Traded
Canada	(5) Toronto Stock Exchange Toronto Futures Exchange Montreal Exchange Vancouver Stock Exchange Winnipeg Commodity Exchange	Puts, calls on shares, gold, silver, platinum, bonds, stock market indexes, bills
Denmark	(1) Denmark Futures	Mortgage bond options, government bonds, puts, calls on common shares
Finland	(3) Finnish Options Brokers	FOX market index
France	(3) Marché à Terme International de France Marché des Options Négociables de Paris (MONEP) OMF Market	French Treasury bonds, puts, calls on shares, bonds, market indexes, three-month Paris Interbank Offered Rate (PIBOR) interest rate futures
Japan	(2) Toyko Stock Exchange Tokyo International Financial Futures Exchange (TIFFE)	Japanese government bond futures, three-month Euroyen futures
Netherlands	(1) European Options Exchange	Put and call options on shares, bonds, silver, platinum, market index, currencies, jumbo dollar contract
New Zealand	(2) New Zealand Stock Exchange New Zealand Futures and Options Exchange	Put and call stock options, Barclays Share Price Index futures, 3-year government stock futures, New Zealand dollar futures
Norway	(1) Norwegian Options Exchange	Put and call options on shares, OBX index

TABLE 3–4 (continued)

Country	Number of Option Markets	Options Traded
Singapore	(1) Singapore International Monetary Exchange (SIMEX)	Puts, calls on Eurodollar futures, German mark futures, Japanese yen futures, Euroyen futures
Spain	(1) El Marcado de Opciones Financieras (MOFEX)	Mibor-90, Spanish Treasury bonds
South Africa	(1) South African Stock Exchange	Put and call options on shares
Sweden	(2) Swedish Options Market Sweden Options and Futures Exchange	Puts, calls on shares, bonds market indexes
Switzerland	(1) Swiss Options and Financial Futures Exchange (SOFFEX)	Puts, calls on bearer shares, ordinary shares, and participation certificates
United Kingdom	(5) London Stock Exchange London Metal Exchange London Futures and Options Exchange London International Financial Futures Exchange International Petroleum Exchange	Puts, calls and double options on common shares, commodities, market indexes, currencies, Eurodollar interest rate futures, short gilts, long gilts, medium gilts, German government bonds, U.S. Treasury Bonds, three-month Euromark futures
United States	(15) Chicago Board of Trade Chicago Board Options Exchange Coffee, Sugar and Cocoa Exchange Commodity Exchange, Inc. New York Futures Exchange American Stock Exchange	Treasury Bonds and Treasury bond futures, Treasury Notes, Treasury Bills, Eurodollar futures, stock market indexes and stock market index futures, economic index futures, commodity futures

(continued)

TABLE 3–4 (concluded)

Country	Number of Option Markets	Options Traded
United States	(15) Philadelphia Stock Exchange Index and Option Market of the Chicago Mercantile Exchange New York Stock Exchange Pacific Stock Exchange Kansas City Board of Trade MidAmerica Commodity Exchange Minneapolis Grain Exchange New York Cotton Exchange New York Mercantile Exchange	(sugar, wheat, corn, soybeans, soybean meal, soybean oil, cattle, cocoa, crude oil, copper, coffee, orange juice, pork bellies, hogs, cotton, heating oil, unleaded gasoline, broiler chickens, oats), foreign currency and foreign currency futures, gold and gold futures and silver futures, platinum, mortgage-backed futures

SOURCE: Eric F. Kirzner and John R. Dickinson, *Guide to International Investing*, CCH Canadian Limited, 6 Garamond Court, Don Mills, Ontario, 1992, para 4760.

The Global Expansion of Futures Markets

Futures contracts are standardized contracts for future delivery or cash settlement of a specified quantity, and quality of an underlying commodity, currency, or financial instrument. Although widely traded by speculators, they are also of interest to hedgers who are attempting to reduce the risk associated with long or short positions in underlying assets. Table 3–5 sets out the major futures contracts traded on world markets.

The Introduction of Market Index Futures and Options

Index futures contracts represent the right to delivery[18] of a specified portfolio of stocks. These innovative contracts made their debut in 1982 on the Kansas City Board of Trade with the Value Line Index futures, a cash settled contract with an

TABLE 3–5
Futures Contracts by Country

Country and Future Exchange	Commodities, Currencies, Financial Instruments, and Stock Indexes Traded
Australia	
Australian Financial Futures Market	Ordinary shares, ASX Securities Index
Sydney Futures Exchange Ltd.	Australian dollars (denominated in U.S. dollars), All-Ordinaries share price index, Eurodollars (traded under a link with the London International Financial Futures Exchange), gold (fungible with COMEX gold futures), live cattle, 90-day bank accepted bills of exchange, U.S. Treasury Bonds (traded under a link with the London International Financial Futures Exchange), Commonwealth Treasury Bonds (2, 3, and 10 year), wool
Bermuda	
International Futures Exchange (Bermuda) Ltd.	Baltic freight index, gold
Brazil	
Brazilian Futures Exchange	Gold, IBV-12 Rio de Janeiro Stock Exchange Index, Japanese yen, Treasury bonds (OTN-nominal), U.S. dollar, German mark
Sao Paulo Exchange	Brazilian Certificate of Deposit, British pound, cattle, feeder cattle, cocoa, frozen chicken, gold, Japanese yen, soybean meal, soybean oil, U.S. dollar, German mark, FGV-100 Stock Index
Bolsa Mercantil & de Futoros	Bovespa Index, Brazilian Treasury bonds, broilers, cattle, Central Bank of Brazil bills, coffee, Domestic CD, gold, hogs, Japanese yen, U.S. dollar, German mark

(continued)

TABLE 3–5 (*continued*)

Country and Future Exchange	Commodities, Currencies, Financial Instruments, and Stock Indexes Traded
Canada	
Montreal Exchange	Gold (cash-settled), bankers' acceptances, Government of Canada Bonds
Toronto Futures Exchange	Toronto Stock Exchange 300 Composite Index, TSE 35 Index, TSE 35 Spot Index, TSE Oil and Gas Index, U.S. dollar, TSE Composite spot index contract, TSE Oil and Gas spot index contract, Canadian T-Bills, long-term Canadian bonds
Winnepeg Commodity Exchange	Barley, flaxseed, oats, rapeseed, rye, wheat, gold, silver, T-Bills, long-term bonds
Denmark	
Copenhagen Stock Exchange	Danish bonds, KFX Stock Index
Denmark Futures and Options Market	2006 Annuity mortgage credit bond
Finland	
Finnish Options Brokers	FOX Index
France	
Marché à Terme International de France	French long-term bonds, French Treasury bills, CAC 40 Stock Index, three-month Pibor, Euro D-mark (three-month), potatoes, Italian government bonds
Paris Commodity Exchange (Open only to members of the French Broker's Association)	Sugar-white, cocoa, coffee-robusta, soybean meal
France Matif Automatique	OMF 50 stock index
Germany	
Deutsche Terminborse	Five-year German Government bonds, three-month domestic interest rates, Euroyen futures, crude oil futures, German stock index (DAX)

TABLE 3–5 (continued)

Country and Future Exchange	Commodities, Currencies, Financial Instruments, and Stock Indexes Traded
Hong Kong Hong Kong Futures Exchange	Soybeans, sugar, gold, cotton, Hang Seng Index, Hong Kong Interbank Offered Rate (HIBOR), Hong Seng properties sub-index
Ireland Irish Futures and Options Exchange	Long gilt, Irish pound/U.S. dollar, three-month interest rate, ISEQ Index
Japan Osaka Securities Exchange	Stock Futures 50, Nikkei 250 Index, Nikkei 225 Futures
Tokyo Stock Exchange	10-year government bonds, 20-year government bonds, Tokyo Stock Exchange Price Index (TOPIX), U.S. Treasury Bond
Tokyo International Financial Futures Exchange	Three-month Euroyen, three-month Eurodollar, Japanese yen/U.S. dollar
Malaysia Kuala Lumpur Commodity Exchange	Crude palm oil, tin, SMR 20 rubber, cocoa
Netherlands Amsterdam Financial Futures Market	Guilder bond futures
Amsterdam Pork and Potato Terminal Markets	Pork, potatoes
Financiele Termijnmarkt	FTA Bullet Index, FTB Bullet Index, EOE Dutch Stock Index, Dutch Top 5 Index, Dutch government bonds, Eurotop 100 Index
New Zealand New Zealand Futures Exchange	Prime commercial paper, U.S. dollar/New Zealand dollar, wool, wheat, New Zealand Treasury notes, bank bills, Barclays share index
Philippines Manila International Futures Exchange	Cane sugar, soybeans

(continued)

TABLE 3–5 (continued)

Country and Future Exchange	Commodities, Currencies, Financial Instruments, and Stock Indexes Traded
Singapore	
Singapore International Monetary Exchange	British pound, Eurodollar, Japanese yen, German mark, gold futures, fuel oil futures, Nikkei Stock Average, U.S. Treasury bonds, Euroyen futures, crude oil futures, Euromark, Eurodollar strip facility. The first four contracts have identical specifications to those listed on the Chicago Mercantile Exchange (CME), and may be traded through the SIMEX/CME mutual offset system
Spain	
Mercado Español de Futuros Financieros (Meffsa)	90-day Madrid interbank offered rate (Mibor)
El Mercado de Opciones Financieras (MOFEX)	Fiex 35 Index
Sweden	
Sweden Options and Futures Exchange	SX 16 Index
Switzerland	
Swiss Options and Futures Exchange	Swiss Market Index, Eurofranc interest rate
United Kingdom	
Baltic International Freight Futures Exchange	Baltic freight index
Grain and Feed Trade Association Ltd. (London)	Barley, wheat
International Petroleum Exchange	Gasoil, heavy fuel oil, leaded gasoline, crude oil
London Potato Futures Association Ltd.	Potatoes
The GAFTA Soybean Meal Futures Association Ltd.	Soybean meal
London Bullion Market	Gold, silver
London Futures and Options Exchange	Rubber, cocoa, coffee, rice, sugar No. 5, sugar No. 6, MGMI Index, property futures

TABLE 3–5 (continued)

Country and Future Exchange	Commodities, Currencies, Financial Instruments, and Stock Indexes Traded
London International Financial Futures Exchange Ltd.	U.K. gilts (20 year), U.K. medium gilts, U.K. short gilts (3 to 4½ years), Eurodollar interest rate (3 month), sterling interest rate (3 month), U.S. Treasury bonds, Financial Times Stock Exchange 100 Index, British pounds, German marks, Swiss francs, Japanese yen, German government bonds, three-month Euro-German mark interest rate, Euromark (three months), ECU (three-month), Japanese government bonds, Euro-Swiss interest rate, FT-SE Eurotrack 100, Italian government bonds
London Meat Futures Exchange	Pigmeat, pig (cash-settled), beef, live cattle (cash-settled)
London Metal Exchange	Aluminum, copper-higher grade, copper-standard wirebars, lead, nickel, silver, tin, zinc
London Rubber Terminal Association	Rubber No. 1A
London Vegetable Oil Terminal Market Association Ltd.	Soybean oil
United States	
Comex (New York)	Copper, gold, silver, aluminum, corporate bond index, high-grade copper
New York Cotton Exchange (New York)	Cotton, orange juice, propane gas, U.S. dollar index, European currency unit (ECU), 5-year U.S. Treasury note
New York Futures Exchange (New York)	NYSE Composite Stock Index, NYSE Financial Stock Index, CRB Index, Russell 2000 Index, Russell 3000 Index
New York Mercantile Exchange	Crude oil, heating oil, unleaded gasoline, propane, residual fuel oil, palladium and platinum, natural gas

(continued)

TABLE 3–5 (continued)

Country and Future Exchange	Commodities, Currencies, Financial Instruments, and Stock Indexes Traded
Chicago Board of Trade	Broilers-iced, corn, oats, soybeans, soybean meal, soybean oil, wheat, crude oil, heating oil, unleaded gasoline, GNMA (cash-settled), GNMA CDR, domestic CDs, long-term municipal bond index, repurchase agreements, U.S. T-bonds, U.S. T-notes, gold, silver, plywood, Major Market Index, NASDAQ 100 index, Corporate Bond Index, Institutional Index, 30-day interest rate, CBOE 250 (traded on the Chicago Board Options Exchange), mortgage-backed securities, Topix, Japanese government bonds, three-year interest rate swaps, five-year interest rate swaps, diammonium phosphate
Chicago Mercantile Exchange	Broilers, feeder cattle, live cattle, eggs, hogs, pork bellies, lumber, SPOC Index, S&P 500 Index, S&P 100 Index, ECU, Nikkei Stock Average, U.S. dollar—Deutschemark differential, U.S. dollar—Japanese yen differential, U.S. dollar—Sterling pound differential
Chicago Rice and Cotton Exchange	Rough rice
International Monetary Market (Chicago)	German marks, Canadian dollars, Australian dollars, French francs, Swiss francs, Dutch guilders, British pounds, Mexican pesos, Japanese yen, gold, U.S. Treasury bills (1 year), certificates of deposit, Eurodollars, one-month LIBOR
Coffee, Sugar and Cocoa Exchange, Inc. (New York)	Cocoa, coffee, sugar-world, sugar-domestic, Consumer Price Index-W

TABLE 3–5 (*concluded*)

Country and Future Exchange	Commodities, Currencies, Financial Instruments, and Stock Indexes Traded
Kansas City Board of Trade	Wheat, Value Line Stock Index, Mini Value Line Stock Index, grain sorghum
Mid America Commodity Exchange Chicago	Corn, wheat, soybeans, soybean meal, oats, live cattle, live hogs, rough rice, gold, silver, platinum, Treasury bonds, Treasury notes, Treasury bills, British pounds, Canadian dollars, Japanese yen, Swiss francs, German marks
Minneapolis Grain Exchange	Wheat, sunflower seeds, corn syrup, oats
Philadelphia Board of Trade	National Over-the-Counter index, Australian dollars, British pound, Canadian dollar, French franc, Japanese yen, Swiss franc, German mark, European Currency Unit (ECU)

SOURCE: Eric F. Kirzner and John R. Dickinson, *Guide to International Investing*, CCH Canadian Limited, 6 Garamond Court, Don Mills, Ontario, 1992, para 4910.

underlying portfolio of the approximately 1700 share Value Line Composite Index. Two other index futures contracts were introduced in that same year on the Chicago Mercantile Exchange and the New York Stock Exchange. Shortly after, a derivative form of the index futures, the index option contract was introduced on the Chicago Board Options Exchange. Index put options allow the holder to sell the underlying index at a specified price (index level) up to a specified expiry date while index call options allow the holder to buy the index at a specified price up to the expiry date. Unlike index futures contracts, index options need not be exercised; if the market moves in the wrong direction the option holder simply abandons the contract, losing the initial premium paid.

The introduction of these exotic instruments has represented a most important development in investment and managerial finance, in providing a wide range of investment and hedging applications. For example, a fund manager worried about a temporary decline in the stock market can sell short index futures contracts or buy index put options to hedge his position. If the market subsequently falls, the loss on the portfolio is partially or fully offset (depending on the degree and precision of hedging undertaken) by a corresponding profit on the futures or options position. If the market rises, however, the increase in the portfolio is offset, again in full or in part, by the loss on the index product. In either case the portfolio manager has essentially temporarily locked-in the current value of the portfolio.

The index products available today range from the broad based such as the Value Line Index or the Australian All Ordinaries Share Price Index, designed to capture a complete market, to the narrow-based types such as the Toronto Futures Exchange's Oil and Gas Index tailored to represent specific market segments.

Scores of new contracts have been introduced in recent years in the United States, Australia, Bermuda, Canada, Hong Kong, Japan, the Netherlands, New Zealand, Singapore, and the United Kingdom. Some, such as the CBOE's S&P 100 option contract have been remarkably successful; others, such as the Philadelphia Stock Exchange's gaming/hotel index, dismal failures. But one thing is certain, the addition of index products has richly expanded the market and the opportunities for investors and hedgers. Table 3–6 provides a listing of these options products currently traded on world markets.

TABLE 3–6
Index Futures and Options Contracts Traded on World Markets

Australia
   ASX Securities Index—futures (Australian Stock Exchange), options on actual (ASE)
   Australian Stock Exchange All Ordinaries Share Price Index—futures (Sydney Futures Exchange) and options on futures (SFE)
Bermuda
   Baltic Freight Index—futures (International Futures Exchange (Bermuda) Limited)

TABLE 3–6 (continued)

Brazil
IBV-12 Rio de Janeiro Stock Exchange Index—futures (Brazilian Futures Exchange)
FGV-100 Stock Index—futures (Sao Paulo Commodities Exchange)
Bovespa Index—futures (Bolsa Mercantil & de Futoros)

Canada
Canadian Market Portfolio Index—options on actual (Montreal Exchange)
Toronto Stock Exchange Composite 300—futures (Toronto Futures Exchange), options on actual (Toronto Stock Exchange)
Toronto Stock Exchange 35 Index—futures (TFE), options on actual (TSE)
Toronto Stock Exchange Composite 300 Spot—futures (TFE)
Toronto Stock Exchange Oil and Gas—futures (TFE)

Denmark
KFX Index—futures (Copenhagen Stock Exchange)

Finland
Finnish Options Index—futures (Finnish Options Brokers Ltd.), options on actual (Finnish Options Brokers Ltd.)

France
CAC 40 Stock Index—futures, options on actual (Marché à Terme International de France)
OMF 50 Stock Index—futures, options on futures (OMF)

Germany
German Stock Index (DAX)—futures (Deutsche Terminborse)

Hong Kong
Hang Seng Stock Index—futures (Hong Kong Futures Exchange)

Ireland
ISEQ Index—futures (Irish Futures and Options Exchange)

Japan
Nikkei 225 Futures Index—futures (Osaka Securities Exchange)
Stock Futures 50—futures (Osaka Securities Exchange
Tokyo Stock Price Index (TOPIX)—futures (Tokyo Stock Exchange)

Netherlands
Dutch Top 5 Index—futures (Financiele Termijnmarkt)
EOE Dutch Stock Index—futures (Financiele Termijnmarkt)
EOE Stock Index—options on actual (European Options Exchange)
Eurotop 100 Index—options on futures (European Options Exchange), futures (Financiele Termijnmarkt)
Major Market Index—options on actual (European Options Exchange, fungible with the American Stock Exchange)
FTA Bullet Index—options on actual (European Options Exchange), futures (Financiele Termijnmarkt Amsterdam N.V.)
FTB Bullet Index—futures (Financiele Termijnmarkt Amsterdam N.V.)

New Zealand
Barclay's Share Index—futures (New Zealand Futures Exchange), options on actual (NZFE)

(continued)

TABLE 3–6 (continued)

Norway
   OBX Index—option on actual (Oslo Stock Exchange)
Singapore
   Nikkei Index—futures (Singapore International Monetary Exchange)
Spain
   Fiex 35 Index—futures (El Mercado de Opciones Financieras or MOFEX)
Sweden
   OMX Stock Index—options on actual (The Swedish Options Market)
   SX 16 Index—futures (Swedish Options and Futures Exchange), options
      on actual (SOFE)
Switzerland
   Swiss Market Index—futures (Swiss Options and Financial Futures
      Exchange), options on actual (SOFFEX)
United Kingdom
   Baltic Freight Index—futures (Baltic International Freight Futures
      Exchange)
   Eurotrack 100—futures (LIFFE)
   Financial Times—Stock Exchange 100—futures (London International
      Financial Futures Exchange), options on actual (London Stock
      Exchange), options on futures (LIFFE)
United States
   Airline Index—options on actual (American Stock Exchange or AMEX)
   Bond Buyer Municipal Index—futures (Chicago Board of Trade or CBOT),
      options on futures (CBOT)
   CBOE 250 Index—futures (CBOT)
   Commodity Research Bureau Futures Price Index—futures (New York
      Futures Exchange or NYFE)
   Computer Technology Index—options on actual (AMEX)
   Consumer Price Index-W—futures (Coffee, Sugar and Cocoa Exchange)
   Corporate Bond Index ($1,000 × Index)—futures (CBOT)
   Corporate Bond Index ($500 × Index)—futures (COMEX)
   Financial News Composite Index—options on actual (Pacific Stock
      Exchange)
   Gold/Silver Stock Index—options on actual (Philadelphia Stock Exchange
      or PHLX)
   Institutional Index—options on actual (AMEX), futures (CBOT)
   International Market Index—options on actual (AMEX)
   Japan Index—options on actual (AMEX)
   Major Market Index—futures (CBOT), options on actual (AMEX, CBT, and
      European Options Exchange)
   Major Market Index Maxi—futures (CBOT)
   Market Value Index—options on actual (AMEX)
   Mini Value Line Index—futures (Kansas City Board of Trade)
   NASDAQ 100—futures (CBOT), options on actual (National Association of
      Securities Dealers)

TABLE 3–6 (concluded)

National Over-the-Counter Index—futures (Philadelphia Board of Trade), options on actual (PHLX)

New York Stock Exchange Beta Index—options on actual (New York Stock Exchange or NYSE)

New York Stock Exchange Composite Index—futures (NYFE), options on futures (NYFE), options on actual (NYSE)

New York Stock Exchange Composite Double Index—options on actual (NYSE)

Nikkei Stock Average—futures (CME), options on futures (CME)

Oil Index—options on actual (AMEX)

Pacific Stock Exchange Technology Index—options on actual (Pacific Stock Exchange)

Russell 2000 Index—futures (NYFE)

Russell 3000 Index—futures (NYFE)

Standard & Poor's 500—futures (Chicago Mercantile Exchange or CME), options on futures (CME), options on actual (Chicago Board Options Exchange or CBOE)

Standard & Poor's 100—futures (CME), options on actual (CBOE)

Standard & Poor's Over-the-Counter 250 index (SPOC)—futures (CME)

Tokyo Stock Price Average (Topix)—futures (CBT), options on futures (CBT)

U.S. Dollar Index—futures (New York Cotton Exchange), options on futures (New York Cotton Exchange)

Utility Index—options on actual (PHLX)

Value Line Composite—futures (Kansas City Board of Trade), options on actual (PHLX)

New Mutual Fund Products

Over the past four decades, financial innovators have expanded the opportunities available to investors through the introduction of other new mutual fund financial products and services. These include global and international mutual funds that invest in foreign securities, specialized country mutual funds that invest in the securities of specific countries, and ethical funds that invest only in the securities of corporations that are morally and ethically acceptable to the fund managers according to a preset of criteria. During the period 1984 to mid-1987, many of the top performing mutual funds were to be found among the international and global groups. As we shall see in Chapter 7, these funds provide a practical avenue to global investing for the individual.

Templeton on Ethical Funds

NB: What do you think about the proliferation of ethical funds?
Do they constitute a useful addition to the investment world?
JT: Ethics is tremendously important in every area of human activity and especially in your personal thoughts and attitudes and
words and deeds. Investment mutual funds avoiding various companies because of ethics do perform a service to certain people,
and their growth should be encouraged.

The Trend toward the Internationalization of World Markets

A major trend of the 1980s in world markets has been the internationalization of investment markets. Stimuli have come
from two sources—national economic and political policies in-
viting foreign participation in domestic markets, and direct
market links among exchanges and bourses. Both have served
to foster and expand international investing opportunities.

From a running start earlier, several occurrences on these
fronts materialized in 1985 and momentum thus steamrolled
into 1987 and beyond. Meanwhile, in an ironic parallel development, competition among countries to become world centers
in the inevitable integration of financial markets has
intensified.

Open-Door Policies
In the 1980s a number of countries, including Australia, Norway, Portugal, South Korea, and Sweden, even China, liberal-
ized their banking laws to allow nonresidents to apply for
domestic banking licenses. Japan, in particular, and as a result
of a 1984 agreement with the United States, took a major step
forward by allowing direct participation by foreign banks in
primary Japanese government bonds, waiving the Japanese-
only rule for the 83 member Tokyo Stock Exchange, and relaxing the Euroyen bond issuance regulations, among other
things.

In an allied development, the London and Tokyo Stock Exchanges both passed amendments allowing foreigners to own or control member firms.

Market Links

Curiously enough, 1984 turned out to be the year that major deregulation and internationalization inroads were made in financial markets. Just the opposite of what Orwell would have predicted (assuming that he had an interest in financial markets). These developments point the way to the possibility of one world market, where all of the 400 or so stock, futures, and options markets are electronically linked, allowing investors and intermediaries immediate access to every security.

The Chicago Mercantile Exchange (CME) and the Singapore International Monetary Exchange (SIMEX) fashioned the first-ever futures link on September 7th, 1984, when dual trading commenced in Eurodollar and West German mark futures. The CME/SIMEX link allowed investors to purchase or sell on one exchange and offset their positions on the other, with one central clearing house for both. Other futures market links, both of which were forged in 1986, include the Commodity Exchange Inc. (COMEX) and the Sydney Futures Exchange for gold futures trading, and the London International Financial Futures Exchange (LIFFE) and Sydney Futures Exchange for linked trading in U.S. Treasury Bond futures and Eurodollar futures.

In 1984, the Montreal Exchange and the Boston Stock Exchange agreed to a two-phase link-up of their trading floors. The initial link allowed traders in Montreal to route their orders for Canadian stocks listed in the United States to the Boston Stock Exchange for execution at the best possible price. The system was expanded in 1985 to allow for automated trade routing in Montreal to be available to the Boston Stock Exchange. Similar market links have been fashioned between the American Stock Exchange and the Toronto Stock Exchange (1985), the Midwest Stock Exchange and Toronto Stock Exchange (1986). Furthermore, as of 1984 some of the major European bourses are linked to provide each other with historic price information and intermarket direct quotations. Other market links include that of the London Stock Exchange and the United States National Association of Securities Dealers (NASD) 1986 agreement to share price quotation information via their respective computerized systems.

These developments have served to change the nature of global investment opportunities. Although markets are still generally segmented and supply challenging obstacles to the international investor, the world is steadily moving, albeit slowly, toward integration.

Templeton on Market Links

EK: Lets talk about some recent developments in investment finance. For example in the last couple of years there has been a number of links between markets.

JT: Stock brokers are now members not only in America but in London and Tokyo, etc., and with the ease of transportation of information, orders can be executed on dozens of markets instantly. The world market is coming. Market makers make markets in stocks not just in North America but anywhere. For example, now Morgan Stanley has lists of market makers that are equipped to buy and sell stocks of many nations, 24 hours a day . . .

The Persistence of Inflation

One of the most important and pervasive phenomenon of the post-war years has been the increase of both inflation levels and inflation expectations. Earlier in this chapter we referred to Templeton's adaptability to changing times. Nowhere can this degree of adaptability be seen more clearly than in Templeton's unique, often articulated views on inflation. Unlike many other contemporary financial pundits, Templeton can easily remember a world in which inflation was the least of society's concerns. The Great Depression struck one year before he began working his way through Yale, in fact; and when he launched his investment career, it was the fear of deflation—inflation's opposite number—that haunted the financial community.

Templeton sensed early in his career the new economic forces that were to be fashioned by World War II. While the Depression had created an economy characterized by too much production and not enough money, the war was to bring demands for more goods and services of practically every type. There would soon come a time, Templeton reasoned, when this situation would be reversed, when there would be too much money chasing too few goods and services—prices would rise constantly as the worldwide economy struggled to catch up to its war-created needs.

It was just this reasoning that led to Templeton's first investment coup. Certain that inflation was about to make itself felt, Templeton scraped together $10,000 and bought shares of every stock he could find that were selling for $1 or less. He bought the shares of struggling companies, even bankrupt ones, the halt and the lame of the post-Depression years.

His reasoning was on target. During the next three years, he parlayed that initial $10,000 investment into a portfolio worth $40,000.

Templeton learned two lessons from the experience, and he has adhered to them ever since. First, that inflation must be viewed as a constant in the modern economic world. And second, that inflation, while it has numerous corrosive effects, can be a positive factor in a well-conceived investment strategy.

Templeton was convinced that the investor who fully understood inflation could derive a bonanza from it. "Because the price of oil rose in seven years from $1.17 to $2.82 a barrel," he said in a 1955 talk, "some oil companies that previously earned little or nothing have become most profitable." Low-grade copper mines that were unprofitable when the metal was 9 cents per pound in 1938 have become most profitable now that copper is selling for 43 cents per pound. "By careful study it may be possible to anticipate other economic areas in which such inflation may lead to similar results."

Obviously, not even Templeton at that point could foresee the extent to which inflation was to affect the oil industry 20 years later. But in 1957, when most investment professionals spoke of a 2 percent annual inflation rate as "the historic norm," Templeton advised his investment-counsel clients:

> For the proper planning of investment programs, it is essential to study inflation. It is a vast and complex subject, and in each case the causes are different and often debatable. For brevity and clarity, it is helpful to group the causes into three categories, namely: a surplus of money, a shortage of goods, and rising wages.

Surplus of money. By the operation of the law of supply and demand, whenever cash becomes excessively abundant inflation of prices is likely to result. In the histories of inflation, a surplus of cash usually was associated with government printing of a flood of currency, as was the case in the United States between 1941 and 1945, when the government sold its bonds to banks in the amount of $70 billion, causing money in the form of demand deposits to rise from $39 billion to $76 billion.

Templeton noted that a surplus of money sometimes results almost immediately in inflation, but there are times when inflation may be delayed for many years. If consumers have no urge to spend or invest their cash, for example, a surplus of cash results; but there's also a reduced turnover of funds, so inflation is slow to make itself felt.

> The most frequent cause of inflation is shortage of goods, often caused by war. There are multitudes of examples of extreme inflation based on war, such as the recent inflations of Greece, Hungary, China, and Korea.

Goods may become short, also, when a nation devotes an unusually large proportion of its resources to the construction of factories and equipment.

> This particular kind of shortage is self-correcting, because it may lead to a surplus of production facilities. The surplus of facilities not only produces more goods; it also increases competition, reduces profit margins, and discourages continuation of expenditures on still more factories and equipment.

At the end of World War II, the shortage of goods was worldwide; but those shortages gradually changed to abundance.

One industry after another shifted from a condition of shortage to a condition of surplus. "The abundance of goods (can be expected to have) a deflationary effect on prices, and especially on profit margins in the majority of industries," Templeton told his clients.

> Rising wages: The prospect for continuing inflation in the United States is not based on a surplus of money or on a shortage of goods, but rather on rising wages. Labor leaders have taught union members to expect higher and higher wages; and they compete with each other in trying to obtain maximum wage increases. Psychologically and politically, it is next to impossible to change this trend. The end is not yet in sight.
>
> Because of new inventions, automation, and more mechanical power, Americans have enjoyed a continuing increase in production per man per hour. If wage rates increased only as much as output per man-hour, then prices would not be forced up. However, the desire for higher wages is stronger than the desire for a stable cost of living. Therefore, inflation is a condition of our present society; and in the long run, the dollar will probably buy even less than it buys today.

Templeton is convinced that in this century at least one of those underlying causes of inflation will be present and active at all times. In the late 1950s, it was wages. During the "guns and butter" presidency of Lyndon B. Johnson, it was an excess of money. In the oil crisis of the 1970s, it was the suddenly disrupted supply of goods—petroleum products.

Today's crowded world pressing ahead on all fronts is far from the point where it can be fine-tuned to a level of balance. In essence, Templeton feels, human attitudes compel inflation; if only for that reason, inflation is the most reliable constant in modern economics.

A question from the floor during a 1984 meeting of Templeton mutual-fund shareholders gave rise to these impromptu inflation-related remarks from the then 72-year-old money manager:

> There have been long periods in world history when there was very little inflation. I don't think that's going to be the case again, at least not in my lifetime or yours; and the reason is

mainly the attitudes of people—or attitudes of governments that reflect the attitudes of people.

At the time that we had little inflation, there was a philosophy that government was not supposed to see to it that everyone is prosperous. Now we demand that.

And so I don't expect ever, as long as any of us lives, to see a year—even one year—of deflation.

I remember in (the Depression year of) 1932 I could say that it cost 20 percent less to live than it did three years earlier. I'd be very surprised if ever again we can say it costs even 1 percent less to live than it did in the prior year.

At that time, we had none of the built-in economic stabilizers, such as Social Security or unemployment insurance or insured bank deposits. Now we have all those things, and more; and we also have an attitude that the government is supposed to prevent deflation. As soon as we get anywhere close to deflation, the voters will demand that the government act.

Most any good economist, including some of us here, could suggest a dozen ways that the government could ward off deflation if it has the voters back of it. And when it looks like we're going to have deflation, the voters will demand that the government act, and the government will act, and the economy will reinflate.

Templeton noted in those 1984 remarks that financial analysts on his staff reexamine the status of inflation worldwide, on a nation-to-nation basis, every few months.

We do make adjustments in our opinions, and our opinions at present are that there may be one or two extraordinarily favorable years, perhaps right away, perhaps next year, in which we'll see inflation as low as 2 percent on an annualized basis.

But we also think that by 1994 there will be a bad year in which inflation will climb as high as 20 percent, averaging out over the years to about 8 percent annually—as it has done over the latest 10 years.

That's the same as saying the cost of living may double every nine years. It's also the basis for our belief that within 36 years the cost of living may reach a level 16 times what it is now.

Templeton, in those comments, limited his analysis to the United States. But, significantly for an investor who has made global markets his long suit, he noted that even at 16 times current levels, the inflation in the United States is likely to be less than it is in almost any other nation.

> And we're talking about normal conditions. If Americans should do anything foolish, such as engaging in a war or electing a socialist government, the rate of inflation would be accelerated.
>
> So what we're talking about is a minimum rate of inflation for the next 10 or 20 years—a minimum rate averaging roughly 8 percent annually.

At the core of the constancy of inflation, in Templeton's opinion, is the fact that almost all governments engage in deficit spending; they spend money they don't have. He doubts that those governmental debts will ever be repaid. Consequently, deficits will be more prevalent than surpluses; and governments will simply print more currency to provide a fool's paradise solution to their monetary problems. The money supply in those countries, therefore, will grow more than will the quantity of goods available for purchase.

"The governments of a few countries, such as the United States, West Germany, and Japan, are doing fewer things wrong, so their currencies are eroding less quickly than are currencies elsewhere," Templeton notes. "Relatively speaking, those countries are economically healthier; but the fundamental problem of governments causing their currencies to lose value is universal."

Characteristically, Templeton sees beyond that truism. To him, deficits and the inflation they bring about are investment facts of life: they are in the long run a force for higher prices in real estate and common stocks.

That Templeton and his organization have mastered the tiger of inflation is evident in Table 3–7. The Templeton Growth Fund has outpaced the U.S. rate of inflation by a factor of about 36 to 1! How Templeton and his staff have achieved this phenomenal and consistent rate of growth is the subject of the latter half of this book.

TABLE 3–7
Rates of Returns and Inflation 1955–1991

Year Ended Dec. 31	Annual Rate of Return— Templeton Growth Fund	Cumulative Total Rate of Return— Templeton Growth Fund	Annual Rate of Inflation— Consumer Price Index	Cumulative Rate of Inflation— Consumer Price Index
1955	− 7.04%	− 0.50%	0.37%	0.37%
1956	4.64	4.12	2.86	3.24
1957	−16.91	−13.49	3.02	6.36
1958	48.80	28.73	1.76	8.23
1959	14.00	46.75	1.50	9.85
1960	13.84	67.06	1.48	11.48
1961	18.29	97.62	0.67	12.23
1962	−13.52	70.91	1.22	13.60
1963	5.14	79.69	1.65	15.47
1964	28.58	131.05	1.19	16.84
1965	22.15	182.22	1.92	19.09
1966	− 5.30	167.26	3.35	23.08
1967	13.74	203.98	3.04	26.82
1968	37.76	318.75	4.72	32.80
1969	19.67	401.11	6.11	40.92
1970	− 6.44	368.84	5.49	48.66
1971	21.93	471.64	3.36	53.65
1972	68.56	863.54	3.41	58.89
1973	− 9.92	767.93	8.80	72.87
1974	−12.07	663.18	12.20	93.96
1975	37.59	950.04	7.01	107.56
1976	46.74	1440.83	4.81	117.54
1977	20.38	1754.78	6.77	132.27
1978	19.21	2111.05	9.03	153.24
1979	26.84	2704.48	13.31	186.95
1980	25.89	3530.49	12.40	222.53
1981	− 0.24	3422.01	8.94	251.37
1982	10.81	3802.65	3.87	264.96
1983	32.91	5086.87	3.80	278.83
1984	2.17	5199.35	3.95	293.80
1985	27.78	6671.77	3.77	308.64
1986	21.24	8109.82	1.13	313.26
1987	3.11	8364.78	4.41	331.49
1988	23.60	10362.19	4.42	350.56
1989	22.56	12722.50	4.65	371.51
1990	− 9.06	11561.42	6.11	400.32
1991	31.33	15214.87	3.21	416.38

SOURCE: Securities Fund Investors, Inc., internal documents and brochures, undated.

ENDNOTES

1. In recent years there has been a remarkable exodus of high profile finance professors from academia to Wall Street. The large brokerage firms obviously are attracted to the idea of having the frontier theoreticians and proven empiricists developing and validating theories in their enclave, while the academics can continue their research with the mammoth resources of the brokerage firms at their disposal. Of course, the big salaries offered by Wall Street may be a modest incentive as well!

2. Although initially presented in 1948, Markowitz's first major publication of the theory was Harry Markowitz, "Portfolio Selection," *Journal of Finance,* March 1952, pp. 77–91.

3. See William F. Sharpe, "A Simplified Model for Portfolio Analysis," *Management Science* 9 (January 1963), pp. 277–293; John Lintner, "Security Prices, Risk and Maximum Gains from Diversification," *Journal of Finance,* December 1965, pp. 587–615; Jan Mossin, "Optimal Multi-Period Portfolio Policies," *Journal of Business,* April 1968, pp. 215–229.

4. In the original form of the CAPM, the market index is supposed to be the market portfolio which contains all of the world's risky assets, both financial and real. However in both empirical testing and application, a representative index such as the Standard & Poor's 500 Composite Index is employed.

5. Stephen A. Ross, "The Arbitrage Pricing Theory of Capital Asset Pricing," *Journal of Economic Theory,* December 1976, pp. 344–360.

6. See for example: Louis Bachelier, "Theóry de la Spéculation," *Ann. Sci. Ecole Norm. Sup.,* vol. 3, no. 1018, Paris, Gauthier-Villars, 1900; Holbrook Working, "A Theory of Anticipatory Prices," *American Economic Review,* May 1958, pp. 188–199.

7. See Harry V. Roberts, "Stock Market Patterns, and Financial Analysis: Methodological Suggestions," *Journal of Finance* 14, March 1959, pp. 1–10; M.E.M. Osborne, "Brownian Motions in the Stock Market," *Operations Research* 7 (March–April 1959), pp. 145–173; Sidney A. Alexander, "Price Movements in Speculative Markets: Trends or Random Walks," *Industrial Management Review* 2 (May 1961), pp. 7–26 and "Price Movements in Speculative Markets: Trends or Random Walks, No. 2," *Industrial Management Review* 5 (Spring 1984), pp. 25–46; Eugene F. Fama,

"The Behavior Of Stock Market Prices," *Journal of Business* 38 (January 1965), pp. 34–105.

8. A filter is a strategy of buying a security and holding it until it declines $X\%$ from its highest point. When the filter is thus activated on the decline, the long position in the security is then sold and a short sale is made as well. The short position is maintained until the stock rises by $X\%$ from a subsequent low point, at which point the short position is covered and a long position established, etc. The level of the filter, the "$X\%$" can be set at various levels such as 5% or 10%. Filter strategies are based on the principle that trends once begun tend to persist. To test whether a filter works, a filter strategy for stocks and portfolios employed over various time periods is compared to a simple buy and hold strategy. If the filter works, it will outperform the simple buy and hold.

9. Some of the complex tests include serial correlation studies and runs tests. See Eugene F. Fama, "The Behavior of Stock Market Prices," *Journal of Business* 38 (January 1965), pp. 34–105; or James E. Lorie, Peter Dodd, and Mary Hamilton Kimpton, *The Stock Market: Theories and Evidence,* Richard D. Irwin, Inc., 1985, Ch. 4, pp. 55–79, for a description of these tests.

10. Sanjoy Basu, "The Investment Performance of Common Stocks in Relation to Their Price-Earnings Ratios: A Test of the Efficient Markets Hypothesis," *Journal of Finance* 32, no. 3 (June 1977), pp. 663–682.

11. Rolf W. Banz, "The Relationship Between Return and Market Value of Common Stocks," *Journal of Financial Economics* 9 (March 1981), pp. 3–18; Donald Keim, "Size Related Anomolies and Stock Return Seasonality: Further Empirical Evidence," *Journal of Financial Economics* 12 (June 1983), pp. 13–32.

12. Kenneth R. French, "Stock Returns and the Weekend Effect," *Journal of Financial Economics,* March 1980. This Day of the Week Effect has been traced as far back as 1928, and has also been identified for other markets including Canadian, Japanese, British, and Australian.

13. Marc R. Reinganum, "The Anomolous Stock Market Behavior of Small Firms in January: Empirical Tests For Tax-Loss Selling Effect," *Journal of Financial Economics* 12, no. 1 (1983), pp. 89–104; Richard Roll, "Vas ist Das?" *Journal of Portfolio Management,* Winter 1983, pp. 18–28.

14. E. O. Thorp and S. T. Kassouf, *Beat the Market: A Scientific Stock Market System,* Random House, New York, 1967.

15. Fischer Black and Myron Scholes, "The Pricing of Options and Corporate Liabilities," *Journal of Political Economy,* May–June 1973, pp. 637–654.
16. One cannot use the Black–Scholes approach or must employ major modifications and extensions when the underlying institution issuing the financial instrument is a risky firm; where the exercise of the outstanding contract affects the structure, distribution policies, and value of the underlying firm; where the distribution of the underlying asset(s) price or value is not lognormal; where there is no unique exercise price; or where there are a large number or tree of options imbedded in the security.

    The issue is particularly interesting when the provisions of an instrument allow the holder of the option to acquire a specific real or financial asset from the underlying company (other than the underlying company's common or preferred shares). In such cases one can easily visualize states of the world where the real or financial asset has substantial value but the option to acquire said asset is worthless due to the technical or real insolvency of the issuer.
17. Investors can create riskless positions in stocks, currencies, commodities, financial instruments, and stock portfolios by buying put options for their long positions and call options for short positions. The down-side risk is thus eliminated for a price, the option premium. The process is analogous to purchasing insurance.
18. With a few exceptions, actual delivery does not take place. Instead the buyers and sellers at the expiry date settle their winning and losing positions with cash.

CHAPTER 4

THE GLOBAL INVESTOR'S WORLD

THE WORLD MARKET PORTFOLIO

The concept of the world market portfolio is important in both theoretical and applied investment finance. Portfolio theory, the pivotal exposition of the value of diversification and the capital asset pricing model (CAPM), the model for pricing risky assets, both hinge on the world market portfolio. The growing trend toward globalization of world markets also means that investors can start to view the entire world, or at least major portions of it, as the eligible opportunity set for their investing.

Ibbotson et al. have provided a rough estimate of the market portfolio.[1] The 1984 total *identifiable* wealth of the investor's world (as shown in Table 4–1) amounts to about U.S. $27,000,000,000,000 (that's $27 trillion). This represents the total assets, including real estate, stocks and bonds, and monetary metals (gold and silver) that one can trade in 20 major industrialized countries outside the former socialist bloc. The authors carefully point out that they haven't really measured the wealth of the world; but instead have presented market values and returns for asset classes that make up a large part of that wealth.

The great preponderance of world wealth still resides in its land; real estate represents by far the greatest arena for investment. By comparison, stocks at some U.S. $3.2 trillion represents a relatively modest amount. Metals holdings, including gold and other precious metals, is a mere 932 billion or 3.4% of the world portfolio of assets.

TABLE 4–1
The World Market Portfolio—Total World Wealth as of
December 31, 1984

Asset	Dollar Value (U.S.$ Billions)	Percentage
Real Estate*	$15,177.9	54.8%
Durable goods	3,479.2	12.6
Equities	3,214.4	11.6
Fixed income	3,692.1	13.3
Metals	932.0	3.4
Cash	776.8	2.8
Crossborder bonds	365.5	1.3
Convertible bonds	22.5	0.1
Venture capital	16.3	0.1
Art	3.8	0.0
Total	$27,680.5**	100.0%

*Estimate only
**Total slightly different to Ibbotson et. al., due to rounding

SOURCE: Roger G. Ibbotson, Laurence B. Siegal, and Kathryn S. Love, "World Wealth: Market Values and Returns," *The Journal of Portfolio Management,* Fall 1985, p. 6.

Still, as investment media, stocks and bonds have proven to provide the best opportunity for a manager to apply his expertise. Real estate is fixed and relatively illiquid. Gold and silver are subject to sudden and vicious price swings on unpredictable events. Stocks and bonds yield far better to analysis, comparision, and study than other assets. That is why Templeton has concentrated the majority of his efforts on this slice of the great world pie.

The global investor in stocks actually deals with relatively few of the world's nations. Private investors faced with limited resources can at best become expert on two, possibly three, countries. Even the globally minded institutional investors tend to concentrate on a small sample from the vast universe of securities and markets. Many markets are just too small, too illiquid, or indeed too imponderable. And many are either blocked or restricted to nonresident investors.

Templeton described the nature of international investing to us in one of our early sessions at his home in Lyford Cay, in

Nassau. Relaxing in his customary spot at the right side of the drawing room sofa, Templeton pointed out that:

> Of the 163 members of the United Nations there are no more than four dozen that can claim to be open, active markets. The others present enormous problems to outside investors. They are so unreliable or so undeveloped that it's just obvious that you couldn't invest prudently in actively traded stocks or bonds. Who would want to invest in the Soviet Union? Who would want to invest in Uganda? Who would want to invest in Ethiopia or Iran, for that matter?
>
> After you get through scratching off all these places, there are only about four dozen countries where practical opportunities exist.

But even those four dozen represent a challenge to the outsider. The Templeton organization has traditionally invested heavily in the stocks of companies of only about 12 countries. However, this is changing. The Templeton network is expanding its operations and investment opportunity horizons. Recognizing the bargains that exist in some of the smaller, lesser-developed markets, the Templeton team is now studying intensively many more markets in a wide range of countries.[2]

The reason for the somewhat restricted span of nations utilized by even the most experienced global investors is the complexity of learning enough about any country to feel confident about the profitable opportunities that can be found there.

Templeton, by now warming to the task of describing the complexity of the global investment world, began to talk in his precise and curiously unemotional manner.

> We have many chartered financial analysts and a staff of excellent people, and over the course of decades we have managed to achieve enough knowledge about 12 countries that we feel comfortable investing in them. Now, we are studying 3 dozen new countries, but the process of understanding a country as an investor is painstaking and time consuming.
>
> Consider all the things you need to know about a country before you can accurately access what's going to happen there.

The Global Trader

The 1980s have represented the watershed for global investing. The deregulation of many of the major capital markets, such as the United Kingdom's "Big Bang" of 1986 and Canada's "Little Bang" in 1987;[3] the internationalization of securities such as Euroyen bonds; the expansion of electronic trading systems; and market links between selected equity, futures, and options markets have moved us closer to the day of pure global trading with limited barriers.

The expansion of world markets now allows traders to participate in some markets on a 24-hour basis. Market links[4] such as those fashioned in the 1984–1986 period between the Boston Stock Exchange and the Montreal Exchange, the Toronto Stock Exchange and the Midwest Stock Exchange (of Chicago) and the Toronto Stock Exchange and American Stock Exchange for equities trading, the pathbreaking Chicago Mercantile Exchange and Singapore International Monetary Exchange link for Eurodollar, West German mark and gold futures trading and the International Options Clearing Corporation Montreal Exchange, Vancouver Stock Exchange, Amsterdam Stock Exchange and Sydney Stock Exchange for gold and currency options trading, now allows investors to place orders overnight for execution while they sleep. Sophisticated electronic trading systems and networks provide global traders with quick—sometimes instant—access to markets that were previously hours or days away through telecommunication devices. Certainly, in the world of financial investment, the borders are rapidly shrinking. The global trader will find Table 4–2, which provides simultaneous trading times for the major world equity markets, useful.

Finally, numerous market indexes of world market performance have been developed and introduced to echo this trend toward global trading. The most widely followed index of international equity market performance is the Morgan Stanley Capital International World Index of returns for 20 countries. The index is calculated as weighted average of total returns (change in index levels plus dividends) and is compiled

TABLE 4–2
Trading Times for Major World Markets

				When the Exchange Opens in . . .				
The Time in—Is	NY/to/Mntrl[1]	Lond[2]	Tokyo[3]	Sydney[4]	LA[5]	Ger[6]	Fr/Ams/ It/Swiss[7]	HK[8]
New York/Montreal/ Toronto	09:30	04:30	19:00p	19:00p	09:15	05:30	04:00	21:00p
London	14:30	09:30	00:00	00:00	14:15	10:30	09:00	02:00
Tokyo	23:30	19:30	10:00	10:00	23:15	19:30	18:00	11:00
Sydney	00:30n	19:30	10:00	10:00	00:15n	20:30	19:00	12:00
Los Angeles	06:00	01:30	16:00p	16:00p	06:15	02:30	01:00	18:00p
Germany	15:30	10:30	01:00	01:00	15:15	11:30	10:00	03:00
France/Amsterdam/ Italy/Switzerland	15:30	10:30	01:00	01:00	15:15	11:30	10:00	03:00
Hong Kong	22:30	17:30	08:00	08:00	22:15	18:30	17:00	10:00

Notes: n = next day; p = previous day
[1]New York Stock Exchange, Toronto Stock Exchange, Montreal Exchange
[2](London) Stock Exchange
[3]Tokyo Stock Exchange
[4]Sydney Stock Exchange
[5]Pacific Stock Exchange
[6]Frankfurt Stock Exchange
[7]Paris Stock Exchange, Amsterdam Stock Exchange, Milan Stock Exchange, Zurich Stock Exchange
[8](Hong Kong) Unified Exchange

Source: Eric F. Kirzner and John Dickinson, *Guide to International Investing*, CCH Canadian Limited, 6 Garamond Court, Don Mills, Ontario, 1992, para 4561.

and published in British pounds, U.S. dollars, and local currencies. A sub-index comprised of Europe, Australia, and the Far East (the EAFE) is also published. Countries included in the index, and their approximate weighting are shown in Table 4–3.

Other indexes of world equity market performance include, the Salomon Brothers, Inc. *Salomon Russell Global Equity Index* (tracking about $3.565 trillion of equities) launched

TABLE 4–3
Country Weights in Morgan Stanley Capital International World Index

Country	Weight	
	MSCI World Index	Europe, Australia, Far East Index
North America		
United States	37.8%	—
Canada	2.6	—
Europe		
Austria	0.3	0.5
Belgium	0.7	1.2
Denmark	0.5	0.8
Finland	0.2	0.3
France	3.4	5.8
Germany	3.9	6.5
Italy	1.3	2.2
Netherlands	1.7	2.9
Norway	0.2	0.3
Spain	1.2	2.0
Sweden	0.9	1.5
Switzerland	2.0	3.3
United Kingdom	10.7	18.0
Pacific Basin		
Australia	1.6	2.7
Hong Kong	1.1	1.9
Japan	28.9	48.7
New Zealand	0.1	0.2
Singapore/Malaysia	0.7	1.2
Other		
South Africa	0.2	—

SOURCE: Market coverage of Morgan Stanley International Indices, *Morgan Stanley Capital International Perspective,* December 1991, Geneva Switzerland, page 5.

in 1987; First Boston Corp. and Euromoney's *Global Index* of 17 markets published in *Euromoney* magazine; and the Goldman, Sachs & Co., Wood MacKenzie & Co., and the Financial times *FT-Actuaries World Indices* published in the *Financial Times* (London).

Templeton points out that although it is educational and interesting to talk about world wealth and world markets, they really are only statistical collections. Although he views favorably moves toward market integration he believes that the task of bargain hunting still remains paramount.

> One of the first concepts to understand about global investing is that the so-called world market for stocks is actually nothing but a collection of various isolated markets with little interdependence. An investor doesn't buy stocks on the world exchange. He buys only in a particular market and the factors that drive that market, that determine the prices of stocks listed there, are almost always peculiar to the environment. There are no worldwide rules and few trends or events that impact in the same manner and degree across the Earth's exchanges.

> As professional investors, we are constantly exploring new markets but we will only enter them after what we consider sufficient study and thought. That should be true for any prudent global investor. The complexity of global investing has limited its appeal until the past few years, when the greater general level of knowledge about other countries has made having investments in them seem less unsettling. Still, the total amount of American money that is invested on a global basis remains less than 5% of American total national investment in stocks. The concept of global investing has become much better known and much more popular in America than ever before, but is still just beginning to achieve its potential.

> The task for the global investor is to educate himself so well in the structure, style and tendencies of several markets that he can accurately gauge the impact of events on share prices in those places. Then, the question becomes, *where does the greatest bargain lie?*

> You have money to invest and you want to receive greatest possible value for it. Where on Earth can that be found? You use yardsticks to compare companies in these different markets, which really don't have much in common at all. For example, you might look to see where in the world can you buy the most

book value for your money? But using your knowledge of international information sources you can find quickly that $1 of book value in Mexico costs only 62 cents. To buy a dollar of book value in Japan, however, you have to pay $3.27. Or you could choose another basis for comparison. How about cash income? Where can you buy the most cash flow for your purchase price? It turns out that for $1.00 you can buy one quarter of a dollar worth of annual cash in Mexico. In Austria, however, it would take $6.00 to get that much yearly cash return. Your dollar will buy six times as much in Mexico as it does in Austria. And you can do the same thing with earnings, and dividends and many other yardsticks of values. Then you can do the same process with industries. You can see where you can buy the most earnings for each dollar you pay in terms of industries. One of my information reports shows that you can buy a gold mine for relatively little money per dollar earned, whereas in shipping you'd pay a lot per earned dollar. That's one of the ways you use information to be successful in world investment.

Underlying this intellectual exploration, however, must be a bedrock of hard facts about the life and times of the countries whose markets you are dealing with. The numbers don't exist in a vacuum. The global investor must see the world not only in terms of p/e ratios and dividends, but as the teeming, turbulent planet-sized village that it is. Often, the root of global investment opportunity lies in understanding the course of world events, rather than just fixating on purely investment oriented issues.

Before you can do an adequate job investing in, say, Mexico, you have to find out what's going on in Mexico. And when you look at this particular country, you see that there are tremendous problems. Because the price of oil has gone down, and three quarters of their exports are oil, the country is suffering. So sometimes you might say, because of what's going on in the world right now, I'd pass up Mexico. I'd have to have prices of better value in order to put money in Mexico because of the state of the place. So, you have to understand what's going on in a nation, you have to understand politics.

You also have to understand the attitudes of the people. Are they socialists? Are they thrifty, are they spendthrifts? Are they feeling optimistic or depressed? Why? Do they want to work hard? Are they facing grave social problems?

Armed with all of this knowledge you can make an intelligent decision about the value of any global investment opportunity. That is a daunting challenge, and the reason why global investment is really the preserve of professionals, not an arena for the amateur dabblers.

Still, even an investor who has a professional manager for global investments, or who participates in a global mutual fund (both of which options we will discuss in more detail in Chapters 7 and 8) should have a general sense of the markets that are available.

Here then is a very brief tour of the global investor's world. As John Templeton notes: "It would, literally, take an entire book on each of these markets to even scratch the surface of how they really work, what their peculiarities are. No one can become an expert on a foreign market by reading a few paragraphs about it." These sketches of different markets should be seen in the light of that understanding. They are interesting and can raise our general level of awareness about global markets, but they can't provide enough detail to be of much practical use. You will need to follow up the information provided here and devote much time and study to any market you genuinely want to understand.

MAJOR EQUITY MARKETS

To get a sense of the information Templeton analysts look for in global markets, here are brief synopses of key factors affecting seven major equity markets.

Australia

Introduction
There are six stock exchanges in Australia, all of which are members of the Australian Association of Stock Exchanges, a central governing body. The largest markets in trading volume are the Stock Exchange of Melbourne and the Sydney Stock Exchange, while the Adelaide Stock Exchange, the Stock Exchange of Perth, the Brisbane Stock Exchange, and the Hobart Stock Exchange are primarily regional in nature. However,

any Australian listed security, regardless of home exchange, can be traded on all six exchanges.

The Australian equity market is known primarily for its concentration of mining stocks, which comprise about one third of the approximately 1,130 companies listed on the six exchanges. For the 12 months ended March 1986, average daily trading volume was 68,000,000 shares, valued at U.S.$76,000,000 (at an exchange rate of U.S.$.735 to A$1.00) and total market capitalization was U.S. $85,000,000,000 as at March 31, 1986.

The Stock Exchange of Perth also maintains a market for junior companies. This "second board market" is aimed at companies that have a minimum issued capital of A$100,000 but which cannot meet the more stringent listing requirements of the Exchange.

Trading Process

Securities trading on the Australian exchanges is by continuous auction using a trading post system. Securities of relatively homogenous nature are listed and quoted at specific trading posts where consecutive buy and sell orders are maintained by stock exchange officials through manual board chalkings. Trading on the floor is direct and between brokers without intermediaries.

There are two daily trading sessions, five days a week from 10:00–12:15 and 14:00–15:00. The Stock Exchange of Perth has an additional trading session from 16:30–17:30. Traders are allowed to make "off-room" trades when the exchanges are officially closed.

As at April 7, 1986, short selling of securities (which had been banned in 1971) is allowed on Australian Stock Exchanges. Short sales must be made on an up-tick and only "approved securities," as designated from time to time by the regulatory body, are eligible for short selling. A number of other limitations constrain the practice.[5]

Transaction Costs

As at April 2, 1984, brokerage fees are negotiated. Most brokerage firms still use the pre-April 2, 1984, Australian Associated Stock Exchange commission schedule as the base for determining actual trading fees.

The schedule is shown below:

A$5.00 plus

On the first A$5,000 of consideration	2.5%
On the next A$10,000 of consideration	2.0
On the next A$35,000 of consideration	1.5
On the next A$200,000 of consideration	1.0
On the next A$250,000 of consideration	.75
On the amount exceeding A$500,000	.50

Minimum commissions are typically A$25 to $40 (A$15 to A$20 for trades of A$500 or less). A .30% contract stamp tax is charged on transactions as well.

Settlement and Delivery
Settlement and delivery are normally five days from the date posted on the contract note evidencing the trade. Ten days' settlement is occasionally allowed. The proceeds from the sale of securities are not paid by the brokerage firm until signed transfer forms and the share certificates are received by the firm.

Restrictions on Nonresidents
Nonresidents may freely purchase up to 15% of the issued shares or the voting rights of Australian corporations. Approval from the Foreign Investment Review Board is necessary if a nonresident wishes to exceed this upper boundary.[6]

Interest and dividend income and the proceeds from the sale of securities in Australia may be repatriated by nonresidents, subject to the approval of the Reserve Bank of Australia, which administers the foreign exchange control. Such approval is normally freely granted.

Interest income earned by nonresidents is subject to a 10% flat withholding tax. Dividend income earned by nonresidents is subject to a 30% withholding tax; where reciprocal taxation exists, the rate is 15%.[7]

Security and Market Peculiarities

Australia is one of the few countries that allows trading in partly paid or contributing shares in which the full issue price has not been fully paid by the holder for value. If the common shares are issued by limited liability companies, the shareholder will be required to pay the deficiency when called by the company; for no-liability shares the shareholder may forfeit his ownership if the shares' deficiency is called.[8]

Deferred dividend shares are also issued by Australian companies. These unusual securities, *temporarily* rank junior to ordinary common shares on distributions, and do not pay dividends until a specified future date.

Futures and Derivative Markets

Stocks, precious metal (internationally linked with the Montreal Exchange and Vancouver Stock Exchange of Canada, and the European Options Exchange of the Netherlands), index, interest rate and currency options contracts are traded on the Sydney Stock Exchange and the Sydney Futures Exchange.

The All-Ordinaries Share Price Index, bank bills, fat lamb, gold, greasy wool, silver, trade steers, treasury bond, Eurodollar, and U.S. dollar futures contracts are traded on the Sydney Futures Exchange. Individual futures contract for delivery of 10,000 ordinary shares are traded on the Australian Financial Futures Exchange. These are unique in world markets.

Belgium

Introduction

There are four stock exchanges in Belgium located in Antwerp, Brussels, Gent, and Liège. The Brussels Stock Exchange is by far the largest, handling well over 90% of market transactions. The three others are regional in nature.

The Brussels Stock Exchange has a relatively high concentration of financial companies, utilities, and petroleum producers. Petrofina alone accounts for over 10% of stock market capitalization. Annual average daily trading volume is about

Bfr 600 million and total market capitalization was over Bfr 1 trillion as at 1985.

In addition to the main or official market, equities are also traded on the "second market" (established in 1985) and the unlisted securities market. The second market is aimed at companies that have a relatively short public trading history (less than five years), and who cannot meet the more stringent listing requirements of the Exchange. The unlisted securities market is a principals market dominated by institutional trading.

Trading Process

Securities trading on the Belgium exchanges is by discontinuous auction using a European call or quotation system. There are two trading processes, the cash market used primarily by domestic retail traders and the institutionally dominated forward market.

On the cash market, trading is constrained by daily price limits of 10% on the ring market and 5% on the floor market. Actively traded securities are traded on the ring market where a number of calls or quotations will take place during a single trading day. Less actively traded securities are traded on the floor market where only one auction-determined call is made per session.

The forward market is the more active of the two. Most major companies' stocks are listed here (as well as the cash market), with the exception of banks and financial institutions. Virtually all international and institutional trading takes place here. There are no daily price limits, although Exchange officials have the power to intervene in the event of excessive stock volatility. Trading on the floor is direct and between brokers without intermediaries. There is one daily trading session on the each of the four exchanges, five days a week from 11:30–14:30.

Margin trading is allowed on the forward market. Minimum margin requirements are set at 25%; however the Exchange can set higher minima for selected issues.

Transaction Costs

Brokerage fees are negotiated on the unlisted securities market. On the official market transaction costs are as follows:

Cash Market
A. Bfr 100 plus
B. For securities trading at Bfr 600 or less:
Up to a transaction size of Bfr 2,000,000

Stock price	Commission
Bfr 1 to 15	10%
Bfr 16 to 100	Bfr 1.50 per share
Bfr 101 to 200	Bfr 2.00 per share
Bfr 201 to 400	Bfr 4.00 per share
Bfr 401 to 600	Bfr 6.00 per share

For securities trading above Brf 600

Transaction size	Fee
Up to Bfr 2 million	1.00%
Bfr 2 to 5 million	.90%
Bfr 5 to 10 million	.80%
Above Bfr 10 million	.60%

Minimum commissions are Bfr 40. Maximum commissions are 10% for stocks at or below Bfr 600 and 6% for stocks above Bfr 600.

Additional fees are
.35% contract stamp tax is charged on all transactions
.04% for handling orders
.025% for acceptance of orders

Forward Market

Transaction size	Commission
Up to Bfr 5 million	.80%
Bfr 5 to 10 million	.60%
Above Bfr 10 million	.50%

Additional fees are:

.17% contract stamp tax on all transactions

.04% for handling orders

.025% for acceptance of orders

Settlement and Delivery

Settlement and delivery on the cash market are normally five days from the date posted on the contract note evidencing the trade. Ten days' settlement is occasionally allowed. The proceeds from the sale of securities are not paid by the brokerage firm until signed transfer forms and the share certificates are received by the firm. Settlement on the cash market is twice monthly.

Restrictions on Nonresidents

Nonresidents may freely purchase Belgian equities. Interest and dividend income and the proceeds from the sale of securities in Belgium may be repatriated by nonresidents.

Interest income earned by nonresidents is subject to a 20% withholding tax, which is reduced for countries with reciprocal tax treaties. Dividend income earned by nonresidents is subject to a 20% withholding tax; where reciprocal taxation exists, the rate is 5–18%. The rate for U.S. residents is 15%.

Security and Market Peculiarities

Shares in Belgium, with one exception,[9] are issued in bearer form only. A shareholder who wishes to vote his shares at an annual meeting must deposit and register the shares in advance.

Canada

Introduction

There are five stock exchanges in Canada. The Toronto Stock Exchange (TSE) is the largest in terms of dollar trading volume, while the Vancouver Stock Exchange leads in share volume. The Montreal Exchange is an important market as well, with an aggressive policy of pursuing international listings.

The two other exchanges are regional in nature and unlikely to be of interest to foreign investors.

The Canadian equity market has a large number of natural resource and mining companies' stocks traded on the five exchanges. For the 12 months ended December 1986, trading volume was 9.9 billion shares, valued at C$84.6 billion.

There is an active over-the-counter market in Canada, recently (April 1986) augmented by the introduction of the Canadian Over-the-Counter Automated Trading System (COATS).

Trading Process
Securities trading on the Canadian exchanges is by continuous auction using a trading post system. Securities of relatively homogenous nature are listed and quoted at specific trading posts where consecutive buy and sell orders are maintained by stock exchange officials throughout the trading day. The manual trading system is augmented by automated trading. The TSE in 1977 pioneered the world's first fully automated trading system, the Computer Assisted Trading System (CATS) which allows for direct access and execution of trades on the TSE trading floor through remote computer terminals. The system now accounts for over 20% of TSE trades, and can be used for over 800 of the securities listed for trading on the TSE. CATS is also used on the Paris Stock Exchange.

The TSE has a linked trading system with both the Midwest and American Stock Exchanges of the United States.

Trading on the TSE and the Montreal Exchange takes place five days a week from 9:30–16:00, Monday through Friday.

Margin trading is allowed on all exchanges. Minimum margin requirements are set at 50%; however the Exchange can set higher minima for selected issues.

Transaction Costs
As at April 1983, brokerage fees are negotiated. Many brokerage firms still use the pre-April 1983, commission schedule as the base for determining actual trading fees.

Typical commissions are 2–3% of the value of the order for trades of $5,000 or less and ¼–1½% for larger trades.

Settlement and Delivery

Settlement and delivery are normally five days from the date posted on the contract note evidencing the trade.

Restrictions on Nonresidents

Nonresidents may invest freely in Canadian securities subject to restrictions under which limits are placed on nonresident holdings of Canadian oil and gas stocks, banks, broadcasting companies, and investment dealer firms.

Interest and dividend income and the proceeds from the sale of securities in Canada may be repatriated by non-residents.

Interest income earned by nonresidents is subject to a 10% flat withholding tax. Dividend income earned by nonresidents is subject to a 30% withholding tax. Where reciprocal taxation exists, the rate is 15%.[10]

Security and Market Peculiarities

Considerable financial innovation takes place in Canada. Commodity-denominated warrants, preferred shares and bonds are available as well as other exotics such as auction preferred shares and piggyback warrants.

A wide range of futures and derivative instruments are traded on Canadian markets, including the TSE 35 Index futures and options contracts. The TSE 35 Index was introduced in 1987 for the sole purpose of providing for trading in the underlying futures and options contracts.

Futures and Derivative Markets

Stocks, precious metal (internationally linked with the Sydney Stock Exchange and the European Options Exchange of the Netherlands), index, interest rate and currency options contracts are traded on the Toronto Futures Exchange, the Montreal Exchange, the Vancouver Stock Exchange, and the Toronto Stock Exchange.

The TSE 300 Composite Index, the TSE 35 Index, lumber, gold, and a number of grain futures are traded on Canadian futures exchanges.

France

Introduction

There are seven stock exchanges in France, the international Paris Bourse, and the regional exchanges in Bordeaux, Lille, Lyons, Marseille, Nancy, and Nantes.

There are three markets on the Paris Bourse, the official list, the second market, and the over-the-counter market. Annual trading volume is about Ffr 61.2 billion and total market capitalization was Ffr 2162 billion as at December 31, 1985.

The Paris Bourse also maintains a market for junior and medium sized companies. This *Second Marché* is aimed at companies that have a minimum issued capital but which cannot meet the more stringent listing requirements of the official list.

Trading Process

Securities trading on the French exchanges is both complex and antiquated.[11] On the *cote officielle*, or the official list, there are two methods employed, one for the cash market and one for the forward market. On the cash market, listed securities are allocated into groups and specific groups are allocated to specific brokers. Orders to buy and sell are placed in compartments or pidgeon-holes located behind the broker's section of the floor. The broker then summarizes the orders and fixes a price that best satisfies supply and demand.

On the forward market, securities are traded *a la crieé* where the securities are divided into groups in which a public or oral auction is held in a predetermined and iterative manner. A price is thus set that best equates supply and demand for each security in turn, and this is deemed to be the first price of the day. The arrival of new orders after this first price is set results in a second auction conducted in a similar manner. There are two daily trading sessions on the Paris Bourse, five days a week, from 10:00–11:30 and 12:30–14:30. An additional session is held for foreign trading in foreign securities on the forward market from 15:00–16:00 in May through October and 16:00–17:00 in November through April.

Transaction Costs
As of July 1986, commission rates are negotiated. Prior to then, commissions were charged on a fixed schedule from .215% to .75%, based on volume and market location. A stamp duty of .15% to .30% is charged on all transactions.

Settlement and Delivery
Transactions on the cash market are settled after each trading session. Forward market transactions are settled monthly by both buyers and sellers.

Restrictions on Nonresidents
Nonresidents may freely purchase up to 20% of the issued shares or the voting rights of French corporations. Approval from the Ministry of Economy is necessary if a nonresident wishes to exceed this upper boundary.

Interest and dividend income and the proceeds from the sale of securities in France may be freely repatriated by non-residents, subject in some cases to the approval of the Bank of France.

Interest and dividend income earned by nonresidents is subject to a 25% flat withholding tax.[12]

Security and Market Peculiarities
Innovative securities including bonds denominated in railway tickets, and gold denominated bonds have been issued in France.

Futures and Derivative Markets
Long-term government bond and 90 day T-bill futures contracts are traded on the Paris Bourse (Matif).

Japan

Introduction
There are eight stock exchanges in Japan. Tokyo and Osaka are the largest markets in trading volume, while the six others are regional in nature handling in the aggregate only about 4% of securities trading.

The Japanese equity market is highly developed. The Tokyo Stock Exchange is as large as the New York Stock Exchange in trading volume, and also ranks with New York and London as the world's most widely followed markets. There are approximately 1,475 companies listed on the Tokyo Stock Exchange. Daily trading volume has averaged about 420,000,000 shares in recent years, and total market capitalization was ¥190,127 billion as of December 1985.

Trading Process
Securities trading on the Japanese exchanges is by continuous auction using the *Zaraba method,* under which the lowest offerings and the highest bids are filled first, with priority of receipt of order honored. Initial prices are determined by the *Iyatose method,* where the opening price is the one that theoretically clears the most orders. Securities on the Tokyo Stock Exchange are divided into three trading floors: first section (largest companies), second section (smaller and new companies), and third section (foreign companies). All stocks listed for trading are subject to daily price limits which constrain the amount by which the security can rise or fall relative to the previous day's closing price.

There are two daily trading sessions on the Tokyo and Osaka Stock Exchanges, five days a week, from 9:00–11:00 and 13:00–15:00. A morning session is held on Saturday as well, except for the third Saturday of the month.

Transaction Costs
Transaction costs are fixed although the schedule is changed from time to time. Transaction costs as of June 1986 are listed in Table 4–4.

Settlement and Delivery
Settlement and delivery are normally three days from the date posted on the contract note evidencing the trade.

Restrictions on Nonresidents
Nonresident foreign investors must appoint a resident of Japan to act as a proxy on his or her behalf. Foreigners may freely

TABLE 4–4
Japanese Equity Brokerage Commission Schedule (Stocks, Warrants, and Subscription Rights as of June 1986)

Trading Value	Commission in Percentage of Trading Value
Up to ¥1 million	1.25%
Over ¥1 million and up to ¥3 million	1.05% + ¥2,000
Over ¥3 million and up to ¥5 million	0.95% + ¥5,000
Over ¥5 million and up to ¥10 million	0.85% + ¥10,000
Over ¥10 million and up to ¥30 million	0.70% + ¥25,000
Over ¥30 million and up to ¥50 million	0.50% + ¥85,000
Over ¥50 million and up to ¥100 million	0.30% + ¥185,000
Over ¥100 million and up to ¥500 million	0.25% + ¥235,000
Over ¥500 million and up to ¥1 billion	0.20% + ¥485,000
Over ¥1 billion	0.15% + ¥985,000

Note: Commission on trading value less than 200,000 yen is fixed at 2,500 yen.
  The schedule applies to preferred stocks and foreign stocks as well.
  If a nonresident sells Japanese equities to a Japanese resident there is a transfer tax of .55% of the value of the trade, levied on the nonresident.

SOURCE: Eric F. Kirzner and John R. Dickinson, *Guide to International Investing*, CCH Canadian Limited, 6 Garamond Court, Don Mills, Ontario, 1991, para 71,980.

trade Japanese securities subject to the restriction that the total nonresident stockholdings of designated companies of eleven strategic industries is limited to an aggregate of 25%.

Interest and dividend income and the proceeds from the sale of securities in Japan may be repatriated by nonresidents.

Interest and dividend income earned by nonresidents is subject to a 20% flat withholding tax.[13]

Security and Market Peculiarities

Japanese securities over the past several years have sold at much higher price/earnings multiples than North American and European securities, reflecting in the main, different securities analysis emphasis plus differential accounting practices.

Futures and Derivative Markets

Although there are scores of futures markets available for commercial interests the only contracts of interest to traders are the 10-year Treasury bond futures traded on the Tokyo Stock Exchange.

Switzerland

Introduction

Switzerland has seven stock exchanges, of which the Zurich, Basel, and Geneva Exchanges account for the bulk of securities trading. The other four are regional in nature.

The Swiss equity market, reflecting Switzerland's banking and global orientation, has a high percentage of bank shares and foreign companies listed for trading. The shares of approximately 315 companies are listed on the seven exchanges. Trading volume was about Sfr 452 billion in 1985, and total market capitalization was Sfr 169 billion as at December 31, 1985.

Listed securities need not be traded on the floor of an exchange, but may instead be transacted over-the-counter. The three major Swiss bourses are linked by an electronic information system and investors automatically receive the best available price on the three exchanges for their trades.

Trading Process

Securities trading on the Swiss exchanges is by continuous quotation with intervention by open outcry among the member/dealers. Trading, with the exception of certain designated companies,[14] follows a process where each stock is called in turn by a stock exchange clerk and an auction is conducted until interest subsides. Shares are thus read out in order and traded twice a day. The first 15 minutes of the auction are subject to price limits and market restrictions; after that trading is unrestricted.

For the actively traded designated companies, continuous trading without clerk intervention is conducted.

Trading takes place five days a week from 10:15–13:00.

Transaction Costs
Transaction costs are fixed per the schedule below:

Price per share	Commission
Equal to or less than Sfr150	1% of the value of the transaction
More than Sfr150	.625% of the value of the transaction

In addition there is a federal stamp duty of .09% (.165% for foreign shares) and a .15% Cantonal stamp duty charged on the total value of the transaction.

Settlement and Delivery
Settlement and delivery are normally for cash on the next business day following the transaction.[15] The proceeds from the sale of securities are not paid by the brokerage firm until signed transfer forms and the share certificates are received by the firm.

Restrictions on Nonresidents
Nonresidents may freely purchase Swiss shares subject to the restriction that purchases of shares in Swiss real estate companies require Cantonal permission.

Interest and dividend income and the proceeds from the sale of securities in Switzerland may be repatriated by nonresidents.

Interest and dividend income earned by nonresidents is subject to a 35% flat withholding tax. Where reciprocal taxation exists, the rate is reduced.[16]

Security and Market Peculiarities
Swiss stocks are available in both bearer and registered form; however only the bearer form is available to nonresidents.

In 1986, the Basel Stock Exchange, the eighth largest in the world in terms of trading volume, moved to a new trading floor which represents state-of-the-art electronic trading, including both dual trading rings to allow simultaneous trading in both Swiss and foreign securities and an electronic screen that displays continuous quotations for all major world equity markets.

United Kingdom

Introduction
Of the 13 stock exchanges in the United Kingdom, only the London Stock Exchange is of interest to nonresident investors. The others are both small and regional in nature. There is also an unlisted securities market, established in 1980 for companies that cannot meet the more stringent requirements of the London Stock Exchange.

The London Stock Exchange is the third largest in the world in terms of trading volume. Approximately 2,700 companies are listed on the Exchange of which the majority are industrial and commercial concerns. Total market capitalization was Bp 1,152 billion as at November 1986.

Trading Process
Securities trading on the London Stock Exchange is conducted by market makers who may act as either principal or agent in their dealings but are responsible for maintaining markets in designated securities. Each of these market makers (31 as of April 1987) are required to maintain markets in one or more securities and to provide continuous quotations into the Stock Exchanges Automated Quotation System (SEAQ) and firm bid and ask prices for both the actively traded "alpha" stocks and the less active "beta" stocks. Stockbrokers act as agents only transacting on behalf of clients for a commission. Although they are not required to trade through market makers they must seek the best price for clients[17] and may take the opposite side of a client's trade as long as they disclose their position.

Transaction Costs
Transaction costs are negotiated as at October 27, 1986. Prior to that time, the commission schedule was as listed in Table 4–5.

TABLE 4–5
Transaction Costs in the U.K. Prior to October 27, 1986

Transaction		Commission
First BP	7,000	1.65%
Next	8,000	.55%
Next	115,000	.50%
Next	170,000	.40%
Next	600,000	.30%
Next	1,000,000	.20%
Excess	1,000,000	.125%

There is also a contract note fee on trades charged as follows:

Transaction	Contract Fee
Less than BP 100	Nil
BP 100 to BP 500	12p
BP 500 to BP 1500	30p
More than BP 1500	60p

Nonresidents also pay a stamp duty of .5% of the value of the contract on the purchase of equities.

Many of the transactions on the London Stock Exchange are "net," i.e., no commissions. However, the shares are traded on a spread basis between the bid and ask and the differential represents the market maker's profit and the client's cost. There is no value-added tax (VAT) on the spread.

Commissions on large trades currently average about .20%.

SOURCE: Eric F. Kirzner and John R. Dickinson, *Guide to International Investing*, CCH Canadian Limited, 6 Garamond Court, Don Mills, Ontario, 1991, para 73,035.

Settlement and Delivery
Stocks are settled by an account settlement procedure, by which the trading year is divided into accounts typically consisting of 14 business days each. Trades during the account period are settled on the "account day," which is normally 10 days after the end of the account period.

Restrictions on Nonresidents
Nonresident foreign investors are free to trade U.K. securities subject to the restrictions that nonresidents (including a group acting in concert) must make disclosure on holdings in excess of 5% in any company, a public announcement on holdings in

excess of 15% and an offer for the remainder of the company's shares on holdings in excess of 30%. Interest and dividend income and the proceeds from the sale of securities in the United Kingdom may be repatriated by nonresidents.

Interest and dividend income earned by nonresidents is not subject to withholding tax since corporations normally pay advance corporation tax (ACT) on their dividend distributions.[18]

Security and Market Peculiarities
Despite a 300 year history of personalized trading characterized by trust rather than documentation ("my word is my bond" originated here), the London Stock Exchange is the first major market to move toward the implementation of the impersonal fully automated trading floor.

Futures and Derivative Markets
Commodity, currency, financial instrument, and market index options and futures contracts are traded in the U.K. market. The principal exchanges are the London International Financial Futures Exchange (LIFFE) and the London Futures and Options Exchange (FOX).

OTHER EMERGING MARKETS

While the Templeton organization focuses its activities on about 50 countries, research goes on constantly among other emerging markets to determine where the next generation of bargains is likely to emerge. Appendix B of this chapter provides capsule looks at some emerging equity markets that are being studied by Templeton analysts.

The preceding material and Appendix B present some of Templeton's views of the investment world. As can be seen, there is no real limit on where he will go. He recognizes no artificial boundaries, and views all barriers and restrictions as opportunities. For Templeton and his team, there are no problems, only solutions.

In the second part of this book we will explore Templeton's stock selection methods and his bargain-hunting approach. The material is drawn extensively from our interviews with Templeton in his Lyford Cay, Bahamas home.

ENDNOTES

1. Roger G. Ibbotson, Laurence B. Siegal, and Kathryn S. Love, "World Wealth: Market Values and Returns," *The Journal of Portfolio Management,* Fall 1985, p. 6.
2. In the spring of 1987, the Templeton organization launched the Templeton Emerging Markets Fund, a closed-end mutual fund that invests in the securities of designated emerging nations of which 42, ranging from Argentina to Zimbabwe, are identified in the fund's prospectus.
3. The effect of the "bangs" was to deregulate markets (for example, the United Kingdom eliminated its fixed commission schedule) and to substantially broaden the list of eligible participants in both principal and agency primary and secondary markets trading.
4. The first inter-country link-up between stock exchanges occurred in 1984 when the Montreal Exchange (ME) of Canada, and the Boston Stock Exchange (BSE) of the United States agreed to a pilot project allowing traders in Montreal to route their orders in Canadian stocks listed in the United States to the Boston Stock Exchange for execution at the best U.S. price. The system was expanded over the next years to allow reciprocal trade routing for BSE members on the Montreal Exchange. Other links followed, including those between the Toronto Stock Exchange (TSE) and the American Stock Exchange (ASE) and between the TSE and the Midwest Stock Exchange (MSE). In general, these links provide interchangeable trading and quotation of inter-listed stocks allowing investors to trade contracts on one exchange and to offset on another, or to search for the best possible execution.

   In April 1986 Britain's London Stock Exchange and the U.S. National Association of Securities Dealers (NASD) agreed to exchange price quotation information via their respective computerized systems, the Stock Exchange Automated Quotation System (SEAQ) of the U.K. and the U.S. National Association of Securities Dealers Automated Quotation System (NASDAQ). The link allows for direct electronic transmittal of price and volume information on a select number of issues on each market. Theoretically, stock exchange trading links should provide benefits in the form of improved liquidity for contracts or operating economies and hence lower transaction costs, or superior information flows leading to better trade executions and improved market efficiency. The future of such links will depend on the demonstration of such "value added" effects.

5. See Rule 6.18 of the Australian Companies and Securities Legislation (Miscellaneous Amendments) Act, 1986, for the full details of limitations on short selling on Australian Stock Exchanges.

6. Investment by nonresidents is regulated under the Foreign Takeovers Act of 1975.

7. Australia has reciprocal taxation treaties with most major industrialized countries. Notable exceptions are Italy and Japan.

8. The shareholder's position is thus described as having written a call option in the former case and owning a put option in the latter.

9. Solvay B Shares are issued in registered form.

10. Investors in most countries will receive a tax credit on their domestic income tax returns for the Canadian interest and dividend withholding taxes.

11. The Paris Bourse is currently revamping its operations. One manifestation is the introduction of the Toronto Stock Exchange's Computer Assisted Trading System (CATS) to augment floor trading.

12. Withholding taxes are reduced to 10–12% for interest income and 15% for dividend income through tax agreements between France and other countries.

13. The rate is reduced to 10 to 15% through the operation of tax treaties between Japan and other countries.

14. These designated shares are the bearer shares and participation certificates of 25 designated companies listed on the Zurich exchange and the bearer registered shares and participation certificates of 58 companies listed on the Basle Exchange.

15. Five days' settlement is usually allowed on request.

16. Withholding rates for treaty companies range from nil to 35%.

17. This so-called best execution rule means that the broker must obtain a trading price for a client that is no worse than that currently displayed on the Stock Exchange Automated Quotation System (SEAQ).

18. On application to the inspector of foreign dividends, dividend payments in certain cases may be made on a gross basis to a nonresident.

APPENDIX A   Selected Sources of Information for the Global Trader

GENERAL ECONOMIC INFORMATION

International Financial
Statistics
   (Monthly & Yearbook)
   International Monetary Fund
   700 19th Street, N.W.
   Washington D.C. 20431

Direction of Trade Statistics
   (Annual & Updates)
   International Monetary Fund
   Same address as above.

OECD Main Economic
Indicators
   (Monthly)
   OECD Publications &
   Information Centre
      Suite 1207
      1750 Pennsylvania Avenue,
      N.W.
      Washington D.C. 20006–
      4582

OECD Economic Outlook
   (Bi-Annual)
   OECD Publications &
   Information Centre
   Same address as above.

OECD Quarterly National
Accounts Bulletin
   (Quarterly)
   OECD Publications &
   Information Centre
   Same address as above.

OECD Observer
   (Monthly)
   OECD Publications &
   Information Centre
   Same address as above.

OECD Economic Surveys
   (Country analysis)
   OECD Publications &
   Information Centre
   Same address as above.

Monthly Bulletin of Statistics
   (Monthly)
   United Nations
   Sales Section
   New York, N.Y. 10017

Morgan Stanley Capital
International Perspective
   (Monthly & Quarterly)
   Morgan Stanley
   1633 Broadway
   New York, N.Y. 10019

The Federal Reserve Bank of
St. Louis Review
(Monthly)
The Federal Reserve Bank of
St. Louis
P.O. Box 442
St. Louis, Missouri 63166

International Economic
Conditions
(Monthly)
The Federal Reserve Bank of
St. Louis
Same address as above.

Monetary Trends
(Bi-Weekly)
The Federal Reserve Bank of
St. Louis
Same address as above.
World Financial Markets
(Monthly)
Morgan Guaranty Trust Co.
of New York
23 Wall Street
New York, N.Y. 10015
Bank for International
Settlements
Buchdruckerei, Basel
Switzerland

WEEKLY BUSINESS PUBLICATIONS (Local)

Canadian Business Magazine
CB Media Ltd.
70 the Esplanade, 2nd floor
Toronto M5E IR2 Ontario
Canada
German Business Weekly
German-American Chamber
of Commerce
666 Fifth Avenue
New York, N.Y. 10103
Far Eastern Economic Review
Centre Point
181 Glouchester Road
Hong Kong
Japan Economic Journal
Tokyo International
P.O. Box 5004
Tokyo, Japan
Beleggers Belanger
P.O. Box 152
Amsterdam 1000, AD
The Netherlands

Financial Mail
171 Main Street
2001 Johannesburg
South Africa

Sweden Business Report
Affarsvalden, Box 1234
S-111 82
Stockholm, Sweden

Finanz Und Wirtschaft
CH-8021
Zurich
Switzerland

The Economist
54 St. James Street
London SW 1A 1PJ
England

The Investor's Chronicle
30 Finsbury Square
London EC 4P 4B4
England

WEEKLY BUSINESS PUBLICATIONS (Local) (*continued*)

Business Week
  McGraw-Hill, Inc.
  1221 Avenue of the Americas
  New York, N.Y. 10020

Forbes
  Forbes Inc.
  60 Fifth Avenue
  New York, N.Y. 10011

MONTHLY BUSINESS PUBLICATIONS (Local)

L'Opinion Vie Francais
  67 Avenue Franklin D.
    Roosevelt
  75381 Paris
  Cedex 08
  France

Asian Business Information
  G.P.O. Box 12507
  Hong Kong

Asian Finance
  Suite 9D Hyde Center
  223 Glouchester Road
  Causeway Bay
  Hong Kong

Asian Business
  Far Eastern Trade Press Ltd.
  15 C Lockheart Centre
  301 Lockheart Road
  Hong Kong

Hong Kong Business Today
  1181 Hong Kong Plaza
  186–191 Connaught, West
  Hong Kong

Toyokeizai Tokei Geppo
  OCS America, Inc.
  27–08 42nd Road
  Long Island City, N.Y. 11101

Kikai Tokei Geppo
  OCS America, Inc.
  27–08 42nd Road
  Long Island City, N.Y. 11101

Sweden Now
  M. Oskogsgrand 11
  Box 27315, S-102 54
  Stockholm, Sweden

Euromoney
  Euromoney Publications
  Nestor House
  Playhouse Yard
  London EC4V 5EX
  England

Business
  Business People Publications
  234 King's Road
  London SW3 5UA
  England

Institutional Investor
  488 Madison Avenue
  New York, N.Y. 10022

LOCAL NEWSPAPERS

The Financial Post
  MacLean Hunter Building
  777 Bay Street
  Toronto, Ontario M5W 1A7
  Canada

Globe & Mail Report On
Business
  444 Front Street W
  Toronto, Ontario M5V 259
  Canada

Toronto Star
  1 Yonge Street
  Toronto, Ontario M5E 1E6
  Canada

AGEFI
  108 rue de Richelieu
  Paris 75002
  France

Handelsblatt
  GLP International
  21 Smith St.
  P.O. Box 9868
  Englewood, N.J. 07631

Asian Wall Street Journal
  G.P.O. Box 9825
  Hong Kong

Denpa Shinbun
  OCS America, Inc.
  27–08 42nd Road
  Long Island City, N.Y. 11101

Nihon Shoken Shinbun
  OCS America, Inc.
  Same address as above.

Nikkei Sangyo Shinbun
  OCS America, Inc.
  Same address as above.

Nikkei Shinbun
  OCS America, Inc.
  Same address as above.

Het Financieele Dagblad
  Gebouw 'Metropool'
    Weesperstraat 85–87
  Postbus 216
  Amsterdam 1000 AE
  The Netherlands

The Financial Times of London
  14 East 60th St.
  New York, N.Y. 10022

Wall Street Journal
  200 Burnett Road
  Chicopee, Mass. 01020

LOCAL STATISTICAL SOURCES

ANZ Bank Quarterly Survey
  (Australian Quarterly)
  ANZ Bank
  355 Collins St.
  Melbourne 3000
  Australia

Canadian Statistical Review
  (Monthly)
  STATISTICS CANADA
  Ottawa K1A OZ8
  Canada

LOCAL STATISTICAL SOURCES (*continued*)

DAFSA
(Monthly)
Societe de Documentation &
   d'Analyses Financieres
125 rue Montmarte
Paris, 2
France

Monthly Reports of the
Deutsche Bundesbank
(Monthly)
Deutsche Bundesbank
P.O. Box 10 06 02
D-6000 Frankfurt 1
Germany

Hoppenstedt Borsenfuehrer
(Quarterly)
Verlag Hoppenstedt & Co.
Postfach 4006
D-6100 Darmstadt 1
Germany

Hong Kong Government
Information Services
(Monthly & Quarterly)
Beaconsfield House, 4th Floor
4 Queen's Road
Central, Victoria
Hong Kong

La Borsa Valori
(Monthly)
Sede Palazzo della Borsa
Piazza delgi Affari, 6
20123 Milano, Italy

Review of Economic Conditions
in Italy
(Quarterly)
Banco di Roma
Viale U. Tupini, 180
00144 Rome
Italy

Balance of Payments Monthly
The Bank of Japan
2–1, 2-chome,
Hongokucho, Nihonbashi
Chuo-ku, Tokyo
Postal Code 103
Japan

Monthly Finance Review
Institute of Fiscal &
   Monetary Policy
Ministry of Finance
Tokyo, Japan

Tokyo Stock Exchange Monthly
(Monthly)
Tokyo, Japan

Economic Statistics Monthly
(Monthly)
Research and Statistics
   Department
The Bank of Japan
2–1, 2–chome,
Hongokucho, Nihonbashi
Chuo-ku, Tokyo
Postal Code 103
Japan

Svenska Aktiebolag
(Monthly)
Kungl. Boktryckeriet P.A.
Norstedt & Soner
Box 2030 S103–12
Stockholm, Sweden

Schweizerische Nationalbank
Monatsbericht
(Monthly)
Orell Fussli Graphische
   Betriebe
8036 Zurich 3
Switzerland

LOCAL STATISTICAL SOURCES (*continued*)

Agence Economique et
Financiere
  4 rue Montblanc
  Geneva
  Switzerland

National Institute Economic
Review
  (Monthly)
  National Inst. for Economic
    & Social Research
  2 Dean Trench Street
  Smith Square
  London SW1P 3HE
  England

Bank of England Quarterly
  (Quarterly)
  Economics Division, Bank of
    England
  London EC2R 8AH
  England

Extel Statistical Services, Ltd.
  (Weekly, Monthly, Quarterly
    & Annual Service)
  37/45 Paul Street
  London EC2A 4PB
  England

Moody's Services Ltd.
  (Monthly)
  6 – 8 Bonhill Street
  London EC2A 4BU
  England

MARKET HANDBOOKS

China Handbook
  Synergy Publishing Inc.
  Suite 603
  New York, N.Y. 10013

French Company Handbook
  1 rue Bourdaloue
  Paris 75009
  France

Japan Company Handbook
  Wako Securities Co., Ltd.
  3 Kitahama 3-chome,
  Higashi-ku
  Osaka
  Japan

Van Oss' Effectenboek
  J.H. DeBussy
  Amsterdam 1000
  The Netherlands

South African Stock Exchange
Handbook
  Flesch Financial Publications
    (Pty) Ltd.
  P.O. Box 3473
  Cape Town 8000
  South Africa

Handbuch der Schweizerischen
Anlagewerte
  Editions Cosmos S.A.
  Bern, Switzerland

APPENDIX B   Emerging Equity Markets

Singapore

Market Founded: 1930 (Malaysia/Singapore), 1973 (Singapore)

Number of stocks: 316

Total capitalization: Sing $79112

Trading volume: Sing $8211

Stock index: Straits Times Index

Description: The Singapore market is one of the largest and most active in Asia, on a par with those in many European countries. Founded jointly with Malaysia, it has been independent since 1971.

Sources for more information:

Asian Wall Street Journal
PO Box 15
Chicopee, MA 01021
$78/year

Far Eastern Economic Review
c/o Datamovers
38 W. 26th St.
New York, NY 10018
$62/year

Stock Exchange of Singapore
702 Hong Leong Building
Raffle Quay
PO Box 2306
Singapore 0104

Malaysia and Singapore Monthly Reports
Arnold & Bleichroeder
30 Broad St.
New York, NY 10004

South Korea

Market Founded: 1920

Number of stocks: 342

Total capitalization: 5148 billion won

Trading volume: 4.35 billion

Description: The original Korean market was dissolved during World War II and the Korean conflict and the modern market became operative in 1968. The value of the market has also exploded in recent years, now almost 300 times as much as its worth in 1968.

Templeton on South Korea

South Korea is poised to become an important trading market. Today, as was the case in Japan some years ago, foreigners can't invest in Korea and take their money out again. But it is likely that the law will be rescinded in the near future. When that law is overturned, then many people will want to invest there. Even before the law changes you'll see much activity in Korea, as local people buy in anticipation of the restrictive law's demise.

The companies in South Korea are issuing so much stock that share prices in 1986 were relatively low, among the lowest in the world. This helps make Korea an attractive prospect: low share prices, one of the highest growth rates in the world over the past 10 years, and soon, the availability of shares to foreigners. The gross national product is growing very rapidly because South Korea's low wages allow it to produce almost anything less expensively than can be done in other countries. The low cost Korean automobile [e.g., the Hyundai] now coming into the United States is a prime example.

Thailand

Market Founded: 1975

Number of stocks: 97

Total capitalization: Baht 49.457 million

Trading volume: Baht 15,334 million

Stock index: SET Index

Description: The Thai market underwent heady growth in the years after its founding, then crashed in 1979. Revived in 1982, the market has since grown steadily.

A comment from John Templeton: This is a nice country with calm people and low costs. Clients of Templeton International invested recently. The CEO of Templeton International is a director of the Bangkok Fund, a new investment mutual fund.

Sources for more information:

Securities Exchange of Thailand
Siam Centre
965 Rama I Road
Bangkok 5

Thai Investment and Securities Co. Ltd.
138 Silom Road Boonmitr Building
Bangkok 5

India

Market Founded: 1877

Number of stocks: 8,000 registered companies; 3,900 listed companies; perhaps 1,000 actively traded companies

Total capitalization: R97,980 million

Trading volume: R100 billion

Description: Stocks have had their ups and downs during India's turbulent 20th Century. Markets exist in Bombay, Calcutta, Madras, Delhi, Ahmedabad, Bangalore, Hyderabad, Indore, Cochin, Kanpur, and Pune. The first four handle virtually all of the trading. Stocks have not played a major role in India since independence, but indications are that the government now is paying increased attention to them. Indian markets are complex and a bit chaotic. Not all listed companies are quoted, and those with good records are quoted at different prices on different markets.

A comment from John Templeton: India may soon be as economically important as it has been culturally important. Right now, India is in the same category as South Korea: foreigners can't buy there. But we expect that law to be repealed, and we've had analysts studying India to be prepared for the change. The CEO of Templeton International is a director of the new India Fund.

Brazil

Market Founded: mid-19th Century

Number of stocks: 607, but few are actively traded

Total capitalization: Cr 447,950 billion

Trading volume: US $18.6 billion

Stock index: Bovespa Index

Description: Brazil has markets in almost every major city, but 90 per cent of the trading takes place in Rio de Janeiro and São Paulo. The São Paulo exchange is among the world's largest and best organized, and the economy behind it is growing very rapidly.

A comment from John Templeton: Fast-growing Brazil has a wealth of natural resources, but is still generally underdeveloped. As in Korea and India, foreigners aren't allowed to invest in Brazilian listed shares directly; but Templeton International has been granted authority to manage a mutual fund in Brazilian shares; which fund is owned by Templeton clients in other nations.

Mexico

Market Founded: 1894

Number of stocks: 188

Total capitalization: P129,993 million

Trading volume: 15,131 million

Description: Trading on the Mexican market has been active only since 1976. Mexican stocks have ridden a roller coaster in the decade since then.

A comment from John Templeton: We have made large profits on many shares in Mexico in the past, but the country today faces grave problems. It remains to be seen whether Mexico can overcome its peso devaluation and a host of other economic difficulties and return to the path of positive growth it was following years ago.

Sources for more information:

Informacion Sobre Valores (English Edition)
Banamex Securities Research Department

Paseo de la REforma No. 397 Third Floor
Mexico 1,DF
$28/year

Lloyd's Mexican Economic Report
Lloyd's Mexican Stock and Bond Report
Allen Lloyd y Asociados
Prisciliano Sanchez No. 220,
Guadalajara, Mexico
$12/year

Bolsa Mexicana de Valores, SA de CV
Uruguay 68, 2–0 piso
Mexico 1 DF

Argentina

Market Founded: 1854

Number of stocks: 235

Total capitalization: A1.6 billion

Trading volume: A379 million

Description: The oldest established market in Latin America, Argentina's exchange has a history as turbulent as the country itself has been. All but dead in the mid-1960s, the market rebounded and had the highest return of any emerging market between 1975 and 1980, an average annual return of 97 percent in United States dollars. It's expected to remain volatile.

A comment from John Templeton: Argentina is intriguing, but we now invest for clients only by the Templeton Emerging Markets Fund. I've taken a chance with some of my own money. This is a good speculation, I think, and will help us get to know the Argentine corporations better. Making comparisons of different markets around the world, we found that the total value of all the stocks publicly traded in Argentina was only 2 billion US dollars in 1987 whereas the value of all stocks traded in New York was $2,500 billion.

CHAPTER 5

STOCK SELECTION

There is a fairly well-regarded theory of security prices and analysis called the Efficient Markets Hypothesis. The theory (which we discussed in Chapter 3), embraced at least until recently as gospel in the academic world, in its grandest form states that security prices reflect all available information, that no amount or type of manipulation of information will yield superior investment results. Neither chart reading (technical analysis) nor analysis of corporate financial statements (fundamental analysis) can provide above average investment returns on a risk-adjusted basis. And, if the theory is correct, mutual fund managers cannot outperform the market.

Driving up to John Templeton's house in Lyford Cay, Bahamas, for our interview on his stock selection techniques, we chatted about the relevance in the real world of the Efficient Markets Hypothesis, particularly since Templeton and his team have a record of over 40 years of outperforming the market on a risk-adjusted basis (not every year but most). Are people like Templeton—and the others who consistently outperform the market averages—statistical anomolies, or are they living refutations of the Efficient Markets Hypothesis? What is the Templeton approach to stock selection? Is it analytic, intuitive, fundamentally or technically based? Is there a set format or procedure for selecting specific companies for inclusion in the Templeton Organization's family of mutual funds and individually managed accounts? These and other questions were percolating as we drove through the streets of New Providence toward the home of the legendary investment counsellor. But before addressing such questions, we need to cover some background information.

STOCK SELECTION TECHNIQUES— A PRIMER

Before disclosing Templeton's insights into successful stock se-lection techniques, we should review as useful background the two widely used approaches: fundamental and technical. The former is more respectable and accepted, the latter more flam-boyant and dramatic. Here is a capsule commentary on the basics.

Fundamental Analysis

The fundamental approach, as the title suggests, involves the use of financial and economic data to assess the liquidity, sol-vency, efficiency, and foremost, the earnings potential of a company. The fundamental analyst's kit-bag includes macro-economic data, corporate financial reports, industry data, com-ments from corporate officers (preferably legal ones), and company memoranda, which he then scrutinizes, looking to de-termine whether a specific company's stock is under- or over-valued. There are different starting points with fundamental analysis and scores of different techniques and measures used, but in general, the five step approach that follows is reasonably representative of the fundamentalist's approach to valuing spe-cific companies and their underlying common shares.[1]

Fundamental Analysis—The Five Steps

Step 1. Economic Projections. Usually the analyst starts with economic projections or forecasts for the perfor-mance of the economy for the next 12 to 24 months. This in turn yields a forecast for stock market performance. Certain economic variables (for example, home construction) called *leading indicators* normally provide signals of important turn-ing points in business cycles and are particularly important at this initial projections stage.

Step 2. Company and Industry Ratio Analysis. The specific company and the industry in which it operates is examined next, typically using ratios. One of the key techniques in fundamental analysis is the ratio or relationship between two or more corporate variables. Various financial measures are identified from the firm's financial statements and then assessed. For example, the *times-interest-earned* ratio—operating profit before interest on long-term debt, divided by interest on long-term debt—is a measure of a firm's ability to meet interest payments and hence an indication of the firm's solvency. Analysts use other ratios to determine the firm's liquidity (its ability to meet short-term financial liabilities), its return on shareholders' capital, and its efficiency.[2]

Most fundamentalists use a dual approach to evaluate a firm: the cross-sectional method, where the firm's performance is compared to other firms of similar size in the same industry and/or to industry averages; and longitudinal analysis, where the trend or direction of the firm's ratios, earnings, and growth rates are examined. Table 5–1 presents an example of a cross-sectional analysis where two companies and an industry

TABLE 5–1
CROSS-SECTIONAL ANALYSIS Example Common Size Statements

Assets	Company "A"	Company "B"	Industry Averages
Cash	4.0%	12.0%	6.0%
Marketable securities	7.8	14.6	2.4
Accounts receivable	9.6	10.4	13.4
Inventories	10.2	10.6	11.5
Plant and equipment	55.6	49.1	60.0
Other assets	12.8	3.3	6.7
Total	100.0%	100.0%	100.0%

Liabilities and Equity	Company "A"	Company "B"	Industry Averages
Accounts payable	6.2%	6.8%	10.2%
Other current liabilities	5.8	4.2	6.6
Long-term debt	35.0	60.6	28.6
Deferred tax	10.0	10.9	11.6
Shareholder's equity	43.0	17.5	43.0
Total	100.0%	100.0%	100.0%

average are compared on the basis of common size financial statements (all three statements are placed on the same base with each balance sheet item expressed as a percentage of the total).

A longitudinal analysis where the trend of sales, cost of sales, operating expenses, income taxes, and net income are expressed as index numbers of the 1983 base period is shown in Table 5–2.

Step 3.   Earnings and Dividend Analysis.   The next step is an earnings and dividend analysis in which a forecast of earnings and dividends for next year and for some reasonable horizon (such as the next five years) is made. Forecasting models used range from the simple extrapolations of past data using scatter diagrams or regression techniques to complex multi-factor models.

Step 4.   Discount Rate or Price/Earnings Multiple Forecasts.   In order to project the future stock price performance, the analyst must make an estimate of how the market will pay for the firm's expected growth rate of earnings and dividends, and hence how the market will capitalize earnings through a required rate of return. Alternatively, and more simplistically, the analyst will estimate the market price/earnings multiple to attach to the latest earnings per share. It is essential to recognize here that the analyst's task is to forecast the *market discount rate,* not his own view. The key to success-

TABLE 5–2
Longitudinal Analysis, Index Numbers: 1983 = 100.0

	Company A				
Year/Factor	Sales	Cost of Sales	Operating Expenses	Income Taxes	Net Income
1983	100.0	100.0	100.0	100.0	100.0
1984	121.7	122.6	109.6	118.6	101.2
1985	145.9	140.9	118.6	129.7	106.6
1986	152.6	161.2	123.5	127.5	99.2
1987	183.8	179.8	131.1	142.9	101.0

ful fundamental investment analysis is the ability to project both future corporate earnings and how the market is likely to capitalize them.

Step 5. Specification of Appropriate Valuation Model. Ultimately, the aim of fundamental analysis is to determine whether a firm is under, over, or properly valued. An appropriate valuation model, which will incorporate traditional dividend or earnings growth measures and possibly capital asset pricing model criteria, is normally used. Valuation models range from the simple, such as a one-year forecast of earnings accompanied by a one-year forecast of the price/earnings multiple, to the complex growth models.[3]

Both Templeton and the Templeton organization have been proponents and pioneers in the use and development of fundamental analysis (especially of the bottom-up type), as we will see here and in Chapter 6. The Templeton organization also uses some technical analysis techniques, the subject of the next section.

Technical Analysis

The technical approach involves the use of past price and volume and other external data to assess the "crowd's" attitude toward the market and specific stocks. Instead of examining the fundamentals related to the market or a specific company and its industry, the technical analyst searches for the truth that is found in the chart patterns such as that in Figure 5–1.

The pure technician believes that all relevant fundamental information about the market or a company is already incorporated in the index level or share price and holds (as does the efficient markets proponent) that no direct manipulation of that information can result in superior stock selection. It is in fact the ebb and flow of the market, the momentum, that is revealed in the skillful analysis of trading data and the likely direction of the next move.

Where the technician differs from the efficient markets proponent is in the interpretation of trends. The technical analyst believes that trends once begun tend to persist, while ef-

FIGURE 5–1

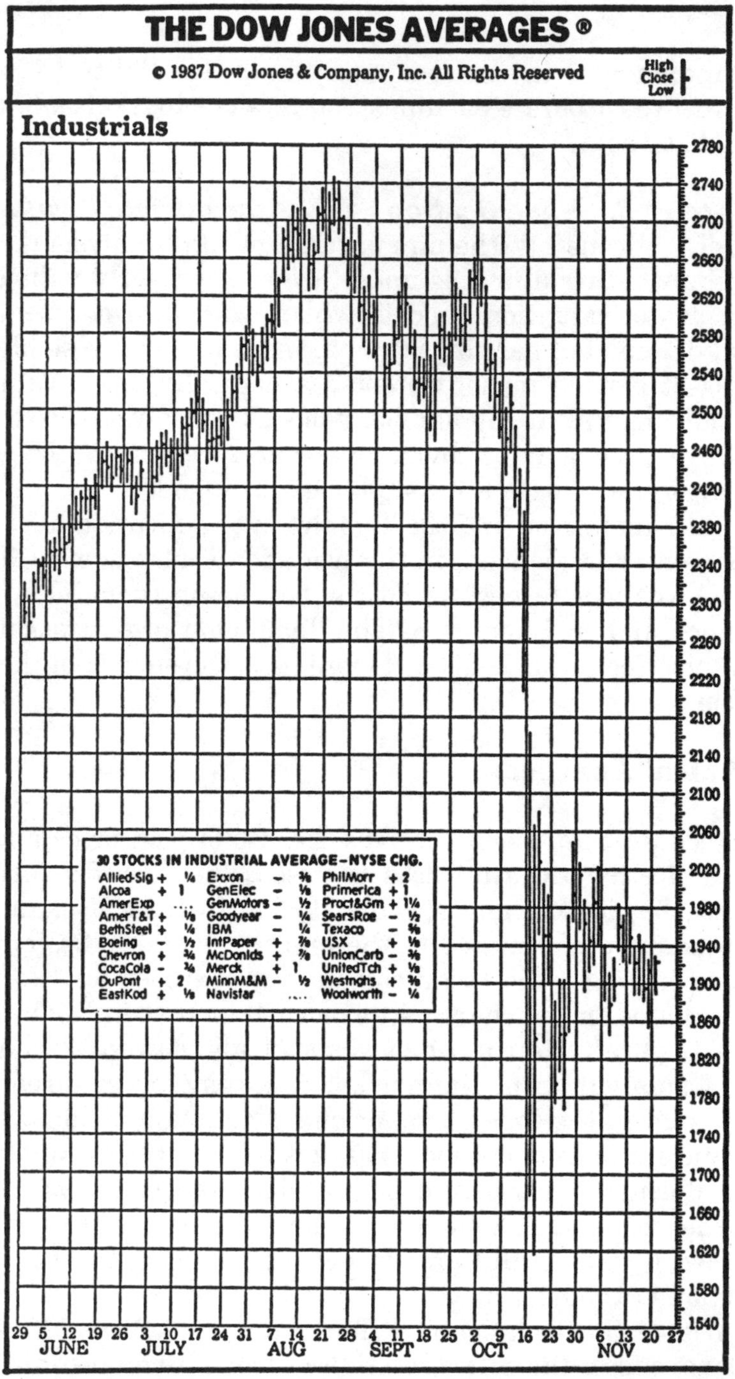

THE DOW JONES AVERAGES ®
© 1987 Dow Jones & Company, Inc. All Rights Reserved
High
Close
Low
Industrials
2780
2740
2700
2660
2620
2580
2540
2500
2460
2420
2380
2340
2300
2260
2220
2180
2140
2100
2060
2020
1980
1940
1900
1860
1820
1780
1740
1700
1660
1620
1580
1540
30 STOCKS IN INDUSTRIAL AVERAGE–NYSE CHG.
Allied-Sig + ¼ Exxon – ⅜ PhilMorr + 2
Alcoa + 1 GenElec – ⅛ Primerica + 1
AmerExp .... GenMotors – ½ Proct&Gm + 1¼
AmerT&T + ⅛ Goodyear – ¼ SearsRoe – ½
BethSteel + ¼ IBM – ¼ Texaco – ⅝
Boeing – ½ IntPaper + ⅞ USX + ⅛
Chevron + ¾ McDonlds + ⅞ UnionCarb – ⅜
CocaCola – ¾ Merck + 1 UnitedTch + ⅛
DuPont + 2 MinnM&M – ½ Westnghs + ⅜
EastKod + ⅛ Navistar .... Woolworth – ¼
29 5 12 19 26 3 10 17 24 31 7 14 21 28 4 11 18 25 2 9 16 23 30 6 13 20 27
JUNE JULY AUG SEPT OCT NOV

Reprinted by permission of *The Wall Street Journal.* © Dow Jones & Company, Inc., November 24, 1987. All rights reserved.

ficient market types believe that trends are identifiable only when they are over!

Many of the present technical theories and approaches are simply variations and extensions of the work of Charles Dow, the creator of the Dow Jones Stock Index. Dow Theory holds that stock prices move together in basic types of trends,[4] and moreover that it is possible to determine these trends from a careful scrutiny of price and index changes.

The classic treatise on the subject of technical analysis is found in Edwards and Magee.[5] They argue that market values of shares are determined by supply and demand; that the factors underlying supply and demand are complex, can influence the market, and are reflected in the market value of shares; that trends in share prices tend to persist for some time; and that changes in these trends are the result of changes in the basic supply/demand relationship. Thus the role of the technician is to spot trends and to do so by gauging market and stock momentum as revealed in chart patterns.[6]

Probably the best known of the modern day technicians is Joseph Granville, famous as much for his flamboyant public presentations, replete with pianos and dancing girls, as for his extravagant recommendations that are either dead right or dead wrong![7]

Research studies have not been kind to the art of technical analysis. Little support for the method, at least as applied to stock selection, has been found.

Templeton on the Stock Selection Method(s)

It takes three minutes or so to gain clearance at the front gates to the Lyford Cay entrance. As we drive up the steep winding driveway in an all pink taxi (interior and exterior), Pinky our cab-driver, who is dressed appropriately in all pink, cautions us to be pleasant to his friend John and not to ask any stupid questions! (We subsequently discover that just about everyone we meet on the island knows Templeton.) We're greeted at the door of the Georgian style Templeton home, aptly called White Columns, by Roy the butler.

We're escorted into the drawing room. John, nattily dressed in blue suit and club tie, appears, offers drinks (club soda seemed appropriate although a major bourbon would have probably looked good at this time), and gets right down to business. No small talk. And indeed all of our attempts to digress from the topics of international investing and money management are deftly and politely thwarted. Two hours of cat and mouse. Of 'who knows what?' If you ask the right question, you get a good answer. Templeton volunteers only when you earn the right.

EK: O.K. Let me get right to the point. How do you pick stocks? Is there a Templeton approach? To what extent is intuition or feelings a part of your fund selection process?

JMT: We avoid intuition. [This is stated emphatically, with steely eyed contact!] We apply arithmetic. What we call a quantitative search. For 47 years we have called ourselves quantitative security analysts. We don't buy something because it feels good, we buy something because we work out the arithmetic and it looks more promising than anything else. That doesn't keep us from being open minded and using far-ranging approaches. The quantitative approach is subject to all kinds of peculiarities. Let me give you an example. A number of years ago I read in the *New York Times* an advertisement for 500 acres of land within 100 miles of New York City at $17 per acre. That's all I needed to know. I bought it that night on the telephone without ever going to see it. With my background of knowledge of the area I knew that the price was so far out of line that it would be snapped up by someone else immediately. I didn't buy it on a hunch; I bought it on the arithmetic; I hadn't seen anything like it within 100 miles of New York at even three times that price. A quantitative approach but not one with any one specific fixed method.

NB: Is there a single, most important strategem that you can cite for long-term investment success?

JMT: Yes. The key to long-term success is to keep an open mind. And by that I mean the willingness to adapt any approach, any technique suitable for the investment. And to explore any type of investment in any place in the world.

EK: O.K., but is there not a spark somewhere? You cannot follow every stock in the world. There has to be an intuitive start somewhere. Somehow you had to decide to invest in say, South Korea. Obviously some quantitative method is used to distinguish South Korean securities. But what got you there in the first place?

JMT: Maybe I can help you with that. In security analysis, we have what are called yardsticks of value. Price/earnings multiples, price/cash flow ratios, etc. They don't all apply to each company. We look for something that is out of line using some yardstick of value. And South Korea is a very good example. I discovered years back with only a casual reading in a newspaper that the South Korean gross national product was growing three times as fast as America's. And then I discovered that South Korean securities could be bought in South Korea at only about four times earnings and a current yield of about 13%. So the combinations of a rapidly growing economy and corporations selling at very low yardsticks of value meant that I should investigate further. So I took a trip to South Korea, met with a banker who had lived there most of his life, and based on that I started studying about South Korea 12 years ago. Having a background of over 100 yardsticks of value, any time that you find something out of line on one maybe two of these yardsticks, you go and investigate and study further. It's not intuitive [emphatically stated again], it's based on value.

EK: You are really looking for anomolies.

JMT: We have many security analysts reading reports and other information constantly. Anomolies may be the technically correct term, but it really isn't the most descriptive word. It would probably be clearer if we called them yardsticks of value that indicate bargains.

EK: Is there a Templeton valuation method? A standardized approach possibly characterized by a set of worksheets?

JMT: No, there isn't. But there are a variety of approaches and worksheets. We think it would be a mistake to adopt any one method. We want our analysts to adopt whatever approaches are appropriate to a particular situation. I cannot be really specific about this. Besides, any method that is particularly successful only works if we keep it to ourselves. So we wouldn't tell people about methods that worked particularly well. Nevertheless I will say this: In 47 years of selecting stocks there is one method that seems to be very useful, works well, and is not likely to become obsolete,

. . . and that is to buy bargain stocks. [*EK to himself*: Darn it, not quite what I was hoping for. But we are getting closer.] We estimate a company's value and then determine if it is selling below its value. But that isn't enough. You need to compare this to all other companies to get relative measures. [*EK*: Just like we were taught in business school . . . cross-sectional analysis.] We call it bargain hunting. It's the major part of our research work. We bought the Mexico Fund below $3.00 a share because it was selling at 40% below liquidating value, a larger discount than we had seen on other closed-end funds. Also, shares of Mexican companies were then very low compared to earnings, net asset value, etc. . . .

EK: Would you describe your approach as earnings-based or asset-based or both?

JMT: Both. You cannot neglect either. But in most cases, in assessing a company, we place more emphasis on future earnings rather than current earnings or assets. Earnings is a complex subject, too. A number of fund managers have adopted the low price/earnings multiple approach. Several books have been written on how you can do well selecting on the basis of low price/earnings multiples. But that's only one method. There are dozens of approaches.

When I was a student under the famous Benjamin Graham, he taught me about using book values and to search for those companies selling for less than net net working capital, i.e., where you subtract the liabilities from the current assets and if the result is higher than market price then you are buying cash at a discount and everything else is thrown in free. And I've used it. But it won't work today. Not in America. Because you won't find any companies selling for less than net working capital. Ben was a very wise man. He had a splendid method. But if he were alive today he would be doing something else, relying on newer and more varied concepts.

The yardstick of value we have used most often is price relative to probable future earnings. Others that we have used include price relative to cash flow, and price relative to true liquidating value, not book value. For different corporations, we look at different things. Most of the time we concentrate on fundamentals over technicals, quantitative over qualitative. Future earnings more important than current or past, etc.

EK: Since you and your team are bargain hunters, to use your expression, would you call yourself a contrarian?

JMT: I think *accommodator* might be more appropriate. When greedy investors jump in to buy at the top of a bull market, I *accommodate* them by selling them my shares. When nervous investors are selling at the bottom, I *accommodate* them by buying. . . [*JMT adds at this point, possibly to temper the somewhat humorous sound of the statement:*] I consider my role as fund manager to be a sacred trust. Investors have entrusted me with their financial future and I carry out this sacred trust . . .

EK: You said that there is no one Templeton method or Templeton valuation worksheet. That there are many. Could we see a typical worksheet?

JMT: No. There isn't a typical one. And they keep changing. Nothing that I want to publish. We are constantly changing the worksheets that we are using. More and more computers are being used. We partially select our security analysts on their ability to use computers in new ways. Each analyst will have a different worksheet. West German companies require different worksheets than Canadian worksheets, analysis of companies in emerging nations such as Thailand and India require an entirely different approach.

EK: Is technical analysis ever used in the Templeton organization?

JMT: Yes, but normally as a supplement. We don't like to restrict ourselves in any way. But we just haven't found much in technical analysis that's worth a lot of study [*John chuckles*].

EK: There have been a number of interesting developments in investment finance in recent years. We'd like to discuss some of these and discuss their relevance, if any, to you and the Templeton organization, and their importance in world capital markets.

For example, the Capital Asset Pricing Model, a theoretical model of how risky assets are priced given some specific assumptions, has had major implications for security analysts and portfolio managers. The critical value of the CAPM is *beta,* a single valued measure that defines how an asset co-moves with the market. High beta securities are aggressive and should outperform (underperform) the market when it is strong (weak). Does the Templeton organization calculate betas for securities. If so, how? And how are they used?

JMT: The beta is of course a major part of modern portfolio management. But we don't rely much on betas because we think that they change. The beta computed for the same corporation five years from now will look quite a bit different from the beta computed now.

EK: How does the Templeton organization select countries? And how do you make geographical portfolio revisions? What are the criteria? Economic growth, inflation, interest rates, people, etc? . . .

JMT: Most of the time we make more money by starting at the bottom, what we call a bottom-up approach. We search for individual shares selling at amazingly low prices, in any nation or any industry. Only after we have selected these unusual opportunities, do we then play our portfolio management role, making sure that we don't have too much in any one country. We found this approach thus far (maybe we'll change in the future) to be more profitable than asking which country and selecting from there. We have always been primarily bottom-up.

EK: Let me see if I understand. The Templeton group visualizes a grand world portfolio. Analysts select from this, using whatever methods and techniques are available to justify their decisions. Then a double check to make sure that you are not overinvested in Japan or Australia or . . .

JMT: That adjustment that you are talking about is what we call diversification. The danger in any bottom-up approach is in the failure to diversify. For example, in December 1986 we were 65% invested in the U.S., not because we had decided that it would be 65%, but simply because that's where we found the opportunities. By the way, that's where CAPM comes into our organization. We do use betas later on as a check on our portfolio manager, to see what the beta of specific fund portfolios is and to make sure that no one portfolio has taken on too much risk.

NB: Now here is something that I think people really want to know. What makes a successful analyst? Could you pin down the criteria?

JMT: That's a real good question. It is crucial to understand, and very few people do, that attaining superior investment performance has nothing at all in common with succeeding in 99% of other occupations. If you were building bridges and a dozen consulting engineers experienced in bridge building all gave you the same advice, you'd be stupid not to build your bridge their way. In all probability, if the experts all agree, their way is the right way to do it. You'd build a better bridge at lower cost if you followed their advice. But the very nature of the investment-selection process turns that scenario topsy-turvy. Let's assume that every securities analyst you see says, 'That's the stock to buy!' You might think that if all the experts are saying 'buy,' you should. But you couldn't be more wrong. To begin with, if they all want it, they'll all buy it and the price will build up enormously, probably to unrealistic levels. By the same token, if all the experts say, 'It's not the stock to buy,' they won't buy it and the price will go down. It's then, if your research and common sense tell you the stock does have potential, that you might pick up a bargain.

That's the very nature of the operation. It's quite simple; if everybody else is buying, you ought to be thinking of selling. But that type of thinking is so peculiar to this field that hardly anybody realizes how valid it is. They say: 'I know you're supposed to look where other people aren't looking,' but very few actually understand what that means.

Templeton takes a fundamental approach to stock selection, one that can be best described as bargain hunting through the use of "yardsticks of value." The Templeton yardsticks of value, the keys to the Templeton approach, and his rules for security selection are the subject of the next chapter. Clearly Templeton is not greatly concerned with theories such as the Efficient Markets Hypothesis. He has been around long enough to see theories come and go. And he has used his yardsticks of value often enough and under enough different market conditions, to know what works and what doesn't. Driving back from our interview with Templeton, we are struck by a curious and disquieting thought. Are business schools teaching students the right things? Are Modern Portfolio Theory, the

Capital Asset Pricing Model, and the Arbitrage Pricing Model really more important than old fashioned bargain hunting and fundamental security analysis? We are also wondering if the anomolies uncovered in recent years (the End of the Year Effect, the Small Firm Effect, etc.) haven't been known, if only intuitively, to Templetons, Buffets, and others of their ilk, for a long time.

ENDNOTES

1. For a detailed examination of fundamental analysis and techniques see: B. Graham, D. Dodd, S. Cottle, *Security Analysis,* 4th ed. (New York: McGraw-Hill, 1962). This is still considered the bible of fundamental analysis. See also: Jack C. Francis, *Investments: Analysis and Management,* 4th ed. (New York: McGraw-Hill, 1986), chaps. 14–17; William F. Sharpe, *Investments.* (Englewood Cliffs, N.J.: Prentice Hall, Inc., 1985), chaps. 14–15.
2. Some of the more widely used ratios are shown below.

Key Ratios

Liquidity

1. Current Ratio $= \dfrac{\text{Current Assets}}{\text{Current Liabilities}}$
2. Quick Ratio $=$
$$\frac{\text{Cash + Accounts Receivable + Marketable Securities}}{\text{Current Liabilities}}$$

Solvency

1. Times Interest Earned $= \dfrac{\text{Profit before Interest and Taxes}}{\text{Interest}}$
2. Times Fixed Charges Covered $= \dfrac{\text{Profit before Fixed Charges*}}{\text{Fixed Charges}}$
3. Capital Structure

   A. Debt Ratio $= \dfrac{\text{Total Debt}}{\text{Total Assets}}$

---

*Includes interest on long-term debt, rent, capital leases and other such fixed commitments.

B. Debt/Equity Ratio $= \dfrac{\text{Total Debt}}{\text{Total Equity}}$

C. Structure $= \dfrac{\text{Long-Term Debt}}{\text{Total Capitalization}}$
$\dfrac{\text{Common Equity}}{\text{Total Capitalization}}$

Efficiency

1. Gross Margin $= \dfrac{\text{Net Sales} - \text{Cost of Goods Sold}}{\text{COGS}} \times 100\%$

2. Net Profit Margin $= \dfrac{\text{Net Income}}{\text{Net Sales}} \times 100\%$

3. Inventory Turnover $= \dfrac{\text{Cost of Goods Sold}}{\text{Average Inventory}}$

4. Total Asset Turnover $= \dfrac{\text{Net Sales}}{\text{Total Assets}}$

Profitability

1. Return on Invested Capital $= \dfrac{\text{Profit before Interest and Taxes}}{\text{Invested Capital}}$

2. Return on Common Equity $= \dfrac{\text{Net Income} - \text{Preferred Dividends}}{\text{Common Equity}}$

3. Return on Total Assets $= \dfrac{\text{Net Income}}{\text{Total Assets}}$

Investment

1. Earnings per Common Share $=$
$\dfrac{\text{Net Income} - \text{Preferred Dividends}}{\text{Avg. Number of Common Shares} \%}$

2. Stock Yield $= \dfrac{\text{Indicated Annual Dividend}}{\text{Current Market Price}}$

3. Payout Rate $= \dfrac{\text{Indicated Annual Dividend}}{\text{Earnings per Share}}$

4. Price/Earnings Multiple $= \dfrac{\text{Price of Common Share}}{\text{Earnings per Common Share}}$

3. Valuation growth models normally are some variation on a constant or variable growth assumption of the following form:

$$P_O = \sum_{T=1}^{M} \frac{D_o(1+g_s)^T}{(1+k)^T} + \sum_{T=M+1}^{\infty} \frac{D_M(1+g_N)^{T-M}}{(1+k)^T}$$

where:

P_O = Value of the share today according to the growth model
D_O = Dividend in period O or latest dividend paid
D_M = Dividend at the end of period M
g_s = Growth rate of dividend during period M
k = Required rate of return of investors
g_N = Growth rate of dividend during period M+1 to N

4. The three trends are primary, secondary, and tertiary. The primary trend is an extensive and basic movement underway (e.g., bull or bear) and has a duration of three months to three years. (Guess what, the 1982 bull market lasted over five years . . . oh well.) Secondary trends set in at some point during the primary and retrace ⅓ to ½ of the latest primary move. If the retracement continues, this may well be a reversal! Tertiary trends are the day-to-day movements and are considered to be random (and unimportant) in nature.

5. R. D. Edwards, and John Magee, *Technical Analysis of Stock Trends,* 4th ed. (Springfield, Mass.: John Magee, 1966). As Graham, Dodd, and Cottle is the bible of fundamental analysis, so is this truly the bible of technical analysis.

6. Other techniques besides chart reading are used by technical analysts. These include the use of external indicators such as odd lot trading indexes, confidence indexes, and the like.

7. Unfortunately for Granville and his followers, he had been dead wrong throughout the 1980s, consistently and stubbornly forecasting a severe market decline. It took until October 1987 for his "prediction" to come true. For Granville's works on the subject of technical analysis see Joseph E. Granville, *A Strategy of Daily Stock Market Timing for Maximum Profit* (Englewood Cliffs, N.J.: Prentice Hall, 1960).

CHAPTER 6

THE TEMPLETON WAY

It takes patience, discipline and courage to follow the "contrarian" route to investment success: to buy when others are despondently selling, to sell when others are avidly buying. However, based on a half century of experience, I can attest to the rewards at the end of the journey.

John Templeton, 1987

INTRODUCTION—THE TEMPLETON WAY IS BASED ON COMMONSENSE RULES (Easy to say, but not so easy to implement!)

Over the past 50 years, the Templeton team, spearheaded by John Templeton, has achieved remarkable success following a set of basic, yet subtle rules of investing. To John Templeton, the worldwide pursuit of profit demands study, patience, and—always—common sense. He leaves it to the more frivolous investment managers to cast the I Ching, track the pattern of Super Bowl wins, or study the behavior of pigeons in Battery Park to find a path to successful investing. Templeton disdains all such spurious or unproven distractions. He has based his career on a set of ever improving basic principles or rules—rules that are reflective of his staunch set of personal morals.

TEMPLETON'S RULES FOR SUCCESSFUL INVESTING

As we return to Lyford Cay in February 1987 to talk with Templeton about his specific stock selection methods, we agree that our goal must be to pin him down on specifics. Like great masters in other fields, Templeton has the ability to see directly to the heart of things, and to express his ideas in disarmingly simple terms. One need not look beyond artists like Monet and Hemingway to be aware of how those who have truly mastered their art tend toward simplicity of form: fewer but more graceful lines on the canvas; shorter but more meaningful sentences on the page. Unfortunately, this makes things more mysterious to the rest of us.

We agreed that we must get him to identify his rules, and then urge him to elaborate on those maxims. We would ask for examples of successes and instances where the rules didn't work. Most of all, we wanted to know how he put the rules to work.

The interview lasted two days, most of it conducted indoors in Templeton's living room, around a small coffee table. Cold drinks were offered on a few occasions, but other than that, it was strictly investment talk. It was 80 degrees outside and the sun was shining, casting the small but beautifully designed room in a hazy glow. The manicured lawns and lush gardens beckoned from beyond the sliding glass doors but business was business and the interview came first.

We found out that there were *many* Templeton rules. And we discovered that these rules really are a major key to both his success and his personality. The rules are constantly evolving and improving, and he freely makes exceptions to any rule when common sense dictates. Some of these rules (or more precisely principles) are described and explained in the following section.

First Rule of Successful Investing: The Rule of the Importance of Price

Purchase an investment only when you can pay less for it than it is worth today, and only if you believe that it will be worth more tomorrow.

Templeton called this his Rule of the Importance of Price. As we discovered, it probably more than any other precept lies behind Templeton's envied reputation. For Templeton, price is absolutely fundamental. He is one of the world's most successful bargain hunters; yet the idea underlying his success is the same as that employed by every coupon-toting food shopper seeking supermarket bargains or every comparison-shopping car buyer.

> *EK:*   This first rule of yours. The key seems to be your ability to predict market directions.

> *JMT:*   No. No. I never ask if the market is going to go up or down next month, I know that there is nobody that can tell me that. Instead, I search, country by country for stocks, asking where is the one that's lowest in price relative to what our securities analysts estimate its worth to be. Usually a stock has to be a bargain or I won't buy it.

Later that day, we found first-hand verification that Templeton rarely buys anything that he doesn't consider a bargain when he drove us to the airport to catch a cab to our hotel. We were loaded into John's 1972 Rolls Royce Phantom VI, and as we tooled over the pock-marked New Providence roads, he turned around and said "I bought this car new in England, and I paid £12,000 for it." He paused. Then, knowing that we were waiting for a punch line, he added: "Now, after 15 years of driving it, I'm told it'd fetch about £50,000."

It is no exaggeration to say that if Templeton had not felt that the Rolls was a genuine bargain, he would have passed it by without blinking an eye. He derives joy not so much from owning prized objects, but from knowing that he got them for less than they were worth at the time—and a lot less than they are worth now. He obviously likes his Rolls, but when a buyer comes along with £50,000, it's clear that he might be pleased to give it a new home.

If Templeton's philanthropies were not so well known, he might be described as penurious (he calls it thrifty). He isn't. His gifts to worthy causes—especially in the field of religion—amount to more than a million dollars yearly and are well-documented. Templeton's ability to adhere to his first rule, the Rule of the Importance of Price, in all financial transactions reveals an understanding of a basic investing process that has eluded many of the more flamboyant but less successful denizens of Wall Street (not to mention Fleet Street, Bay Street, etc.). His steadfast adherence to that Rule has caused Templeton to follow paths totally divergent from those of his peers. Let's take a brief odyssey through Templeton's early years to explore the role of his first rule in fashioning his unique investment approach.

In 1939, when Templeton was ready to start his own business and the Great Depression had left investors discouraged, he borrowed $10,000—something he has not done since—and plunged into the stock market. With this borrowed stake, he bought $100 worth of every stock then listed on the two major exchanges at $1 or less per share. That was 104 stocks in all, 34 of them representing companies already in bankruptcy. Within four years, as the demands of war spurred production and sales, his borrowed $10,000 quadrupled.

At the end of World War II, when Europe lay in ruins, Templeton again saw great opportunity. Rather than concentrate on the rejuvenated U.S. economy, as most other investors did, he bought heavily into the large European companies that the war had floored. Their stocks, as might be expected, were selling at prices that anybody with an eye to the future had to view as ridiculously low. Yet, if Europe were ever to rise again, and Templeton surmised that the United States would take steps to assure that it did, it would have to be those very companies that would lead the way. The introduction of the Marshall Plan proved his thinking to be correct, of course, and profits again flowed Templeton's way.

Similarly, in the 1960s, when Americans viewed Japan and Japanese-made products with disdain, Templeton was actively investing in the Japanese economy. Now that the United States is awash in Toyotas and Nissans, and Mitsubishi and Kawasaki have become household names, American investors are in awe of the powerful Japanese industrial establishment. But Templeton is long gone from Japan. In 1986/1987, Japanese holdings represented less than 1 percent of his investment total; instead, his money is backing companies in the resource-rich Canada and in industrially awakened Australia—areas in which global investors still can find bargain stocks.

Call it contrarianism or special-situation investing, Templeton's ability to cut across the grain profitably extends to individual companies as well. Templeton calls it simply bargain hunting, or recognizing price advantages.

The Templeton bargain-hunting principles aren't always well understood, even among the investment community cognoscenti. Most investors are more oriented toward romantic investment opportunities rather than to what they see as mundane bargains. They are fascinated by insider information, scenarios, fancy tax wrinkles, what "they" are saying on Wall Street—all of which Templeton dismissed long ago as unprofitable. Such superficial interests make for fashionable stocks, stocks that stimulate the herd instinct latent in investors. But when herd activities are brought to bear on a fashionable stock, the resulting stampede produces nothing but excessive prices.

The very popularity and relative stability of U.S. markets limit the prospects for investment bargains, Templeton believes. The tight market controls needed to assure that stability virtually assure that information about any reasonable investment opportunity will be widely disseminated.

It was thinking such as this that early led Templeton into exploring investment prospects where the herd did not graze. It put him on the path toward global investing 40 years before very many other investors warmed to the idea because he was willing to abide by the first rule. While there might be greater risks in the hurly-burly of largely unregulated foreign markets, sticking to his rule of price has greatly limited that risk.

If, in other words, the investor tried to make certain that he was paying less for a property than it was worth at the time—whether in dollars, marks, kroner, yen, or prayer beads—his chance of substantial losses would be rather slim. The first rule might mean that he would miss some potential opportunities, simply because he would have difficulty in proving whether they were bargains. But Templeton recognized that what was important were the opportunities acted on, not those left aside.

"Nobody's going to be able to take advantage of all opportunities," Templeton says, "and nobody should fret about having missed some of them. The very nature of investing is that there will be many opportunities that you don't take part in; your job is to participate in a few good ones.

"What's important is that you be right more often than you're wrong. When you're right, you should be very right, at least once in a while. And when you're wrong, you should recognize that before you become very wrong. An investment advisor makes his record in the long run by not making *huge* mistakes—and by making some mistakes that prove to be fortuitous, such as having a few stocks that rise in price more than he thought they would."

Templeton estimates that one third of the securities his firm buys don't perform as well as the overall market averages. Usually, however, about two thirds of them do better than the market "largely because we bought them at bargain prices."

Templeton's Second Rule of Successful Investing: The Good News–Bad News Rule

Look for situations where short-term factors temporarily affect a company's performance or investor's perception of the company.

This could also be called the "buy on bad news, sell on good news" rule.

NB: You are known as a contrarian. Is the second Templeton rule just a statement of a contrarian approach?

JMT: Not quite. We try to be apart from the crowd. You know that you will never attain a superior record by buying the same stocks that the crowd is buying. You have to do something different.

EK: How about some examples . . .

JMT: Well, one of my best trades was Union Carbide. Remember back in 1985 when there was that horrible accident at the Union Carbide plant in Bhopal [India]? The stock came crashing down to $32.75 from $50 on the New York Stock Exchange on fears that legal suits filed by family and relatives of the victims would put the chemical producer out of business. And we were sitting with a lot of stock. But you know what we did? We bought some more and when the price fell further we bought more again. Some people thought that I had become unglued! But here was the situation.

First, we figured that the insurance settlements would absorb much of the Bhopal sting. And second, Union Carbide, a company that we considered to be well-run, would continue to turn out the products that the public needed. In short, we believed that the Bhopal effect would have to wear off sooner or later. Either the company would rally again to profitability or its undeniably useful business units could be sold off to a number of anxious buyers.

EK: And . . .

JMT: Please allow me to finish. By the end of 1986 GAF Corporation had offered to buy the company for almost $69.00 a share, and we just happened to have 3,000,000 of the shares! That's what I mean by buying on temporary bad news!

John Templeton's Third Rule of Successful Investing: The Broaden-Your-Knowledge Rule

Where the possibility of a bargain appears present, the investor has the responsibility to acquire the expertise to evaluate the situation.

This could also be called the, "if the situation warrants it, get the facts," rule.

This third rule extends subtly beyond the popular brokerage firm dictum to "investigate then invest." Templeton believes that a lack of understanding of a country's economy, society, and form of business should not be a permanent impediment to finding and exploiting a bargain. He argues that if there are attractive opportunities in a particular country, then you must either become an expert on that country or hire yourself one.

NB: How do you go about acquiring the expertise to evaluate foreign investments?

JMT: There are many ways. First and foremost, learn about the country that you are interested in. Investigate the customs, habits, social values, and mores of the people. Learn about the political and social structure, the geography, and the land. Build up contacts with knowledgeable people from that country. Then you can turn your attention to the capital markets and the financial system. Explore the tax system, the financial reporting criteria, and the trading methods and rules.

Templeton obviously delights in becoming informed about the countries that interest him. His home is filled with remarkable items that he has gathered from his countless trips.

He collects first-hand information through extensive travels. And it is no accident that he and his wife Irene live in a town that has attracted one of the tightest concentrations of international leaders on earth. Each dinner party there, each chance encounter, provides an opportunity for him to learn more about financial and political developments in other countries directly from those who influence such events.

NB: You mentioned other methods of developing expertise.

JMT: That's right. There will be times when personal expertise is not enough to evaluate a potential bargain properly. Then you have to use outside resources to get the information needed.

The Templeton organization has its own staff of analysts and specialists on various geographic areas, but in addition it makes extensive use of contacts throughout the world. These contacts not only bring many bargains to Templeton's attention, but provide input for the analysis process. This understanding of local markets and business practices is an important check on the Templeton stock selection process.

Templeton's Fourth Rule of Successful Investing: The Quantification Rule

A bargain can be expressed in terms of its true current earnings (or likely future earnings) as compared to the cost of its shares or the price it could bring on the current open market.

Templeton's fourth rule reflects his deeply pragmatic nature. All aspects of an investment are to be quantified to provide a method of comparing it with other possible investments. A bargain can be found in the earning power of a company as compared to the price that the investor must pay for it. This is called *bottom-up* investing, an outgrowth of fundamental analysis that discourages speculation.

EK: Your fourth rule implies that the key Templeton yardsticks of value for assessing companies are earnings ratios, price/earnings multiples, price/cash flow, etc. Is that right?

JMT: Well, true. But I still want to stress that there are many yardsticks of value and scores of methods, and that you have to stay flexible. Nevertheless, the earnings yardsticks generally are the most important.

EK: How about an example . . .

JMT: I was reading a publication a few years back and discovered that the average price/earnings multiple for Dutch stocks was just 6.2 while U.S. stocks were at 10 and Japanese at around 26. I don't remember the exact numbers, but Dutch price/cash-flow ratios also were relatively low while dividend yields were high. So I had a starting point. But none of this was of any value unless I could find a good specific stock to take advantage of this.

EK: Let me interrupt for a moment. Couldn't you simply find a Dutch stock with a beta of one . . .

JMT: Conceptually, yes. But studies show that North American betas aren't stable, and I haven't seen anything on Dutch company betas. I'm not saying that we won't use betas but, until there is a history of use in a country, we prefer to use our traditional measures.

EK: So you looked for a specific situation . . .

JMT: I started with shipping, one of the industries that is traditionally undervalued, where companies are among the least expensive in terms of book value and cash flow. I zeroed in on Ned-Lloyd. It's the largest, best-managed shipping company in the Netherlands, and it was still a bargain. Its share price was less than 100 florins, whereas the book value per share was over 600 florins. In five of the past six years, the annual cash flow per share had been above 100 florins! So it was selling below cash flow, and at only one sixth of book value. That's a bargain.

EK: Where do dividends fit into the scheme of things? Do you use discounted dividend models in evaluating securities?

JMT: I know that it is customary to compare share prices with dividends. However, we find it more sensible to compare price to earnings instead, because earnings determine the firm's ability to pay dividends. And instead of comparing the customary 12-month earnings figure, we prefer to use figures from the latest five years. This largely eliminates normal cyclical distortions. So we compute aggregate price to average five-year earnings data and then determine whether the resulting price/earnings ratio is high or low by comparison to historical price to earnings ratios. This is one of the yardsticks by which we calculate that prices are above or below normal, and that stocks may be either bargains or overpriced.

EK: Is this a technique applicable to the valuation of U.S. securities only . . .

JMT: Definitely not. This is the very essence of our approach. We make similar calculations for other countries in which the figures can be determined. This allows us to deduce which countries at any given time offer the better bargains.

EK: What about balance sheet data? What yardsticks do you look for?

JMT: If you study stock markets in free enterprise countries, you'll find that there is no better measure than asset value, or book value, to determine when share prices for a nation as a whole are too high or too low. In a speech that I gave in 1984 to a group of security analysts, I pointed out that in the 32 years prior to 1984, share prices for companies making up the S&P 400 stock index averaged 66% above their historic book value. In 1984 that index was only 38% above book, indicating that stock prices were well below the historic norm.

But more important than historical book value is a study of replacement book value, the cost of reproducing assets (after depreciation) at today's cost levels. One simple way to estimate replacement book value is to assume that the average age for all nonmonetary assets of U.S. corporations is about five years. On that basis, our analysts constructed an index of replacement book value for the S&P 400 for the 32 years prior to 1984. In those years, the price index averaged 143% of the replacement book value, whereas in 1984 the price index averaged only 104% above replacement book. This indicated that prices might be considered to be 27% below normal.

While book value in this context is a vital tool for digging toward price relationships, it can be just as valuable as a measure of liquidation value. In world markets, it is possible to search out investments selling at half the worth of their assets; therefore, for every $1 invested, liquidation might bring you $2 or even more. Book value considered in this way could show even a bankrupt company to be a good investment.

Templeton's Fifth Rule of Successful Investing: The Hard Work Rule

Investing is hard work, and short cuts produce second-class results.

Templeton is convinced that investing is hard work; and it should be, given the potential for reward. It is a difficult and demanding profession. Templeton believes that most people try to oversimplify investing. They try to jerry-rig short cuts; and they find that the short cut they've sought to a "hot" market usually is a false route.

"When your friends say such things as 'I'm going to buy semiconductor stocks because they have a great future,' you have to recognize that they're talking investment nonsense," he says. "It's true that semiconductors are going to have a great future, but the price of shares usually reflects that obvious expectation. So if all you know about any particular stock is that the product behind it is going to have a great future, you're nowhere near knowing whether you should buy shares."

Templeton insists that you have to find out how many other people are making the product, whether it is semiconductors or jellybeans. You must assess the competition, determine who—if anybody—is coming up with new types or new processes; you must study the stock price in relation to per-share earnings, in relation to dividends, to assets, to sales. "You have to do all those things before you can make a sound judgment," he says. "Yet, most investors, including many Wall Street professionals, don't want to work that hard. They become excited about something and they buy it without fully understanding the situation."

By the same token, some real bargains go begging simply because not enough digging has been done to unearth them. A classic example lies behind the bargain price Templeton's group paid for shares of Rupert Murdoch's News Corporation, Ltd. While the company is based in Australia, it owns publications in Great Britain and in the United States. "But in relation to the Murdoch company's earnings," Templeton recalls, "we paid about one third the price we'd have had to pay for some publishing companies based in Great Britain or the United States. The price was well out of line because people weren't making an international comparison."

A more current example can be found in Australia also. Says Templeton: "In 1987, you could buy bank shares in Australia for 5 times earnings. At the same time, prices of comparable shares in the United States were 10 times earnings, and in Japan over 80 times earnings. Buyers were following the crowd, and the crowd had not bothered to compare Australian banks."

If hardly anybody will even consider buying some certain asset then that is the asset to consider. That's a principle of utmost importance to Templeton. "It goes beyond just not following the crowd," he says. "If you're building a house, developing a golf course, or running a doctor's office, you're not in a contest with anybody. But you can't buy a stock unless there's somebody wanting to sell it. And because you can't buy unless somebody sells, it's likely that a year later, or five years later, one of you will wish you hadn't done it."

Templeton concludes, "Because it is a contest, and is therefore different from almost every other business activity on earth, you must not go with the majority. You can gain opportunities in investing only by doing something that the majority are against doing or something they don't know about."

He points to high-tech stocks in 1983 as an example. "In June 1983, high-tech stocks were the hottest items on Wall

Street. Many were selling at 30 or 40 times earnings; that was the time investors should have been selling them, not buying them.

"The high-tech stocks have gone way down now," he said [early in 1986], "but they still aren't low enough for me. Some day they will be, when everybody's against them or forgotten about buying them. A wise investor can go in and study them and find bargains then. But not now."

Study and hard work are central to Templeton's bargain hunting. He uses few technical stock market indicators, no one formula, and, he insists, no intuition in his stock selection process. He selects his investments the "prudent" way; he studies them.

"It's very difficult to tell what a company is truly worth," he says. "If you've invested in a company, you and your analysts are continually reexamining it. Is the stock you thought was worth $75 a share now worth $85? Or is it perhaps worth only $65? Sometimes you find new information that will radically change your opinion."

In short, the bargain-hunting investor must ask the fundamental question every day: "What is the stock, anywhere in the world, that is selling at the lowest price in relation to what our analysts estimate its worth to be?" Only study and hard work reveal the answer.

THE TEMPLETON WAY—HOW TEMPLETON AND HIS ORGANIZATION PICK STOCKS

John Templeton's investment enterprises were incorporated in January 1986, into a public firm called Templeton, Galbraith, & Hansberger, Ltd. Under that umbrella are advisors in the U.S., Bahamas, Canada, England, and Hong Kong for the Templeton global mutual funds, the distribution company marketing them, and—of growing significance—Templeton Investment Counsel, a Fort Lauderdale-based operation that manages portfolios for individuals as well as corporations. In 1987, the Templeton Organization included 11 open-ended mutual funds and unit trusts, two closed-end mutual funds, and about 80 managed accounts (at a minimum asset value of $10,000,000 each). In the aggregate, some $U.S. 12 billion were under administration as of June 30, 1987, of which about $9 billion were in the Templeton mutual funds.

The Templeton team selects stocks on the basis of certain principles: global perspective, value orientation, flexibility, and discipline, using many different approaches.

Global perspective has been a principle with Templeton right from the start. Templeton was one of the first to recognize how global investing means an expanded investment opportunity set, diversification, and special opportunities with emerging nations. Global investment is a principle for the entire Templeton organization, not just the funds. Templeton himself puts it this way:

> Some institutions decide that they will invest 10% or more outside America and then employ an investment counselor to handle just those foreign investments. Experience has shown that better results are achieved if instead, the counselor is given discretion to invest either inside or outside the United States, wherever the best bargains might lie. That is our global approach.
>
> Also, some institutions employ a Japanese investment counselor to invest in Japan, a British counselor to invest in Britain, etc. Again, experience has shown that better results are achieved if a counselor with the global approach is engaged.

On the global scene, the Templeton counsel firm uses the same bargain-hunting philosophy found throughout the Templeton organization. "We look for the pearls," says Jim Hocking, a senior vice president of the firm, "and when we find them, they're often with us for a long, long time."

The value orientation refers to the search for stocks selling for less than their true worth or intrinsic value based on a set of universal yardsticks of value, of which price/earnings multiples, price/cash-flow ratios, consistency of earnings growth, and other earnings-based measures are paramount.

Flexibility means a willingness to accept new ideas, new models, and new investment opportunities; to adopt a contrarian approach where necessary; and to analyse securities on the basis of the current environment rather than what has worked in the past.

Discipline is synonymous with patience at the Templeton organization, both for the mutual funds and the pension funds. The team will buy stocks that are apparently selling at bargain levels, possibly because they are out of favor or obscure, and will patiently wait for the fundamentals to take hold, propelling the stock to new heights. As evidence of this, the average holding period for a security selected for inclusion in the Templeton empire of funds and managed portfolios is five years. Many professional investment managers lack either conviction or patience since on the average, they hold their stocks less than one year. As stated in a Templeton fund brochure:

> It takes patience and understanding to place funds on a discretionary basis with a manager who will generally be at odds with the rest of the investment community, in both the way it operates and the types of investments it makes.
>
> A disciplined approach demands disciplined clients.

Stock Selection—The Templeton Filter Process

When you are committed to global investing, you have a big problem; it is a big world. With thousands of stocks to pick from in dozens of national markets, sorting the wheat from the chaff is a major challenge.

The Templeton organization regularly receives investment suggestions from more than 100 financial firms worldwide. These ideas are funneled through the Templeton team of security analysts in five nations who then evaluate the suggestions based on fundamental Templeton yardsticks of value and other measures. The availability of computers and financial data bases helps to expedite this process. From this universe of over 3,000 stocks, about 80% are quickly eliminated. As Templeton describes it "our 45 years of experience tells us that these are not bargains—not at the moment anyway." Thus, the 3,000 is whittled down to a continually changing list of about 600 by the organization's active data bases.

The stocks are then ranked on the basis of relative undervaluation, with the 20% most undervalued stocks selected for possible portfolio inclusion. Both the current selection of acceptable stocks and the universe of stocks are constantly reevaluated and reexamined. Some 10 to 12 times a year the Templeton valuations are compared with changing market prices and if a nonincluded stock is deemed to be undervalued relative to an included stock, then a revision is made.[1] The system is a moving average filter where the objective at all times is to have only the world's biggest security bargains in place. As a result no specific holding period is designated for a new stock purchase. A decade ago, Templeton's average holding period was six years, not very different from today. But he has always made it clear that maintaining a certain average holding period for stocks is not part of any system he has developed as an investor. Templeton himself raised the issue of selling at the end of one of our long discussion sessions. It had been a long day and we were about to pack it in and go exploring for some good native conch chowder, and maybe after to go see Peanuts Taylor at the Drum Beat. But this was an important issue and so, with visions of yet another steak sandwich and fries back at the hotel casino's snack shop we settled in for the response. The answer turned out to be short, sweet, and inexorably intertwined with the filter process, so we still managed to get our Nassau jollies in as well.

NB: That's right we haven't talked at all about when you sell . . .

JMT: Ben Graham felt that if he bought a stock thinking that it was the best, and two or three years later it hadn't proved to be a bargain, he would sell it—but too much turnover is expensive.

   The time period isn't really the thing that guides me in making a decision. If you find something that's an excellent bargain, in order to buy you usually have to sell something else. And so I look over my list to see what stock that I own is the least good bargain—and I sell that—any new suggestion should have 50% better profit prospects than the stock replaced. But in the whole process I haven't asked myself whether I've owned the stock for one week or 20 years. It makes no difference! It's only when I look at the history of what I did that I find that I have an average holding period of five years.

In developing their global bargain-hunting strategies, one key operating policy has been to search for information gaps.[2] Templeton has a story from the 1950s that illustrates what the information gap policy means. In those days, despite the technological advances given impetus by World War II, science was still largely preoccupied with finding peaceful applications for atomic power and a massive device called Univac, for which incredible powers of memory were being claimed. "High-tech" was a term that had not yet entered the collective vocabulary; and technology was not a real factor on Wall Street.

It was then that Templeton began to invest in Haloid, a lightly traded photographic-supply company that—because of Eastman Kodak's dominance—seemed always to harbor feelings of inferiority. "They'd just contracted for a new process," Templeton recalls, "and not many securities analysts had ever heard of it—or them." Somehow, information about the breathtaking potential of the new process had slipped past Wall Street's sharp-eyed eagles. But Templeton realized that Haloid's stock was woefully undervalued and took advantage of the bargain.

Templeton portfolios eventually scored a 1,000% gain on their investment in what is now called xerographic copying, pioneered by Xerox Corporation, formerly the Haloid Company.

The key point of that story, as Templeton tells it, is not that Haloid/Xerox achieved a technological breakthrough, but that simply by recognizing a gap in the flow of public information, an outstanding investment bargain was found.

Templeton used the same principle to make his mark in Japan in the early 1960s, before most of the West had awakened to that industrious nation's potential.

> I was buying Japanese stocks because most investors outside Japan didn't know about them, and those in Japan didn't have enough experience in investing to know how to analyze them. So here was a situation where I was applying the same kinds of analytical techniques everybody else was using, but in an area where they hadn't thought to look. It was a wide open field.

The field was wide open for another reason. Even those investors who might have sensed profits in Japan opted to go elsewhere because of Japanese laws that forbade taking profits out of the country. "They had to protect their foreign exchange," Templeton explains.

But the profit potential was so great, as was the likelihood that international pressures would soon cause Japan to ease her restrictions, that Templeton began buying Japanese stocks for his personal portfolio. "I could take a chance with my own money on the law's being changed," he said, "but not with other people's money."

The law was changed, and Templeton's personal holdings benefited as expected. Having ventured into Japan well ahead of the pack, Templeton could move quickly—before prices were run up—to take positions that benefited his mutual funds and clients. Emerging giants such as Nissan and Hitachi were selling at prices equal to only 2 or 3 times their per-share earnings.

Templeton still likens some foreign securities markets to those in the United States 30 years ago, when informational loopholes ("inefficiencies," he calls them) made bargain hunting relatively easy. "Even now," Templeton says, "the amount of meaningful information available to Americans on many foreign corporations is so small that there are still many foreign stocks prices way out of line with their true value."

But, he says, it's becoming more difficult all the time to find those bargains. And the difficulty is rapidly increasing as U.S. investment houses such as Merrill Lynch gain seats on what once were chauvinistically sacrosanct foreign stock exchanges. It is no secret, either, that the fast-paced markets of 1985, 1986, and 1987 spawned a proliferation of mutual funds that, following Templeton's early lead, have concentrated on global stocks.

Despite mounting competition, however, Templeton is confident that foreign markets, like the domestic ones, will always hold bargains for those competent—and well enough informed—to seek them out.

Stock market bargains can be found only in specific issues. "We never ask ourselves what nation or what industry or what currency offers the best value," Templeton says. "We just search among thousands and thousands of companies, trying to find those whose stocks are selling for a small fraction of what we estimate their worth to be. An investor can not buy a nation or an industry but he can buy a selected stock."

Price. Templeton always comes back to price; whether the potential investment is stocks, bonds, gold, art objects, or real estate, price relationships are crucial.

Templeton owns Caribbean real estate on the remote British island of Grand Cayman. He was led there by chance when a friend interested in Bahamas real estate commented that Bahamas prices were high. "He said he could buy good land in the Cayman Islands for $100 an acre," Templeton recalls. That was in the mid-1970s, when the Caymans, to most outsiders, were just three fly specks on a map known primarily as an idyllic outpost for scuba-diving enthusiasts. "British government, a stable economy, and an excellent climate surrounded by ocean, all for $100 an acre; that had the makings of a bargain," Templeton says. Characteristically, he flew into Grand Cayman within a few weeks. In Georgetown, he sought out a real estate agent—"actually, he was just somebody who knew a lot of the landowners on the island" and the more he was shown, the stronger the scent of bargains became.

"I bought more than 50 different pieces of real estate," Templeton says. "Today, that land is worth at least 10 times what I paid for it. Eventually," he adds in typical understatement, "it should be very valuable land." He allows that he might be persuaded to sell it when the price reaches 100 times what he paid for it.

In real estate as in securities, Templeton insists, bargains await only those willing to seek them out, learn about every aspect of the property and of the market, and make sure that they're buying at the right price, the lowest possible price.

There are undoubtedly land bargains to be had in Florida, but thousands of people who've bought there over the years haven't found them.

They've bought land some salesman had to offer them. He'd come to them in the north and say that Florida has a great future and the land there will become more valuable. Both statements were true; but he was *selling,* and he was getting whatever price the traffic would bear for land he may have bought at $100 an acre.

If his buyers were true investors, they should have concentrated on *buying*. They should have visited Florida, seen the land, taken time to talk to real estate people and study newspaper ads to make price comparisons. They should have bought only after assuring themselves that the price they were offered was the lowest possible one.

Price to John Templeton is more than a dollar amount. It is the amalgam of an investment's past, present, and future. It is, like Einstein's relativity, a measure that ties all forces together and provides them with a comparable weight in the financial cosmos. To paraphrase another concept from physics, price to Templeton represents the binding curve of profit.

But Templeton himself doesn't bother with pretentious phraseology. He is straightforward in describing the role of price in his work:

> I travel in many nations and areas looking for things that are unknown. Where others may specialize in odd securities, I specialize in odd corners of the earth.
>
> If you work at looking for bargains, you'll find them.

ENDNOTES

1. Templeton portfolio managers usually have some three dozen "buy" orders in the hands of brokers at any given time. They may offer the going market price or bid a fraction over or below the market, depending on their own assessment of the stock's worth.

   "If nobody sells to us at what we think is a bargain price," Templeton notes, "we'll instruct the broker involved to pull the order. If further study indicates that the shares are bargains at yet a higher price, we'll resubmit. Otherwise, we'll simply find better bargains elsewhere on the planet. Gradually, we accumulate the stocks we want."

2. Templeton has consistently managed to earn excess returns on a risk-adjusted basis. One explanation for this is that he sets out to deliberately exploit market inefficiencies through these information gaps.

APPENDIX

Templeton's guiding principles of investment selection, originally published in an authorized biography by William Proctor, *The Templeton Touch,** are reproduced below. Some of these principles are really just statements (e.g., #1), others difficult to implement (e.g., #6) while others are provocative and worthy of examination (#13 and #16 might be suitable topics for business school masters theses!).

1. For all long-term investors, there is only one objective— "maximum total real return after taxes."
2. Achieving a good record takes much study and work, and is a lot harder than most people think.
3. It is impossible to produce a superior performance unless you do something different from the majority.
4. The time of maximum pessimism is the best time to buy, and the time of maximum optimism is the best time to sell.
5. To put "Maxim 4" in somewhat different terms, in the stock market the only way to get a bargain is to buy what most investors are selling.
6. To buy when others are despondently selling and to sell when others are greedily buying requires the greatest fortitude, even while offering the greatest reward.
7. Bear markets have always been temporary. Share prices turn upward from one to twelve months before the bottom of the business cycle.
8. If a particular industry or type of security becomes popular with investors, that popularity will always prove temporary and, when lost, won't return for many years.
9. In the long run, the stock market indexes fluctuate around the long-term upward trend of earnings per share.
10. In free-enterprise nations, the earnings on stock market indexes fluctuate around the replacement book value of the shares of the index.
11. If you buy the same securities as other people, you will have the same results as other people.

*Excerpt from *The Templeton Touch* by William Proctor, copyright © 1983 by William Proctor. Reprinted by permission of Doubleday, a division of Bantam, Dell, Doubleday Publishing Group, Inc.

12. The time to buy a stock is when the short-term owners have finished their selling, and the time to sell a stock is often when short-term owners have finished their buying.
13. Share prices fluctuate much more widely than values. Therefore, index funds will never produce the best total return performance.
14. Too many investors focus on "outlook" and "trend." Therefore, more profit is made by focusing on value.
15. If you search worldwide, you will find more bargains and better bargains than by studying only one nation. Also, you gain the safety of diversification.
16. The fluctuation of share prices is roughly proportional to the square root of the price.
17. The time to sell an asset is when you have found a much better bargain to replace it.
18. When any method for selecting stocks becomes popular, then switch to unpopular methods. As has been suggested in "Maxim 3," too many investors can spoil any share-selection method or any market-timing formula.
19. Never adopt permanently any type of asset or any selection method. Try to stay flexible, open-minded, and skeptical. Long-term top results are achieved only by changing from popular to unpopular the types of securities you favor and your methods of selection.
20. The skill factor in selection is largest for the common-stock part of your investments.
21. The best performance is produced by a person, not a committee.
22. If you begin with prayer, you can think more clearly and make fewer stupid mistakes.

CHAPTER 7

GLOBAL MUTUAL FUND SELECTION

GLOBAL INVESTMENT—THE OLD ANALOGY OF EGGS

"Don't put all of your eggs in one basket" is probably the oldest and most hackneyed expression in the investment world. But it is a very true one nevertheless. Most investors know that the maxim translates into a technique called diversification, a strategy of allocating your investment funds into assets of different types and maturities to capture different movements in the economy and to protect against "gambler's ruin," the risk of a particular investment turning sour and destroying your savings. This means that, in addition to fixed-income investments such as government bonds and insured bank deposits, investors should hold some stocks, bonds, and gold; and most important, some foreign securities. Diversifying one's portfolio internationally should, in the long run, lead to higher returns at a lower risk exposure.

In Chapter 2 we discussed the merits of global investing; how, in addition to diversification, it offers an expanded investment opportunity set, foreign currency exposure, and superior risk-adjusted investment performance. The concept of international or global investing is compelling. But it isn't easy to do, at least directly. It's hard enough keeping up with local stocks, let alone tens of thousands traded worldwide.

There are a number of roadblocks to global investing, also outlined in Chapter 2. To invest intelligently in foreign companies, one needs access to quality information. But current and valuable information on foreign companies can be both expensive and hard to obtain. And differing accounting and reporting standards make comparisons difficult.

The actual process of buying and selling can be aggravating. One's local broker may have to deal with a foreign broker or bank which adds to the trading complexity, as well as the cost. It may take hours, even a day, to get market quotes. The movement toward exchange interlistings (the Tokyo Stock Exchange and the Montreal Exchange, for example, have foreign security sections) and intermarket electronic links (such as those between the Toronto Stock Exchange and American Stock Exchange and the Montreal Exchange and Boston Stock Exchange) has mitigated the problems of trading in foreign securities. But the day that traders will have direct access to all traded foreign securities—the so-called global marketplace—is still far in the future.

Trading fees, including commissions, stock turnover taxes, value added taxes, stamp duties, and the like, vary widely from country to country, and add to the complexity and cost of trading. In some cases, these transaction costs are much higher than American costs, and lower in other cases. Commissions vary from below 1% to as much as 7%. Furthermore, some countries levy withholding taxes on dividend income earned by nonresidents. These withholding taxes range from 10 to 30% and are deducted from the proceeds at the source when the dividend is paid, although in most countries the investor is eligible for a foreign tax credit when he files his income tax return.

Other problems of direct international investment include thinly traded markets; custody (in some countries a custodian must be appointed before you can trade); time zone differences (if one wishes to call a broker in London directly to trade a security, the call must be made before 10:30 A.M. Eastern time at the latest); and political and sovereignty risk, the danger of a foreign government taking some action that reduces the value of one's holdings or the ability to trade. And finally, in some countries investors are prohibited from direct trading. Brazil, India, and South Korea are among those that currently restrict trading by nonresidents. These impediments or barriers make it difficult for all but the truly tenacious investor.

BUYING GLOBAL AND INTERNATIONAL MUTUAL FUNDS—THE PRACTICAL ALTERNATIVE

What is the alternative? Investors can buy professional management and avoid the headaches of selecting and trading foreign securities directly (let alone selecting the right countries) by buying shares in global, international, or foreign single country mutual funds. Mutual funds sell shares to investors and invest the proceeds in a portfolio of securities of which the investor owns a pro rata share. Each fund is managed by an advisor or team of advisors who select securities in a manner that is consistent with a published statement of objectives or investment policies of the fund.

Investment companies in the form of pooled and managed portfolios originated in Scotland in the 19th century and were introduced in the United States in 1923. Today there are thousands of investment companies available worldwide, although only a relatively small percentage are international or global in outlook.

There are two classes of investment company funds; open- and closed-ended. Open-ended funds (often referred to as mutual funds) sell shares to the public and also redeem on request on a continuous basis and invest the proceeds in a portfolio of securities. In many countries, such funds are accorded special tax treatments such as tax deferment on income and capital gains not distributed to shareholders. The term open-ended refers to the continuous distribution of new shares (subject only to a limit of authorized shares outstanding) and the fact that the issuing fund will always buy back (redeem) shares at the current *net asset value* (assets minus liabilities divided by the number of shares outstanding). Shares of open-ended funds are sold to the public at this *net asset value* per share, plus, in some cases, a load or commission and are sold back to the fund by the fund holder at the current net asset value at the time of redemption. Some funds are specifically no load; some have exit loads. Unit trusts is the name commonly used in Europe for mutual funds.

Closed-ended funds, on the other hand, do not sell shares continuously to the public. Like any public corporation, they may, with regulatory approval, engage in new share financing from time to time. Like the open-ended fund, the closed-ended investment company invests its assets in a portfolio of securities according to an investment plan or strategy.

Closed-end fund shares are traded on stock exchanges and over-the-counter markets and prices are determined by the usual auction process applicable to stock trading. Prices at any time may be well above or below net asset value, with the latter more usual in recent years. The premium or discount at which these funds trade represents an intriguing and challenging analytic problem, discussed later in this chapter under the subheading "Closed-End Funds: The Discount Issue."

Mutual funds are classified by objectives, as stated by the fund management or the prospectus. Performance ranking publications normally list the surveyed funds by these stated investment objectives, allowing investors to conduct their analysis on a comparative basis within fund groupings.[1]

Global, International, and Single Country Funds—Classification

Mutual funds specializing in overseas investment are classified by the investment community as either international or global. There is an important distinction. International funds are those that limit their investments to markets and countries outside the domestic country. They might even restrict their investment activities to a specific region, country, or continent. By contrast, global funds have no geographic bounds; they invest anywhere that their management believes a bargain can be found—including the host country. Global funds thus offer greater diversification than international funds because of the lack of restriction on investment activities. An investor can, however, combine ownership of a diversified domestic portfolio with ownership of international funds to replicate a global portfolio.

Global and International Mutual Fund Selection—Performance Measures

An international or global fund does not free the investor from the burden of attaining knowledge or making a decision. He still must determine, for example, whether an Australian-oriented fund is a better value at a given time than a Canadian-oriented one; whether he agrees with the fund manager that prospects are better in Europe than Asia; how to select from a universe of global funds; etc. The careful international investor still has the burden of becoming, if not expert, at least knowledgeable. To select from the large universe of global, international, and specialized single country and regional funds, an investor must develop a set of criteria for evaluating and ranking specific funds. These criteria will be both quantitative and qualitative, reflecting both the historic returns and variances, as well as the quality of management.

To compare mutual funds, the basic computations listed on the following pages should be used. The underlying data and indeed most or all of the calculations can be found in the industry source data such as *Forbes, Johnson Charts,* the *Lipper Report, Standard & Poor's Mutual Fund Summary,* the *United Mutual Fund Selector, Barron's Weekly, Money Guide Mutual Funds* (the preceding are all U.S. publications); *The Financial Post,* the *Financial Times* (Canadian publications); the *Financial Times of London* (United Kingdom) and *Euromoney* (international), all of which publish periodic and annual tallies of mutual fund performance.

The prospective investor should first obtain a set of performance data, possibly from a number of sources, in preparation for a careful analysis using the criteria set out below. Investors may discover that they have to add to their data as each performance publication has different criteria and rankings. A sample from the U.S. publication "The Lipper Analytic Service" is shown in Figure 7–1.

FIGURE 7-1
Sample Page from Performance Rating Publication

| Total Assets in Millions | | | | | | Percentage Changes | | | | | Rank | | Yield |
6/30/87	3/31/87	6/30/86	Mutual Fund	OBJ	Closing NAV	10 Yrs Sept. 77 Sept. 87	5 Yrs Sept. 82 Sept. 87	12 Mos Sept. 86 Sept. 87	1987 To Date	3rd Qtr 1987	5 Yrs Sept. 82 Sept. 87	1987 To Date	12 Mos
			Global Funds Range of Assets .1 to 25.0 Million										
$10.6	$ 4.4	$ *	Criterion Global Growth	GL	15.19	*	*	*	51.90	9.44	*	45	*
21.6	7.0	*	MFS Lifetime Global EQ	R GL	12.39	*	*	*	47.50	4.38	*	55	*
1.6	1.0	0.2	Newport Global Growth	R GL	13.43			37.89	34.30	10.72		232	0.0
15.5	14.1	4.9	Principal World	GL	10.77			35.20	27.33	7.38		439	1.0
11.8	10.3	3.3	Alliance World Equity	GL	12.13			24.01	20.27	5.66		614	0.3
3.2LO	#	#	Dreyfus Strat World	LP GL	17.55	#	#	#	35.00#	11.50	#	#	#
16.3	9.3	#	Simms Global	GL	11.91	#	#	#	25.37#	9.97	#	#	#
2.9	#	#	GT Worldwide Growth	GL	11.61	#	#	#	16.10#	11.85	#	#	#
1.2	#	#	GT America Growth	GL	10.96	#	#	#	9.60#	5.28	#	#	#
12.7	#	#	Lexington Global	GL	11.02	#	#	#	8.79#	9.11	#	#	#
0.4	#	#	UST Master International	GL N	8.23	#	#	#	2.88#	#	#	#	#
12.9	#	#	Mackay-Shields Global	R GL	10.17	#	#	#	1.70#	1.80	#	#	#
1.9	#	#	Templeton/Tatt Phil	R GL	10.17	#	#	#	1.70#	0.89	#	#	#
15.6	#	#	AMA Inc-Global Sht Term	GL	10.09	#	#	#	1.40#	0.80	#	#	#
$ 128.2	$ 46.1	$ 8.4	TOTAL 14			0.00	0.00	32.36	36.26	6.83	0	277	0.4
			Global Funds Range of Assets 25.0 to 100.0 Million										
$ 69.2	$ 46.3	$ 29.0	First INV International	GL	5.24	*	227.58	74.20	58.81	13.42	56	29	0.2
64.7	58.4	*	Freedom Global	GL N	15.23	*	*	*	55.27	19.26	*	38	*
99.5	91.0	43.7	Van Eck World Trends	GL	16.16	*	*	26.25	23.43	6.09	*	548	1.7
26.7	25.7	9.8	Gam Global	GL	118.39	*	*	16.08	13.09	1.00	*	747	0.0
52.6	#	#	IDS PAN Pacific Growth	R GL	5.09	#	*	#	1.80#	5.82	#	#	#
$ 312.7	$ 221.4	$ 82.5	TOTAL 5			0.00	227.58	38.84	37.65	9.12	56	340	0.6
			Global Funds Range of Assets 100.0 to 500.0 Million										
$ 321.8	$ 260.1	$218.0	Painewebber Atlas	GL N	22.14	*	*	46.65	38.90	10.70	*	133	4.5
101.8	79.0	*	Scudder Global	GL	16.44	*	*	46.49	34.47	8.39	*	227	0.2
158.1	121.2	52.9	J Hancock Global	GL	19.21	*	*	41.30	31.75	5.20	*	301	0.0
105.1	91.9	*	Thomson McKinnon Global	R GL	12.87	*	*	32.68	29.74	4.89	*	352	0.0
495.5	469.5	325.8	Dean Witter World Wide	R GL	18.78	*	*	33.98	26.58	8.37	*	457	0.6
268.7	278.5	295.1	Shearson Lehman Glbl	OPP GL	31.99	*	*	34.69	25.95	12.15	*	477	0.3
359.2	332.4	282.3	Merrill Lyn Intl Hldgs	X GL	15.22	*	*	32.44	25.51	5.84	*	488	1.4
337.0	335.8	321.7	Templeton Global I	GL +	49.03	#	222.43	24.15	20.14	1.96	66	620	2.2
136.2	115.9	#	AMA Global Growth	GL	22.82	#	#	#	15.11#	6.37	#	#	#
$ 2283.4	$ 2084.3	$ 1495.8	TOTAL 9			0.00	222.43	36.55	29.13	7.10	66	381	1.2

Assets	Assets	Assets	Fund	R	Obj	Mk									
Global Funds															
			Range of Assets 500.0 Million +												
$ 517.1	$ 477.8	$ 379.2	Oppenheimer Global Fund		GL	N	38.29	797.15	286.66	52.59	41.87	14.13	15	94	0.3
831.0)	810.5	300.7	Fru-Bache Global FD	R	GL	N	13.44	*	*	41.01	39.42	9.54	*	124	0.0
1118.6	1052.9	865.7	New Perspective Fund		GL		13.73	635.72	251.13	50.09	38.47	10.19	25	143	1.6
1446.5	1343.7	1781.7	Templeton Growth		GL		17.06	522.79	230.51	39.94	32.56	10.14	48	279	1.1
611.5	526.3	322.1	Putnam Intl Equities		GL		34.98	699.54	378.17	39.97	32.28	7.07	5	288	0.5
4199.0	4063.2	3207.8	Templeton World		GL		18.90	*	228.35	32.65	28.22	8.25	53	403	2.3
587.0	583.3	521.6	Templeton Global II		GL	+	15.28	*	*	22.32	20.13	4.02	*	621	2.1
$ 9310.7	$ 8857.7	$ 7378.8	TOTAL			7		663.80	274.96	39.80	33.28	9.05	29	278	1.1
$ 12035.0	$ 11209.5	$ 8965.5	GLOBAL TOTAL			35		663.80	260.69	37.36	33.24	7.69	38	323	1.0
International Funds															
			Range of Assets .1 to 25.0 Million												
$ 7.2	$ 5.8	$ 3.3	GT Japan Growth		IF		29.29	*	*	49.42	57.21	25.39	*	30	0.0
15.9	13.1	4.9	Ivy International		IF		18.84	*	*	61.06	54.69	13.43	*	40	0.0
4.1	3.7	2.4	Newport Far East		IF		28.97	*	*	53.44	43.77	8.75	*	76	0.0
17.5	15.4	6.4	GT Europe Growth	R	IF		25.77	*	*	56.53	42.44	14.48	*	90	0.0
23.9	16.8	4.3	GT International Growth		IF		24.46	*	*	40.91	37.84	13.72	*	153	0.0
10.7	10.4	7.0	Sigma World		IF		20.66	*	*	43.63	31.18	9.60	*	310	0.0
9.0	5.4	*	Colonial Intl Eq Index		IF		17.27	*	*	35.90	30.46	3.94	*	335	0.1
4.2	2.5	0.2	Financial Port-European		IF		10.51	*	*	26.86	19.84	4.16	*	628	0.0
1.7	0.9	#	Lepercq-Istel Intl		IF	N	12.79	#	#	#	27.90#	8.48	#	#	#
1.8	2.0	#	GAM Tokyo		IF		122.68	#	#	#	22.68#	1.41	#	#	#
2.4	1.8	#	European Fund		IF		12.01	#	#	#	20.10#	8.30	#	#	#
1.6	#	#	GAM Pacific Basin		IF		115.51	#	#	#	15.51#	13.11	#	#	#
0.7	0.4	#	Intl Heritage Ovsea Gr	R	IF		11.43	#	#	#	14.30#	6.23	#	#	#
11.8	#	#	IAI International Fund		IF	N	10.63	#	#	#	5.98#	5.35	#	#	#
0.1	#	#	Boston Frgn Gr & Inc	R	IF		9.75	#	#	#	-2.50#	#	#	#	#
$ 112.6	$ 78.2	$ 28.5	TOTAL			15		0.00	0.00	45.97	39.68	9.74	0	207	0.0
			Range of Assets 25.0 to 100.0 Million												
International Funds															
$ 91.3)	$ 40.5	$ 29.9	DFA United Kingdom SM Co		IF		31.75	*	*	110.51	85.62	9.78	*	7	1.1
62.0)	50.9	43.9	DFA Japan Small Company		IF		24.18	*	*	73.21	66.41	15.97	*	23	0.0
58.8)	43.9	4.8	Financial Port-Pacific		IF	N	19.19	*	*	62.34	51.22	10.99	*	46	0.2
36.4LO	33.1	*	Flag International		IF		14.46	*	*	*	40.39	11.75	*	110	*
29.9	29.8	18.6	Intl FD for Institutions		IF	N	20.75	*	*	41.23	36.64	9.21	*	185	0.2
95.8)	86.6	55.2	Fenimore International		IF	N	16.27	*	*	45.82	35.78	12.67	*	199	0.0
27.3	27.0	24.9	Alliance Canadian Fund	R	IF		9.60	277.53	129.40	40.01	35.52	7.00	324	203	0.9
59.6	57.2	48.5	GT Pacific Growth FD		IF		28.44	456.56	284.49	29.27	33.59	10.66	16	249	0.0
34.2	26.9	23.5	GAM International		IF	N	212.81	*	*	38.54	32.83	4.51	*	272	0.6
28.2	15.5	6.5	Fund Source Intl Equity		IF	N	18.02	*	*	36.49	25.40	6.50	*	490	0.1
52.6LO	17.0	#	Fidelity Intl GR & Inc	R	IF		13.18	#	#	#	18.33#	7.92	#	#	#
$ 576.1	$ 428.4	$ 255.8	TOTAL			11		367.05	206.95	53.05	44.34	9.72	170	178	0.3

SOURCE: From "Lipper-Mutual Fund Performance Analysis—Ranking by Objective," September 30, 1987. Reprinted by permission of Lipper Analytic Services.

Performance

The historic performance of mutual funds should reflect both the returns and the risk. The appropriate measure of return is the annual compounded rate of total return, comprised of the change in net asset value plus dividend and capital gain distributions, which are assumed to be reinvested in the month distributed from the base to terminal period.

Measuring Return

Suppose that Fund A's initial net asset value was $1.00. Assume that over the next five years, the dividends and capital gain distributions per share allow for the purchase of 25% more units. The net asset value at the end of the period is $1.60. The annual compounded rate of total return, R, is calculated as 14.87% as below:

$$1(1+R)^5 = (1.25)(1.60) = 2.00$$
$$R = 14.87\%$$

No sales charges, commissions, or loads are considered in the calculations, as presented in the published performance tables.

Average annual compounded returns provide an appropriate measure of comparison to returns on other investments. However, both risk, as measured by the standard deviation, and consistency, as indicated in the annual simple returns, are important measures as well.

Wherever possible, the careful investor should select funds on the basis of an examination of annual performance over an extended period, such as 10 or 20 years, rather than on the basis of a one year or shorter period. Templeton, in fact, suggests an examination of performance over two or more market cycles (each cycle being 4 plus years). Returns should be compared to the average of the funds in the objective class and to an appropriate market benchmark index.

Risk

Risk measures that can be used to evaluate fund performance include the standard deviation and beta.

The standard deviation measures the degree of total variability about the rate of return on the investment and provides a measure of the risk inherent in the fund. It is an indication of the ups and downs. The higher the standard deviation, the greater the variability of returns. For comparability, the standard deviation of an appropriate benchmark index should be determined. Since most investors wish to minimize risk and earn consistent returns, funds with very high standard deviations on both an absolute and a relative basis should be avoided, everything else being equal. Standard deviation is an appropriate measure of risk for investors who hold small non-diversified portfolios of funds.

The beta is calculated by regressing the return on the fund against an appropriate market index. In nontechnical terms, this means that it is an indicator of how a fund's value has fluctuated relative to past changes in the general market. The higher the fund's beta, the greater the degree of fluctuation for a given change in the overall market.

Combined Performance Measures

Both return and risk measures can be combined to create a single measure of fund performance. One such indicator is the reward/risk ratio which is calculated as the fund's return divided by the standard deviation.[2] This reward/risk ratio measures the past return per unit of risk undertaken and is a relative measure of risk. Comparisons among mutual funds and between the funds and a benchmark index are measures of past reward to variability. Another useful measure is the reward per systematic risk measure or the excess return divided by beta of the portfolio.[3]

An Analysis in Action—Examining Returns

For illustration purposes, seven representative global international and single country mutual funds domiciled in Canada are identified in Table 7–1. For each of the funds we've provided

TABLE 7-1

International Global and Single Country Mutual Funds and the TSE 300—5 and 10 Year Performance (After estimated load or commissions)

Mutual Fund	Average Annual Compounded Rate of Return		Value of $5000 Investment	
	10 Year (%)	5 Year (%)	10 Year ($)	5 Year ($)
Bolton Tremblay International	20.36	26.49	31,899	16,191
Montreal Trust International Fund	16.60	24.20	23,225	14,777
Investors International Mutual	15.37	20.44	20,889	12,672
Templeton Growth Fund	20.62	24.96	32,606	15,234
Guardian World Equity Fund	19.59	20.16	29,905	12,525
Royal Trust A Fund-NL	14.40	19.40	19,197	12,134
AGF Japan-high var	23.73	34.15	42,037	21,720
TSE Composite 300 Index	17.68	25.17	25,470	15,360

the annual compounded rate of return for 10 (1977–1987) and 5 (1982–1987) years, as well as the value today of a $5,000 investment made 10 and 5 years previously. For both calculations we've assumed that the maximum sales charge was paid at purchase. The results are contrasted with the performance of the TSE 300 Composite Index, a representative index of Canadian equities, which has also been adjusted for commissions (both buying and selling). As can be seen, these funds on average, performed about the same as the TSE 300 over this period. If, for example, an investment of $5,000 was made in the Templeton Growth Fund in 1977, and all dividends were reinvested in the fund as received, the investor would have $32,606 today (1987) or an annual compounded rate of return of 20.62%. That same amount invested in a representative portfolio of Canadian common shares, as approximated by the TSE 300 Index, with dividends reinvested, would be worth only $25,470. Of course there is no guarantee that the past performance of global and international funds will be duplicated in the future.

NB: Each one dollar Canadian invested in Templeton Growth Fund when it started 33 years ago with distributions reinvested has grown to $105 by August, 1987. In the future, what percentage do you hope to average each year in a growth fund?

JMT: Values of our shares will go up and down with the stock market. We don't know what the future holds, and I can't make any predictions about what we'll achieve in the long run. We have been working publicly with mutual funds for over 30 years, and the performance has averaged out to 7% per year better than the stock market; but in those years, there have been 7 years when our performance lagged behind the stock market average. In the short range you can't expect that you're going to be better than the market, and you can't expect us to have a positive result when the stock market is in a bad phase. The closest answer is to say that our objective is to be much better on average than the stock market or the average results of similar funds.

SELECTING THE RIGHT FUND

How do you choose from the long and growing list of available funds? Two major sources of information are the prospectuses of the funds themselves and the published performance data as found in the various newspapers and periodicals mentioned above. The prospectus will outline the general investment philosophy of the fund managers, the current structure of the investment portfolio, including the geographic breakdown of its investments, the management fees, the names of the advisors, and so on. In the performance data, the investor can find the annual compounded rate of return on each fund, its variability class (the higher the variability the wider the swings in net asset values and returns), the initial launch date, etc. The following are the major issues that an investor should consider.

Management's Objectives

This is found in the fund's prospectus, along with details on the kinds of investments management is empowered to make. Portfolio revisions can be followed by reading the quarterly, semi-annual, and annual reports. Investors want to select funds that are congruent with their tastes.

Consistency

Studies have shown that high performing funds one year are sometimes the big losers the next year. Some funds outperform the averages in strong markets, but underperform in weak ones. Often mutual funds on average do not outperform a randomly selected portfolio of securities.[4] A key criteria in selecting a good global fund is *consistency*[5] of performance, how well the fund performs in bad markets as well as good. As a result, the firm's beta, variance, and reward/risk measures are all important measurement variables. As an example, the Bolton Tremblay International Fund has achieved an annual compounded rate of return of 20.4% over the 1977 to 1987 10-year period. Over this same period, the fund achieved positive returns in 9 of the 10 years (the only losing year was 1977 in which the fund lost 1.6%) and showed reasonably consistent performance over this period.

In analyzing performance, the investor should first examine the 10-year record which usually represents two, sometimes three, market cycles. A good starting point is a fund which has been in the top 5% of performers over at least a 10-year period. Then the investor looks to see how it has performed relative to a benchmark index and relative to the other funds available, in strong as well as weak markets. One should check to see if the same advisor who achieved the results is still in place. The objective is to find a fund with a consistent track record, preferably the same manager, and with a history. Some of the funds that have been issued recently look very interesting but one must keep in mind that there isn't a long-term record to examine.

Then the performance measures should be used to reduce the long selection list to a short one. From the prospectuses of the fund in this list, one can discover the firm's investment philosophy and the current geographical composition of the portfolio (for example, in late 1986 Bolton Tremblay had about 25% of its portfolio in the United States, 35% in Europe, and 14% in the Pacific rim; while the Templeton Growth Fund, a global fund, was by contrast heavily invested in the dollar currency countries: Australia, Canada, and the United States).

Stability of Management

Next, one should determine the tenure of the fund's manager and whether the person who managed the fund's portfolio when it produced big gains is still at the helm. "Hot" managers are sometimes lured into a better paying competitor's camp. Often, the portfolio is managed by an advisory firm with a defined strategy. That can be a plus; it provides a degree of consistency, at least, even when there's a coming and going of individual managers. Mutual fund prospectuses generally do not detail such things, but the Wiesenberger Service's *Investment Companies* annual report does provide management information.

Loads and Costs

There are two types of potential costs borne by fund holders; loads or sales charges payable at purchase (front-end) or much less commonly at sale (back-end), and management fees. Sales charges are levied by what are called load funds; firms that charge no sales fees are called no-load. However, over 600 American no-load funds instead pay salesmen out of annual 12b-1 fees deducted yearly from the funds' assets. With the exception of speculators, who are planning to actively trade mutual funds (and frankly there are much better media for speculating than mutual funds) investors should, in general, base their selection of funds on the performance and management criteria.

Most funds with a sales charge set 8.5% as the maximum load for the first $10,000 to $25,000 of an investment. The $100,000 investor, however, can be charged as little as 2.75%. Also, the fund's distributor might accept a "letter of intent." Such letters allow an investor to make smaller investments at the lower rate that applies at the $100,000 breakpoint, as long as the total invested over a 13-month period reaches $100,000, or the breakpoint.

Templeton funds, for example, would allow a $5,000 investment to be made at a sales charge of only 4.5%, the charge that applies once a $50,000 breakpoint is reached; but the investor would have to sign a letter stating that he intends to invest at least an additional $45,000 during the subsequent 13-month period. The Templeton funds' sales load is ½ of 1% for investors who fulfill a $2 million letter of intent.

These criteria should allow the investor to select a fund (or funds) that meet his tastes and risk preferences.

Some Mutual Fund Selection "Side Issues"

Other criteria for fund selection can be identified. However, despite popular belief to the contrary, there is as yet either little or no proven relationship between fund performance and the variables outlined below.

Operating Expenses
The funds' operating expenses can be measured as total operating costs per $100 of assets. Although studies indicate that in general, high expense ratio funds tend to slightly underperform low expense ratio funds, the relationship is not a strong one and is likely to be dominated by other factors. Investors are thus cautioned that a low expense ratio does not necessarily imply above average performance.[6]

Size
There is a belief, possibly as a result of confusion with the small firm effect, that small mutual funds outperform large ones. Research studies are mixed on the relationship between size of fund and performance, but in general they show that small funds earn similar returns to large funds.[7]

Portfolio Turnover and Timing
Researchers have similarly been unable to detect any strong relationship between fund performance and the frequency and degree of portfolio revision, and timing of purchases.[8]

> *NB:* Isn't it harder to manage a portfolio with over a billion in assets? Is there a point when a portfolio becomes unmanageable?

> *JMT:* It is a popular question, and there's good common sense in it. An outstanding result is much easier to produce with a

hundred thousand dollars than it is with a billion dollars. But, that's only one factor of many. For example, if you look at the list of mutual funds that had the top performance, you will find that perhaps 8 out of 10 are small funds. You could conclude that a small fund can perform better.

NB: And you might think that you're better off moving into smaller funds, from one fund to another smaller fund. I've met people with that mentality.

JMT: Many people have that idea but that's an illusion. There are almost two thousand mutual funds in America. Ninety percent of them are quite small. So if you took the average of all mutual funds, 90% of the best performers would be small and 90% of the worst performers would be small because 90% of all the funds are small. So it doesn't prove anything to see that 80 to 90% of the good performers are small. At one time, we had a statistician take the 50 largest mutual funds that had a long-term record and the 50 smallest mutual funds to see which performed better. The large funds performed better than the small ones. If you take a fair statistical comparison, comparing the best 20 or best 50 with the worst 20 or the worst 50, you will find that the smaller ones have not done as well in the long run as the big funds. There are so many other factors involved in performance, such as the ability to attract superior security analysts by higher salaries.

Valuation of Closed-End Single Country Funds

Country specific closed-end funds were steadily introduced to the market over the 1981 to 1987 period. These single country or regional funds are interesting but much more volatile than the global and international funds. And they certainly have a checkered history, with many of the issues selling well below issue price.[9] The funds of countries that are otherwise blocked to nonresidents (such as South Korea, Taiwan, and Brazil) are particularly valuable in allowing investors major diversification opportunities. A representative list of closed-end mutual funds was previously shown in Table 2–6.

One of the most interesting of this genre is the Templeton Emerging Markets Fund which made its debut in May 1987. The fund is described below.

The Templeton Emerging Markets Fund
The Templeton Emerging Markets Fund commenced operations on March 5, 1987. As of May 31, 1987, they had invested 17% of their paid-in capital of $107 million in the portfolio listing shown in Appendix A at the end of this chapter. The fund has investments in 35 companies listed on 6 emerging stock markets and operating in over 20 emerging nations. Direct emerging stock market investments include those in Singapore, Malaysia, Hong Kong, Mexico, Thailand, and the Philippines. Other investments in firms listed on major world stock exchanges include companies with operations primarily in Brazil, Chile, The People's Republic of China, the Republic of China, Colombia, Costa Rica, Ivory Coast, Dominican Republic, Ecuador, El Salvador, Greece, India, Mexico, Nigeria, Papua New Guinea, Portugal, Sri Lanka, Turkey, Venezuela, Zambia, and Zimbabwe.

As Mark Mobius, President of the fund, points out, "Investing in emerging markets offers high rewards, but aligned with those rewards are high risks. In view of these risks, the fund's investment approach will be to adhere to the Templeton principles of *value* investing, seeking the best long-term investment bargains in emerging markets and nations. In many emerging markets, the fund is the pioneer foreign portfolio investor and is thus breaking new ground."

Templeton puts it this way, "Where we invest is a real service to nations, we will be helping them to get more capital so they may grow faster. We'll be helping them to have their stock exchanges grow with wider share ownership. We're helping the American owners of this fund to opportunities for greater results. We're helping both sides on this. This is the first fund (of its kind) available to the public. There will be more."

Closed-End Funds—The Discount Issue

Closed-end fund shares sell at a market-determined price which is rarely the net asset value. And typically at a discount to net asset value. In the United States, for example, the discount has *averaged* 10 to 20% in recent years.

At first blush, one might immediately conclude that a well-managed fund of high quality reasonably liquid securities, selling at, say, a 20% discount to net asset value represents a good buy. The investor is paying 80¢ on the dollar for value. And if the underlying portfolio contains a high proportion of dividend paying securities, then the investor has a higher dividend yield than the implicit rate in the secondary market. But it is interesting to note that the discount to net asset value can prevail indefinitely.

The question of why closed-end funds typically sell at prices other than net asset value (and usually a discount) has perplexed researchers and practitioners for years. Numerous reasons have been put forth, some simplistic, others more subtle.

To explain this anomaly we must first start with a paradox. Assume that a closed-end fund is selling at a price other than net asset value. Whether it is a premium or discount, it is easy to see that this introduces an additional element of uncertainty into the investment, since the *amount (or percentage)* of the premium or discount can change over time in a random fashion. The investor has two sources of risk and return; that associated with the portfolio itself, and that associated with the variance about the premium or discount. A fundamental concept of investments is that of risk aversion: when faced with two investments offering identical expected returns the risk averter selects the one with the smaller risk or variance. Studies indicate that the vast majority of investors are risk averters. Thus if we compare two funds with identical portfolios, one open-ended, the other closed-ended, we would expect the closed-ended to sell at a lower price. But this doesn't fully explain the discount or premium.

Arguments that have been put forth to explain the typical prevailing discount include the following:

1. The closed-end fund discount reflects the cost of liquidating the portfolio and distributing the proceeds to investors. However, this cannot explain a discount of the magnitude of 10–20%, nor would it explain the differential pricing of open and closed-end funds since

the former is also subject to (identical) liquidation costs.

2. Closed-end fund discounts reflect the implicit management/advisory fees or other expenses of the fund. If so, we would expect to find higher percentages of such expenses in the closed-end fund over the open-ended counterpart.

3. Since commissions are typically lower for closed-end funds than for open-ended funds, brokers have an incentive to sell the latter, thus reducing the relative demand for closed-end funds. An interesting argument, although difficult to test.

4. Closed-end funds are not promoted by a sales team, as with their open-ended counterpart.

5. Closed-end funds are not awarded the favorable tax treatments of their open-ended counterparts. This however is certainly not the case in a number of countries.

6. Closed-end funds have pent-up tax liabilities associated with unrealized capital gains. Hence the net asset value is a before-tax measure that doesn't reflect the tax liabilities.

These arguments are still at this stage, conjecture. And none would explain the *premium* over net asset value observed for some funds. For example, both the Korea Fund and the Taiwan Fund, publicly traded in the United States, have traded for substantial premiums (often over a 100% premium) over net asset values since their introduction, while the France Fund has been at a perpetual discount. Did the relative pricing of the three funds reflect aggregate investor outlooks for these three markets, or possibly a bonus for ability to invest in blocked country markets, the case of the two premium funds?

Nevertheless, numerous studies have pointed out that market inefficiencies may exist for closed-end funds. One of the more recent concluded that ". . . investors can improve the likelihood of trading profits by employing strategies using closed-end fund shares similar to those tested and found successful here."[10]

WHERE TO BUY AND SELL GLOBAL, INTERNATIONAL, AND SINGLE COUNTRY FUNDS

The global and international funds described in this chapter are open-ended funds (shares sold continuously to investors). One can buy them in some cases directly from the issuer, in others through stock brokers. Investors should not buy global funds for quick trading. It takes some time just to recover commissions. The single country funds are often closed-ended funds traded on stock exchanges. One can buy and sell them in the same manner as common shares. A representative list of global and international funds is found in Table 7–2.

CONCLUSION

The performance record of mutual funds is mixed. Studies of relative performance, spanning the 1960 to 1975 period,[11] indicate that mutual funds did not on average outperform the market. Examination of performance data indicates, however, that some funds consistently outperform both the general market and the majority of other funds. These are the ones that you should identify and purchase. More recent studies are ambiguous. Little real evidence on global and international funds performance exists, since researchers have paid little attention to them thus far because they represent such a small spectrum of the mutual fund world. For example, at year end 1985, international funds represented only about 3% of total U.S. mutual fund assets, and about 1.5% of total United States mutual fund sales.[12]

The key principle is to recognize that global and international funds provide investors with instant diversification and professional management—two valuable features that most investors cannot achieve on their own.

TABLE 7-2 U.S. Global and International Funds—Recent Change in Net Asset Values

Name/Address	Global, % Change Net Asset Value				Minimum Investment
	Jan–Mar 1987	1986	1981–1986	1976–1986	
Dean Witter World Wide One World Trade Center New York, NY 10048 800 221-2685	+12.2	+31.9	—	—	$1000
First Investors Int'l 120 Wall Street New York, NY 10005 800 221-3846	+24.8	+45.1	95.8	—	200
Merrill Lynch Int'l Box 9611 Princeton, NJ 08540	+13.8	+30.2	—	—	1000
New Perspective 333 Hope Street Los Angeles, CA 90071 800 421-9900	+17.8	+27.1	157	429	250
Oppenheimer Global Two Broadway New York, NY 10048 800 221-9839	+16.6	+46.4	146	503	1000
Paine Webber Atlas 140 Broadway New York, NY 10005 800 544-9300	+16.8	+39	—	—	1000
Pru-Bache Global One Seaport Plaza New York, NY 10292 800 872-7787	+24.3	+43.7	—	—	1000

Putnam Int'l Equities 265 Franklin St. Boston, MA 02110 800 225-1581	+14.6	+37.6	221.4	483	500
Shearson Global Opp Two World Trade Ctr. New York, NY 10048 800 451-2010	+11.5	+30.9	—	—	500

Templeton Funds
  Global II
  Growth
  World
P.O. Box 33030
St. Petersburg, FL 33723
800 237-0738
	+13.4
	+14.8
	+16.3
		+10.3
		+21.2
		+18.3
			—
			133
			158.7
				—
				433
				—
					500
					500
					500

International, % Change Net Asset Value

Euro Pacific Growth 333 South Hope St. Los Angeles, CA 90071 800 421-9900	+ 9.5	+39.9	—	—	250
Fidelity Overseas 82 Devonshire St. Boston, MA 92109 800 544-6666	+32.5	+69.2	—	—	2500
G.T. Pacific 601 Montgomery St., #1400 San Francisco, CA 94111 800 824-1580	+11.6	+70	121	339	500
Kemper Int'l 120 So. La Salle St. Chicago, IL 60603 800 621-1048	+ 7.3	+44.1	62	—	1000

(continued)

TABLE 7–2 (concluded)

Global, % Change Net Asset Value

Name/Address	Jan–Mar 1987	1986	1981–1986	1976–1986	Minimum Investment
Keystone Int'l 99 High St. Boston, MA 02110 800 633-4900	+17.1	+46.7	144	282	250
Merrill Lynch Pacific 633 Third Av. New York, NY 10017	+27	+78	257	640	300
Rowe Price Int'l 100 East Pratt St. Baltimore, MD 21202 800 638-5660	+10.7	+61.2	201	—	1000
Scudder Int'l 175 Federal St. Boston, MA 02110 800 225-2470	+10.9	+50.7	191	417	500
Templeton Foreign P.O. Box 3942 St. Petersburg, FL 33731 800 237-0738	+18.8	+28.7	129	—	500
Transatlantic Growth 100 Wall Street New York, NY 10005 800 223-4130	+16.5	+52.6	125	340	1000
Vanguard World Int'l Vanguard Financial Center Valley Forge, PA 12948 800 662-7447	+ 7.9	+56.7	256	—	500

Source: Derived from Lipper Analytic Services, March 1987.

Templeton on Portfolio Allocation to International Investments

Templeton's suggested allocation is about 20% to 60% of your funds to international investments. He is not a strong believer in diversifying among a number of different mutual fund managers, arguing that "if you have faith in the ability of a fund manager, stay with him. Why increase your probability of a losing position or a poorly managed fund by buying a pack of them? I know all about modern portfolio diversification, but you get that in a properly constructed global portfolio. Buying a package of equity funds means double diversification."

ENDNOTES

1. The various types of mutual funds by classifications include:

Equity Growth Funds: The funds of the portfolio are invested in shares that are expected to have above average earnings and growth potential.

Balanced Funds: The fund manager maintains a balanced portfolio of stocks and bonds, normally within a specified range. The primary objective is stability of returns. Balanced funds are either formalized, where the portfolio is fixed in some proportion such as 40% bonds and 60% equities, or semi-discretionary, where proportions can be changed when the advisor thinks it wise.

Dividend Income Funds: The portfolio is invested primarily in higher yield equities.

Global and International Funds: Funds that invest a substantial portion of their assets in securities outside the country of domicile.

Single Country Funds: Funds that invest all of their assets in specific countries.

Specialty Funds: Funds that invest in a defined industry or asset including gold, high technology, and oil and gas.

Fixed Income Funds: Fixed income funds have virtually all of their assets in fixed income securities, including bonds, mortgages and money market instruments. The primary objective is stable and regular income.

Money Market Funds: Money market funds invest virtually all of their assets in money market instruments, including treasury bills, certificates of deposit, deposit receipts, government short-term bonds, and commercial paper. Money market instruments, in general, mature in one year or less.

Real Estate Funds: Funds that invest all or most of their assets in real estate.

Index funds: Funds whose objective is to replicate the performance of some market index such as the S&P 500 Index. These funds buy the securities that make up the index.

2. Sometimes this is expressed as the excess return (return above the risk-free rate) divided by the standard deviation of the excess return. This is referred to as the Sharpe measure. See, for example, William F. Sharpe, *Investments,* 3rd ed. (Englewood Cliffs, N.J.: Prentice-Hall Inc., 1985), pp. 688–689.

3. This is known as the Treynor measure.

4. See, for example, as evidence, William F. Sharpe, "Mutual Fund Performance," *Journal of Business,* Supplement (January 1966), pp. 119–138; J.C. Bogle and J.M. Twardowski, "Institutional Investment Performance Compared," *Financial Analysts Journal,* January–February 1980, pp. 33–41. Note that most of the academic studies of mutual fund performance concentrate on domestic rather than international or global funds.

5. See Robert C. Klemkosky, "How Consistently Do Managers Manage?" *Journal of Portfolio Management* 3, no. 2 (Winter 1977), pp. 11–15.

6. See United States Securities and Exchange Commission, "Institutional Investors Study Report," Government Printing Office, March 10, 1971.

7. See United States Securities and Exchange Commission, "Institutional Investors Study Report," Government Printing Office, March 10, 1971.

8. An extensive study of 116 mutual funds spanning the period 1968 to 1980 found that virtually all of the managers of the funds surveyed showed no significant ability to time their purchases for superior performance. See Roy D. Henriksson, "Market Timing and Mutual Fund Performance: An Empirical Investigation," *The Journal of Business* 57, Part 1 (January 1984), pp. 73–96.

9. The Mexico Fund, for example, was launched in June 1981, but quickly fell from its issue price of $12.00 after the major peso devaluation in early 1982. It traded as low as $1.50 a share in 1985 and then recovered to the $14.00 level in late 1987. The Scandanavia Fund, floated in 1986, at $10.00 still sells for below its issue price. On the other hand, the Korea Fund launched in 1984 at $12.00 a share traded as high as $87.00 in 1987. Even the Templeton Emerging Markets Fund, a fund that invests in the securities of companies of designated emerging countries, was issued at $10.00 and ranged between 9¼ and 15½ in the first six months after issue.

10. S. A. Anderson, "Closed-End Funds Versus Market Efficiency," *The Journal of Portfolio Management,* Fall 1986, pp. 63–65.

11. More recent studies of the 1975–1985 period show ambiguous results.

12. Investment Company Institute, *1986 Mutual Fund Factbook,* p. 28.

APPENDIX

The portfolio holdings as of May 31, 1987, of the Templeton Emerging Markets Fund is shown below.

Portfolio Listing:

	Number of Shares	Value
Aberfoyle Holdings P.L.C.: Multi-industry holding company with activities in clothing manufacturing, equipment sales and service, and agriculture in addition to a portfolio of listed Zimbabwe firms	650,000	$614,321
Atlantic, Gulf and Pacific Industrial Corp.: The Philippines' largest construction company with affiliates manufacturing cables and prestressed concrete components	100,000	408,852
Antofagasta Holdings P.L.C.: Railway and water distribution services in Chile with subsidiaries in banking, wire and cable manufacturing, mining, and communications	215,000	882,863

(continued)

Portfolio Listing (*continued*):

	Number of Shares	Value
Astra Compania Argentina de Petroles S.A.: Petroleum exploration, petrochemical product manufacturing and distribution in Argentina	180,000	$268,301
Avimo Singapore Ltd.: Manufacturing of electro-optics, electro-optic instruments, night vision equipment, laser equipment, and related subsystems and components in Singapore		
Brazil Fund: One of the few funds by which foreigners may invest in Brazilian securities, this Fund is managed by a subsidiary of the NMB Bank of the Netherlands and has investments in over 50 Brazilian listed firms	27,000	48,060
Cable and Wireless P.L.C.: Telecommunications company with activities throughout the world, particularly in the emerging nations, with most important operations in Hong Kong	246,000	1,571,359
Ceteco Trading and Industrial Corp.: Multi-industry company active in international trading, manufacturing, distribution, and services in South America, Central America, and the Caribbean	2,575	218,561
Cheung Kong (Holdings) Ltd.: Hong Kong property company with major holdings in wholesaling, import and export, shipping terminal operations, electricity generation, hotels, and manufacturing	175,000	246,953
Cifra S.A. de C.V.: Mexico's largest retail organization with activities in supermarkets, department stores, restaurants, and hotels	77,000	263,658
Collins and Leahy Holdings Ltd.: A Papua New Guinea trading, retailing and wholesaling company with interests in coffee plantations, hotels, engineering, and timber	60,000	289,193
Eastern Produce (Holdings) P.L.C.: A producer of tea, coffee and citrus fruits with plantations in Malawi and Kenya	100,000	570,325
Federal Flour Mills Bhd.: A leading Malaysian flour milling, feed milling, and grain trading firm	48,000	102,005

Portfolio Listing (*continued*):

	Number of Shares	Value
Foremost Friesland: Producer and distributor of dairy products in Thailand	10,100	318,197
Henderson Land Development Co. Ltd.: Property development firm in Hong Kong with specialization in apartment construction and sales	200,000	$164,208
Hongkong and Shanghai Banking Corp.: Hong Kong's largest bank with operations in other emerging markets such as China, Taiwan, Korea, the Philippines, Sri Lanka, Pakistan, Brazil, Chile, and Jordan	500,000	519,564
Hopewell Holdings Ltd.: Property management and development company in Hong Kong with major infrastructure projects in China	109,000	58,380
India Fund Inc.: Presently the only vehicle for non-Indians to invest in the Indian stock market	500,000	721,054
International Cosmetics Co. Ltd.: A leading Thai distributor and importer of cosmetics, garments, sports equipment, toys, and other consumer goods	8,000	324,451
James Finlay P.L.C.: Multi-industry international company with particular emphasis on management of tea plantations in Africa and Asia	625,000	1,130,466
Jardine Matheson Holdings Ltd.: One of Hong Kong's oldest firms with operations in marketing and distribution, financial services, engineering and construction, transport, property, and hotels	89,600	204,603
Lonrho P.L.C.: Multinational company with the largest single portion of activities in Africa including such nations as Malawi, Kenya, Zambia, Swaziland, Nigeria, Zimbabwe, Mauritus, Angola, and Ghana	220,000	1,050,376
Malaysian Airline System Bhd.: Malaysia's national airlines with domestic and international routes in addition to subsidiaries in trucking, coach transportation, helicopter services, aircraft overhaul and maintenance, and properties	166,000	439,294

(*continued*)

Portfolio Listing (*continued*):

	Number of Shares	Value
Malaysian International Shipping Corp. Bhd.: Malaysia's national shipping line with 40 vessels including container ships, dry bulk carriers, liquid bulk carriers, and LNG carriers	300,000	908,180
Mexico Fund Inc.: Investment company with holdings of Mexican listed securities in a wide range of activities including shares in firms not normally available to foreigners	55,000	$371,250
McLeod Russel P.L.C.: Plantation company with tea and coffee plantations in India and Kenya in addition to other interests in Australia and the United Kingdom	100,000	622,469
Ocean Wilsons (Holdings) P.L.C.: Tug boat and stevedoring operations in Brazil in addition to other interests in truck distribution, petroleum exploration services and ship repair	600,000	684,390
Philex Mining Corp.: One of the Philippines' oldest and largest copper and gold mining companies with subsidiaries engaged in motor tire production, oil exploration, and banking	28,900,000	734,886
Philippine Long Distance Telephone Company: The Philippines' largest telephone company with domestic as well as international services	50,000	1,118,750
Polly Peck International P.L.C.: Fruit processing and packaging operations in Turkey and Northern Cyprus in addition to paper and carton box manufacturing, consumer electronics manufacturing, and water bottling in Turkey, and other operations in Hong Kong, the United Kingdom, and the United States	300,000	1,398,111
Steamships Trading Company Ltd.: Multi-industry company in Papua New Guinea with operations including trading, retailing, wholesaling, hotels, shipyards, coffee plantations, and other areas	27,200	60,120

Portfolio Listing (*concluded*):

	Number of Shares	Value
Swire Pacific Ltd.: Diversified Hong Kong holding company with interests in the airline industry, hotels, property, shipping, offshore petroleum services, dockyards, manufacturing, and trading	1,680,000	748,942
Thai Farmers Bank: Thailand's second largest commercial bank with 280 branches throughout the country	45,600	659,342
Universal Matchbox Group Inc.: Manufacturer and marketer of toys with primary manufacturing operations in Hong Kong, the People's Republic of China, and the Republic of China in addition to distribution facilities in the United States, the United Kingdom, and other countries	28,000	$399,000
Winsor Industrial Corp. Ltd.: One of Hong Kong's leading textile manufacturers with integrated operations in cotton and wool spinning, weaving, dyeing and finishing, as well as garment manufacturing	230,000	318,666
		18,461,930
Short-Term Obligations:	*Principal Amount*	
U.S. Treasury Bills with various due dates to July 9, 1987, 5.00% to 5.32%	$94,300,000	93,536,086
Total Investments		111,998,016
Other Assets, less Liabilities		(2,429,501)
Total Net Assets		$109,568,515
Net Asset Value per Share		$9.52

Chapter 8

WHAT MAKES A GREAT PORTFOLIO MANAGER?

IS IT LUCK OR SKILL?

John Templeton's oldest mutual fund, the Templeton Growth Fund, has been in the top 25% in the performance rankings of mutual funds in 14 of the past 30 years. It has ranked first in three of those years and has **on average** over that period been in the top 33%.[1] What are the chances of these results being attributable to chance? Statistically nil! Consistent portfolio management performance of this type can only be achieved through superior analytic skills and applications. Templeton is not the only fund manager to demonstrate superior performance over the long term. Immediately, Warren Buffett and his extremely successful closed-end fund Berkshire-Hathaway[2] spring to mind. What then makes a great portfolio manager? Why do a few individuals seem to have the capability to produce investment results that are significantly better over the course of time than those of their compatriots?

One way to explore this question is to examine these two widely acclaimed investment managers, John Templeton and Warren Buffett. Their investment interests and styles differ. Their personalities are miles apart. But both have produced bountiful returns for their faithful investors over the years.

Templeton and Buffett—Two of the Legends

It is an interesting coincidence that these two legendary investment managers launched their flagship investment portfolios at practically the same time. In 1955, Templeton started the Templeton Growth Fund in Toronto, with $7 million in assets, much of it from a public offering of shares. In that same year, Warren Buffett, with money provided by relatives and friends, began his investment partnership. Since then, the two have set a pace that few others could match. They are the Magic Johnson and Larry Bird of security analysis, different in style, but each expressing in his own way a unique excellence at what he does. The accomplishments curiously enough, can be described in the context of a series of similar characteristics as follows.

Strong Results in Isolated Surroundings

The foremost characteristic that the two men share is an ability to get results. As Templeton has said, "The first duty of a security analyst is to discover investment opportunities that result in superior total real returns, net after-tax, for his client." They have accomplished this despite (maybe even because of) a complete physical separation from Wall Street. Buffett has always operated out of Omaha, Nebraska, hardly a major financial center, while since 1969, Templeton has produced his investment results from the remote little New Providence Island in the Bahamas. In this world of instant communications and air travel, physical distance isn't as important a separator as it once was; but for both Templeton and Buffett the physical isolation bespeaks a state of mind that bears heavily on their investment outlook and their strategies. Templeton's investment performance, in fact, improved when he left Wall Street for Lyford Cay, and he has had only one year, 1982, where he failed to be ranked in the top 40 percent of investment portfolio managers.[3]

Templeton explained it this way, "With the advantage of hindsight now, I think that there are two reasons for this success. One is that if you are going to produce a better record than other people, you must not buy the same things as they. If you are going to have a superior record, you have to do something different from what other security analysts are doing. And when you are a thousand miles away in a different nation, it's easier to buy the things that other people are selling, and to sell the things that other people are buying."

Buffett agrees that a key element for outstanding investment success is mental aloofness from the crowd, which the
relative quiet of an isolated locale can help create. In response
to a question about remaining in Nebraska during his investment career, he once said, "Well, believe it or not, we get mail
here, and we get periodicals, and we get all the facts needed to
make decisions. And unlike Wall Street, you'll notice that we
don't have 50 people coming up and whispering in our ear that
we should be doing this or that this afternoon. I like the lack
of stimulation. Here we get facts, not stimulation."[4]

Successful Investing Is Done by Individuals
Not Committees

In his excellent book *Preserving Capital and Making It Grow*,
John Train, who has made a life's work of studying the investment process, says, "Stock picking is really not that over-
whelming a subject. A superior man, not a committee, is
needed to set the policy; and assuming he has access to good
information, which can certainly be arranged, one man can set
the 'buy list' for even the largest firm.

"The whole thing will stand or fall on whether once or
twice a year or so he can spot a potential Schlumberger (a
stock exhibiting great profit potential at the time) and then
avoid being pressured into selling it. If a Churchill can preside
over a nation—indeed, an empire—at war, cannot one man
pick a number of stocks and hold them? Neither Napoleon nor
Wellington asked for advice or held 'councils of war.' They
would have regarded a general who required such councils as
incompetent. Similarly, no first-rate investor wants to filter his
ideas through a committee."[5]

Both Templeton and Buffett agree on this. There are no
committees managing their portfolios. Templeton says:

> Whatever happens to the Templeton organization, the invest-
> ment decisions will be made by individual chartered financial
> analysts, never by a committee. It's extremely difficult for a
> committee to do anything that stands apart from the crowd. Af-
> ter all, a committee is a small crowd unto itself. Also, the time
> that is wasted waiting to get committees set up and reaching
> consensus, puts you at a disadvantage to someone who can react

to things more quickly. Most investment firms with the best records don't rely upon committees.

You can invest superbly, or run a company; but not both. Templeton believes, as does Buffett, that an investor seeking the best possible results must be free to spend his time on investment ideas and research, rather than on the actual trivia of trading shares or running an investment company. Buffett in fact, became so disenchanted with the nagging demands of his original 1955 partnership that he actually dissolved it and quit investing for several years. When he went back into securities analysis and portfolio management it was with a small company, Berkshire-Hathaway, whose size, direction and destiny he entirely controls. It has one investment manager and one client—Warren Buffett.

Templeton, too, found that he was beset by distractions during his Wall Stroot years. While his ultimate reaction was not as severe as Buffett's, it did mark a watershed in his career.

> One of the major reasons why my investment performance improved since I came to Lyford Cay (1963), is that so much of my time in New York was taken up with administration and in serving hundreds of clients, that I wasn't left enough time for the study and research essential to a financial analyst, and that was the area in which God may have given me some talents. So now, in the Bahamas, I have more time to search for the best bargains.

But unlike Buffett, Templeton didn't turn into a solo act. Instead, he sought out young investment counselors whom he believed would have the talent and ambition to maintain the administration, leaving him free to pursue his investment research and ideas. As John Galbraith, one of the principles in the Templeton organization notes, "The difference between Mr. T. and Warren Buffett is that John is a fiduciary; he lives to help other people through investing. Warren Buffett invests primarily for his own account." Over the years the organization has grown to the point where today, much of what Templeton does is to apply the research of many of the younger people that he has brought along over the years.

Many of them have become leading investment analysts in their own right.

Consistency, Not Flash

Both men, although no strangers to winning the occasional portfolio manager sweepstakes, believe that being first is not always the best. Being first in performance among over 500 mutual funds may imply that one's portfolio has taken substantial risk. One of the most interesting similarities that surfaces in studying Templeton and Buffett is the fact that their success is truly long-term. Consistency is the operative word. Measured over a one- or five-year period, you will normally not find either leading the pack. But, over the long haul, the ability of these masters to outperform other talented investment managers becomes self-evident.

Barton Biggs, head of international research for the investment firm of Morgan Stanley, noticed this unusual performance characteristic of great investors. "The fascinating thing," he wrote in his newsletter, "is that these superstars underperformed the Standard & Poor's index in 30 percent to 40 percent of the years studied. The only exception was Warren Buffett, whose partners had just one down year out of 11 when he dissolved his partnership in 1969. None in the group always beat the S&P, probably because no one thought that was the primary objective. However, the underperformance in the down years was generally (but not always) small, and the positive differentials were large."

"Furthermore," Biggs continued, "with only two exceptions, all of the great investors had long bouts (defined as three straight or three out of four consecutive years) of underperformance. Almost invariably, these bad periods were either preceded and/or followed by sustained bursts of spectacular returns. Relative performance runs in three-to-five-year cycles, probably related to the manager's style and the dominant themes of a particular market."

Templeton has made it clear that the only view he considers worthy of a true investment manager is the long-range perspective. "We are long-term investors, we buy to produce the greatest gain over the longest period," he says. "We aren't traders. Trading stock is an excellent way to lose money. Holding stocks, the right stocks, is an excellent way to make money."

Buffett concurs. In typically blunt style, he says: "Most of the professional investors focus on what the stock is likely to do in the next year or two, and they have all kinds of arcane methods of approaching that. But they do not really think of themselves as owning a piece of business. The real test of whether you're investing from a value standpoint or not is whether you're one who asks if the market will be open tomorrow. If you're making a good investment in a security, it shouldn't bother you if they closed down the stock market for five years."[6]

Psyche More Important Than Savvy

The key to success lies in temperament or attitude. Buffett once was asked what he considered to be the most important quality for an investment manager to have. He answered that it was a temperamental rather than an intellectual, faculty:

"You don't need tons of IQ in this business—I mean you have to have enough IQ to get from here to downtown Omaha, but you do not have to be able to play three-dimensional chess or be in the top league in terms of bridge playing or something of that sort. You need a stable personality. You need a temperament that neither derives great pleasure from being with the crowd or against the crowd, because this is not a business in which you take polls. Rather, this is a business in which you think. And Ben Graham (the father of modern security analysis) would say that you're not right or wrong because 1,000 people agree with you, and you're not right or wrong because 1,000 people disagree with you; if you're right, it's because your facts and reasoning are right."[7]

With his Oxford training and Rhodes Scholar background, Templeton takes a more scholarly approach than Buffett. Still, he feels, along with Buffett, that successful investing requires more than being smart. While Templeton, with characteristic humility, will only say that an "open mind" is the principal personality trait behind his investment success, peers who have known him well, point out more dramatic traits. John Schroeder, chairman of the Axe-Houghton Funds, now a competitor but once a close associate of Templeton's, describes one of these qualities that sets the investment master apart; he calls it courage. "I've met all kinds of great analysts and great brains who never made any money because they never had the courage of their convictions," Schroeder says. He points out that Templeton has shown the fortitude to do whatever he felt was right, regardless of opinion popular at the time. As an example, he recalls Templeton's bold move as a fledgling investor—his confident fling as a buyer of $1 stocks in the depressed 1930s.

> It took as much courage to do that then as it would today. It takes a lot of gumption to put yourself on the line like that and John has a lot. To me, he has three dimensions. First, he is a brilliant man. Secondly, he's a spiritual man, which gives him stability and a long range sense of purpose and hope. And thirdly, he's a courageous man. You have to put all three of these together to understand him. And it's the courage part of him that permitted him sometimes to take huge risks. There were times when he lost money, but he never changed course out of fear. As a result, when he made money the gains were so much bigger than those of other managers that his long-term performance has been exceptional. Of course, courage without brain power is worthless. But so is brain power without the courage to back it up.

The contrast between Buffett's and Templeton's styles is illustrated by their attitude toward that ultimate blue chipper, IBM. Neither has ever bought IBM. But the reasons behind their decisions and their perspective on technology stocks in general, show how different their approaches actually are.

Buffett stated his view on Adam Smith's "Money World" television program:[8]

> *Host Adam Smith:* Have you ever bought a technology company?
>
> *Warren Buffett:* No, I really haven't.
>
> *Smith:* In 30 years of investing, not one?
>
> *Buffett:* I haven't understood any of them.
>
> *Smith:* So you haven't ever owned, for example, IBM?

Buffett: No, I haven't — marvelous company, I mean it's a sensational company; but I haven't owned IBM.

Smith: So here is this technological revolution going on and you're not going to be a participant.

Buffett: It's gone right past me.

Smith: Is that all right with you?

Buffett: It's okay with me. I don't have to make money in every game. I mean, I don't know what cocoa beans are going to do. You know, there are all kinds of things I don't know about, and that may be too bad; but you know, why should I know all about them?

Templeton's reaction to Buffett's remarks was direct and spoken with feeling. "I would part company with Buffett on this. I think you should try to understand companies or you should hire someone who understands any company, any industry, where there appears to be a good buy. It would be a mistake for somebody to say 'I am not going to buy high-tech stocks because I don't understand them.' If you think that a high-tech stock could really be an investment, a real bargain, you should investigate it." It is the duty of an investment manager, Templeton insists, to become as knowledgeable as necessary to find various opportunities in various nations.

As for avoiding IBM, Templeton's rationale points up his unwavering support of his First Law, his "rule of price." "I've never owned any IBM," he says, "because it has never been cheap enough."

Quick and Decisive Actions
Another trait, clearly common to all great investors, stands in counterpoint to their long-range, steady-at-the-helm investment perspective. When the time comes to make a pivotal decision (such as a major portfolio revision, or a change in portfolio composition) they each make it quickly, often with seemingly minute bits of information. Part of this is a practical manifestation of Benjamin Graham's advice to security analysts to "buy stocks like you buy groceries, not like you buy perfume." Part is the overt demonstration of the mental cour-

age a great investor must have. And, in Templeton's view, most of it is nothing more than "... simple, everyday common sense applied to investment situations."

John Schroeder tells of a time in the early 1960s when Templeton visited a small company located in North Carolina. The Templeton Growth Fund had made a modest investment in the company, after the usual painstaking research of the financial fundamentals and Templeton decided to meet the principals, with an eye to possibly increasing the Growth Fund's investment stake in the firm.[9] Generally on such trips, Templeton delayed any decision making until he returned home. But in this case, Schroeder said, "He called me right after the meeting and said, 'Jack, sell that stock immediately.' I said, 'Why? I thought that it was such a great company.' 'I thought so too,' he said, 'but I've just interviewed the president and he has a great big bar in his office and a ticker tape machine and I don't trust him. Sell all of our stock!' After all of the numbers we had run and all the work we had put into finding this company he gave it the bounce as soon as he had this new slant! I'll tell you, that is decisiveness!"

There is no room for sentiment or ego when you are running a successful investment program.

Not Intuition—Common Sense, Hard Work, and Other Fundamentals

Beyond any specific personality trait, however, there still appears to us to be a kernel of mystery about the process of superior investment selection and portfolio management. The principles of success, elucidated by Templeton and Buffett, are elusive and nebulous. You almost expect to hear, "buy low, sell high and use your common sense." But, no matter how pressed, the tune is the same. "I have no intuitive ability," Templeton insists. "Investment success has nothing to do with intuition or creativity. It is a combination of hard work, common sense, and an open mind."

Buffett, as noted earlier, emphasizes his belief that the key to investment success "is a temperamental quality, not an intellectual one." He feels that his methods work largely "because they are so simple." What you need to do, he says, isn't something magical; it's simply a matter of developing stoic patience and knowing your limits.

> There are no called strikes in this business. The pitcher stands there and throws balls at you, and if you were playing real baseball and it's between the knees and the shoulders, you either swing or you get a strike called on you. If you get too many called on you, you're out. In the securities business, you sit there and they throw U.S. Steel at 25 and they throw General Motors at 68, and you don't have to swing at any of them. They may be wonderful pitches to swing at, but if you don't know enough, you don't have to swing. And you can sit there and watch thousands of pitches and finally you get one right there, where you want it, something that you understand. And then you swing.[10]

But the view that great investors are somehow more naturally attuned to profitable opportunities is universally held by those who watch them in operation. Barton Biggs has said with awe: "The returns achieved by the superstars cannot be attained by us mortals." And John Schroeder insists that "whatever Templeton feels about his abilities, others see him as a true visionary, a man with the ability to see the future with a clarity that very few people can achieve."

Schroeder says Templeton "always talks about being right two-thirds of the time," implying that's the best to be hoped for. "But when John's wrong, he's never very wrong; and when he's right—that two-thirds of the time—he's often very right, like a tenfold increase or better. That's where the brilliant record comes from."

Schroeder recalls a seminar held for the Young President's Organization in New York at a time when world currencies were under strict international controls.

> A vice president of the Federal Reserve was talking about a policy of managing world financial affairs, about stabilizing currencies. This, he argued, would establish more stable relationships between countries. And John got up, just as a member of the audience, and said, "What about just letting currencies trade freely and let the market be the judge of what they're worth?" The audience was stunned. They thought he was crazy, talking about unleashing currencies without any controls.

That's why he's different. All the financial hotshots in that room weren't as capable as John of seeing that deregulation of currency was what was really going to happen. The Federal Reserve didn't understand, the audience didn't understand. But John could see that the future was going to bring "floating" currencies. He just has a better grasp of what's going to happen than anyone else I've ever known.

It Really Boils Down to an Art

Both Templeton and Buffett have pursued their arts for over 40 years. There is an aspect that has long baffled those who try to unravel their success, to find the philosopher's stone, the mystical set of equations used to achieve their success. The assumption made is that there must be some single method that produces the results. But in truth, there have been many. Both Templeton and Buffett have explained that their refusal to become wedded to any particular way of doing things is a crucial aspect of their achievements.

For example, a Canadian financial consultant, Keith P. Ambachtsheer, who has worked with Templeton's Counsel firm in Ft. Lauderdale, Florida, sums up neatly the quandary those studying Templeton face.

> A great deal of discussion about professional investment management today focuses on "style." Investment consultants have built an entire industry out of studying and categorizing the differing approaches to professional investment research and portfolio management in use today.
>
> There are growth stock managers, and junk bond managers. There are low p/e managers and small cap managers. There are top down managers, and bottom up managers.
>
> Investment consultants would have great difficulty, however, deciding which of these categories best describes the Templeton style. None is capable of capturing the essence of what has made that style so successful. While it is tempting to simply say the Templeton style defies categorization, such a statement would not be accurate. It would be more accurate to say that the Templeton style is a category unto itself.
>
> The financial and economic tests that Templeton uses are applied with a great deal of flexibility. Sometimes, depending on the country, the phase in the economic cycle, or the type of

stock, balance sheet tests might be emphasized. Other times, earnings growth and earnings stability would be deemed most important. In short, the Templeton style suggests that there is no standard way of identifying potential winners and losers in the stock markets of the world. Experience and common sense dictate how the formula must be adapted to time, place and type of security.[11]

CONCLUSION—NO REAL UNIVERSAL TRUTH

Despite their similarities and all that those reveal about the requirements of superior investment performance, at the heart of matters Templeton and Buffett are very different men with vastly different attitudes and approaches to investing. And they are widely dissimilar from dozens of other top-flight analysts and managers whom an investor could choose today.

Buffett buys only American stocks; Templeton shops worldwide. Buffett manages only his own investments; Templeton invests the money of hundreds of thousands of people. Buffett tends to focus his investments in areas he has long known and fully understands; Templeton sends his analysts to India, Thailand, Korea, Brazil, Spain, and other exotic locales and savors learning new things, expanding his investment horizons. Buffett works almost entirely on his own; Templeton works closely with a large worldwide organization.

The differences can be seen when both men state the philosophy underlying their work. Buffett is more prosaic and bounded in his views. "The first rule of investment is, don't lose. And the second rule is don't forget the first rule. And that's all the rules there are. I mean, if you buy things for far below what they're worth and you buy a group of them, you basically don't lose money," Buffett says. "It's an intellectual process, a matter of defining your area of competence in terms of valuing businesses, and then within that area of competence finding whatever sells at the cheapest price in relation to value. And there are all kinds of things I'm not competent to value, but there are a few that I am competent to value."[12]

Templeton expresses a broader, more scholarly view. "My own philosophy has long been that any individual with God-given intelligence, independence of mind, and patience can avoid the mistakes made by many of those experts who are swayed by the emotions of the crowd. I have maintained that the best buying opportunities come at what appears to be the worst of times. This applies to the general market and to particular securities. I've often invested in companies with poor records and performance when our research indicated that their problems were likely to be temporary," Templeton says. "I search for just such investments. Usually these securities are selling for less than their true worth. These may be any type of security, in any industry, in any part of the world. To find such securities and reap their worth, the investor's first and last touchstone must be value."

These statements back up one final conclusion upon which all great investment managers certainly would agree: superior investing and portfolio management are not tied to a formula. There is no pat answer, no single path. While there are characteristics that the great investment managers and analysts share, they can be combined to create an infinite number of personalities and approaches to the sometimes treacherous journey that investment success represents.

ENDNOTES

1. From Wiesenberger's *Investment Companies' Service* (Boston: Warren, Gorham and Lamont, 1987).
2. The shares are traded on NASDAQ, The National Association of Securities Dealers Automated Quotation system, the world's largest over-the-counter or principals market.
3. From Wiesenberger's *Investment Companies' Service*.
4. "Adam Smith's Money World," April 28, 1985, "The Three Greatest Investors of Our Time," by permission—Guests: Warren Buffett, John Templeton, Robert Wilson, WNET, Box 862, New York, N.Y. 10101. "Money World" is a popular PBS television series featuring Adam Smith, the author of the "Money Game" and "SuperMoney," two delightful and easy-to-read books on the investment scene.

5. Reprinted from *Preserving Capital and Making It Grow* by John Train. Copyright © 1983 by John Train. Used by permission of Crown Publishers, Inc.

6. "Adam Smith's Money World," April 28, 1985.

7. "Adam Smith's Money World," April 28, 1985.

8. "Adam Smith's Money World," April 28, 1985.

9. Templeton, in fact, until the early 1980s, often made such in-person field trips to back up decisions on what to hold, what to buy more of, and what to sell.

10. "Adam Smith's Money World," April 28, 1985.

11. Personal correspondence between Keith Ambachtsheer and John Templeton.

12. "Adam Smith's Money World," April 28, 1985.

CHAPTER 9

LOOKING AHEAD—THE FUTURE FOR GLOBAL INVESTORS

John Templeton always points out to investment clients that no one can predict the future—certainly not he. Change is inevitable and necessary and the serious investor must be prepared for it. That's only common sense, the intellectual asset that Templeton deems requisite for successful investing.

"The future of investors" and "change" were the topics for discussion as we returned to Lyford Cay for our last two-day session with Templeton. The ritual is repeated. We are greeted by Roy, escorted into the drawing room, and offered drinks. As usual, Mr. Templeton appears on the stroke of two; but this time there is no tie and the greeting is casual and friendly. We are near the end and we are clearly on a topic close to Templeton's heart.

JMT: Let's leave aside some time for a stroll around the garden. I've some interesting plants and 14 varieties of citrus trees.

EK: (Somewhat intrigued by the notion of the garden tour, shakes his head and proceeds): You have described your fundamental bargain-hunting approach using yardsticks of value for stock valuation, and we have also talked about some recent developments including capital asset pricing, arbitrage pricing, and option pricing models. What do you see for the future?

JMT: Every method used for predicting stock market trends or for selecting stocks eventually will become obsolete. And that includes what everyone is talking about today—global investing.

It's possible that in the long run global investing may not be the wisest thing to do, but since in America we're only in the very early stages of it, that seems a long way off.

Here's the logic. At present, the Americans have some $27 billion of tax free funds invested outside the United States. That's a pittance when viewed in relation to world markets and when compared to the amount of money sitting in American pension funds. Only 2% roughly of American funds are invested outside the United States, whereas almost 65% of all available securities are outside the United States. So I don't think that there is any danger that the concept of global investing is going to become obsolete soon. But it will, undoubtedly, change; it must.

Roy brought in the drinks at this point and while we sipped our club sodas, Templeton, who as we had often observed, really doesn't like to stop work when he is rolling, talked about a Henry Ford quotation on that subject. The quote, from Ford's 1922 book, *My Life and Work,* was:[1]

If to petrify is success all one has to do is humor the lazy side of his mind; but if to grow is success then one must wake up anew every morning and keep awake all day.

I saw great businesses become but the ghost of a name just because someone thought they could be managed just as they were always managed. And though the management may have been most excellent in its day, its excellence consisted in its alertness to its day—not in slavish following of its yesterdays. Life, as I see it, is not a location but a journey. Even the man who feels himself 'settled' is not settled—he is probably sagging back. Everything is in flux, and was meant to be. Life flows. We may live at the same number of the street, but it is never the same man who lives there.

NB: Very true. But you are a skilled and experienced observer of world financial affairs. Surely you can perceive the broad trends and tendencies developing as that change occurs, trends and tendencies that appear certain to flow strongly into future events.

JMT: Here, let me give you the text of a talk that I gave in London early last year [1986]. It will set out my views on the future.

Templeton then presented us with his talk which we proceeded
to read on the spot. Templeton's future was indeed one of great
promise, based to a large extent upon the increasingly global
aspects of investing. It was a future with challenges for the
investor; and one that promised very positive economic and social aspects for the countries sharing it. Maybe a bit one-sided
and rosy but thoughtful nevertheless. Here is part of the text
of that London talk:[2]

> The future for investors, and for people in general, is exciting.
> Several powerful trends are leading the way.
>
> First, the world continues to move to economic *interdepen-
> dence*. Companies are recognizing this trend and adjusting their
> strategies accordingly. In addition, more and more investors are
> beginning to see the advantages of "cross-border" investing.
>
> This trend to a global-scale market, so to speak, is very posi-
> tive. It will lead—and, indeed, is leading—to more competition
> and, thus, to more efficiency. I would also suggest that these in-
> ternational business trends—such as corporate diversification
> and cross-border investing—are vehicles for greater cooperation
> and harmony between peoples and nations.
>
> The seeds are being sown already for major changes in secur-
> ities markets around the world. Thirty or 40 years from now, it
> is likely that domestic securities markets will be replaced by an
> efficient technology-driven international market with a set of
> uniform rules and regulations. We are currently witnessing a
> shift by major banks, insurance companies, and investment
> firms towards a globalization of their activities. Financial insti-
> tutions with a high degree of domestic concentration will in-
> creasingly find themselves facing severe international compe-
> tition.
>
> The trading floor as we know it today may gradually disap-
> pear, giving way to the computer. Automatic transfer systems
> are already in place in Toronto, the over-the-counter markets in
> the United States, in Japan, and, just recently, on the Paris
> Bourse. This trend may continue until most exchanges, both in
> developed and developing countries, will be computer-linked on
> a worldwide basis. Security analysts may evaluate a company's
> shares more on the basis of its quality and prospects by inter-
> national standards, and less on the basis of what country it is
> domiciled, or listed, in.

A second powerful worldwide trend is the rise of capitalism. In fact, we are seeing a renewed belief in Adam Smith's natural law of economics, economic theory advanced by Smith 210 years ago. Smith believed that the economic system was harmonious in itself; the less interference by government, the better. He held that free competition was basic to an efficient economy.

Today, governments and individuals are coming to recognize that the forces of free enterprise are best left alone to produce economic well-being. In the free world, socialism is receding and trade unions are accepting productivity incentives and share-ownership programs for union members.

Democracy, deregulation, decentralization, denationalization are today's watchwords—not just in the United States, but here in the United Kingdom and in Western Europe as well. Even the Peoples Republic of China is moving to favor individual initiative, even though it does not acknowledge free enterprise as such. Numerous nations are sending delegations to London to learn how to transfer ownership from governments to people.

We believe that this is a long-term trend, one that provides greater prospects for economic growth worldwide. Common sense alone tells us that prosperity is more apt to flow from nations that have:

- Less government ownership.
- Wider personal share ownership.
- Free movement of capital across national borders.
- Less government regulation.
- Less quarrelsome labor unions.
- Better schools for management studies.
- Lower corporate and personal income tax rates.
- Incentives for thrift and entrepreneurship.

For proof, we have only to look at the east Asian countries where growth incentives exist. These countries' economies have prospered at an outstanding rate of 7.5 percent annually over the past two decades.

Such progress will not only continue, it will accelerate. I believe this to be true because of several key factors. Among them is the increasing commitment of governments and corporations to funding research and development.

I'm sure you will agree that investment in research and development and technological innovation has a positive long-term effect on productivity and economic growth. Fortunately, most modern governments do not seem to share the old view of the U.S. Patent Office at the turn of the century. Management there seriously planned to close up shop because they felt there was very little left to invent.

Modern industry believes there still is room for new and better products. Last year, the free world collectively spent over £156 billion on research and development. An additional £70 billion was spent by the Communist bloc. This means a world expenditure of £226 billion on research and development in 1985—close to a billion pounds sterling every business day.

Consider some examples of research-and-development spending around the world: In recent years, Japan has been increasing its financial commitment to R & D by about 10 percent per annum. The United States and most European countries have been stepping up their R & D programs by more than 6 percent per year.

For those interested in the actual number of dollars spent, I can tell you that in 1985 the United States spent $107 billion on R & D. And, to put that figure in perspective, consider that in 1953, United States R & D funding totaled $5.1 billion. That's almost a *21-fold* increase in 32 years! What increase will we see in the *next* 32 years?

It is particularly interesting to note the increase in the number of scientists and engineers engaged in R & D over the past 20 years in countries outside the United States. Since 1965, the proportion of R & D scientists and engineers in the labor force has grown by 70 percent here in the United Kingdom, and by more than 100 percent in Germany and Japan.

Another reason that I am optimistic about the future is the steady improvement in management skills and tools. When I was born, there were only 2 graduate schools of business. Today, there are some 600 in the United States, and approximately 800 worldwide. In fact, business schools today attract some of the brightest young university students, and the number of graduates from these schools is escalating. In 1984, there were more than 50,000 graduates from programs offering the master of business administration (MBA) degree in the United States alone, an increase of 150 percent over the number in 1970. MBA programs continue to grow at an accelerated pace.

As for business tools, I think we can all agree that new computer technologies have revolutionized the business world. Their impact extends from processing plants and factory floors to automated offices and the international stock exchanges. They give today's manager instant access to vast pools of detailed information.

These systems will allow managers to make more and better high-level decisions. Furthermore, the capacity of computers is increasing at an astounding rate. Today's systems will seem archaic five years from today. To prove this point, ask any recent computer-course graduate to work on a system that is five years old and listen to his comments!

Given this scenario and assuming world freedom, we believe the free-world economies will grow in real terms by at least 3.5 percent per annum. In other words, production is likely to quadruple in only 40 years.

Of course, rates of growth will differ from country to country, with some of the developing nations showing the most dramatic economic growth. At the same time, the comparative advantages enjoyed by various industries will shift as more countries participate to a greater degree in the global market.

This is one reason the Templeton organization has made a long-term commitment to the study of emerging stock markets in places such as Thailand, Brazil, Argentina, India, Jordan, and Korea—and in dozens of other countries as well. The higher growth-rate possibilities and the opportunities to fund undiscovered and undervalued situations make these markets attractive.

What about the long-term future for equity investments in general?

The prospects are excellent. For example, let's focus on the United States: Assuming that over the *next* 40 years corporate earnings grow at the same 6.4-percent annual rate that they've averaged for the *past* 40 years, the combined earnings of the stocks making up the Standard & Poor's 500-stock index would be $30 in 10 years, $55 in 20 years, and $191 in 40 years. If we were to assume that the S&P-500 sells at only its average price/earnings multiple of 14 over the next 40 years, then the S&P-500 would rise from its current level of 211 to 416 in 10 years, 775 in 20 years, and 2,630 in 40 years.

Turning to the United Kingdom, if you make the same assumptions the Financial Times Index would be 3200 in 10 years, 6000 in 20 years, and 20,600 in 40 years. It's now at 1412.

Growth of corporate earnings is not the only reason for higher share prices, of course. An even more important factor is the availability of cash. Consider that the total market value of all the wealth is roughly £19 trillion in 19 major noncommunist nations. That's $27 trillion. Equities, or stocks, represent only 23 percent of world wealth, and even less if one includes the value of private businesses plus the assets of 140 other nations. What might happen to the price of shares, one wonders, if equities become more popular than bonds!

According to the Intersec Research Corporation, world private and public pension plans now exceed £1.5 trillion. It is estimated that within 10 years world pension funds will total approximately £5 trillion ($8 trillion), and that total ignores such things as the United States' Social Security promises. Assets of the pension funds will become so large that the funds could more than buy up the total of common stocks now available— unless share prices rise.

To these potential demands, we can add the stimulus coming from governments for their taxpayers to invest. More and more nations are providing incentives that encourage individuals to save a portion of their earnings for retirement. Quite likely a meaningful portion of these funds will find their way into equities.

If local pension funds invest more in their own markets, the impact could be significant. Incentives so far put in place have been designed primarily to encourage private investors to put money into the equity markets, and will make these markets a more useful part of the financial system. While there has not yet been a real equivalent to the United States' individual retirement account (IRA) legislation, or to Canada's similar RSPs, proposed United Kingdom legislation will greatly increase the involvement of U.K. pensioners with their own investments. Switzerland and Denmark also have made encouraging moves in this area.

The individual retirement accounts in both the United States and Canada are exciting examples of what can be done. In the U.S. alone, the potential impact of IRAs is staggering, even when the impact of the 1986 tax-law changes is considered. More than 100 million Americans are eligible to create their own retirement accounts. About half of those eligible are likely to do so. And if only half the number of eligible Americans choose to buy stocks with just half of the $2,000 they're allowed to invest, more than $50 billion worth of shares could be purchased for IRAs each year. I would venture to say that the amount of money available for buying securities is so large that in some future year there may conceivably be a shortage of shares.

A recent study by the Financial Analyst Research Foundation shows that stocks in the United States historically have returned 6.2 percent, compounded annually, more than Treasury bills, and 5.8 percent more than long-term corporate bonds. The study concludes that such premiums paid for taking greater risk may continue.

Also worth mentioning is the historic boom we are witnessing in unit-trust participation and sales. An increasing number of individual investors are turning to fund managers for help. In America, new net sales of non–money market mutual funds rose from $1.8 billion in 1980 to $72.4 billion to the end of November 1985. The 1985 rise alone (to the end of November) represented a 180 percent increase in mutual funds other than the money market variety.

The same phenomenon is occurring in the United Kingdom. The net new money put into unit trusts in 1980 was £108 million, and in 1985 it was in the region of £2,600 million—an increase of 2,400 percent in only five years.

It appears that the City itself [London's financial district] is the center of a growth industry. The trend toward global investing will bring new activity to this traditional hub of international finance.

NB: Let's explore some issues that you didn't address directly in that talk. For example, in the last couple of years there have been a number of links between markets.

JMT: Stock brokers are now members of exchanges, not only in America, but also in London and Tokyo and so on. With the ease of transportation of information, orders can be executed on dozens of markets instantly. The world market is coming. Market makers make markets in stocks not just in North America but anywhere. Major stock brokers are now equipped to buy and sell stocks of many nations, 24 hours a day.

NB: For all of your career you have been known as an investor in shares . . .

JMT: That's true. Our studies have usually indicated that stocks represent the best possible long-term bargain for the investor.

NB: What about other forms of investment: real estate, gold, . . .

JMT: If the present enthusiasm for stocks continues or grows more intense, then perhaps stocks will no longer represent the great value they traditionally have. In such a situation, the prudent thing for us to do would be to go where we believe the greatest bargain could be found, wherever that might be.

EK: Let's talk about these other forms of investment. Your views on alternative [investment] forms will be revealing to say the least. Let's start with real estate. Can you generalize sufficiently to provide an opinion on its investment merits?

JMT: Throughout history, real estate has been by far the best way to protect yourself against inflation and by far the biggest investment across the globe in terms of the dollar invested. As such, real estate is an important subject for anyone who wants to invest. There is a saying among real estate people that we subscribe to. There are three important things in real estate, location, location, location. . . . That's the key, I think, to understanding real estate investments. Land is the most local commodity there is. It is inextricably tied to its location and its value is wholly determined by the factors that apply at that place. As a result, real estate requires that the investor have a large knowledge base of the area. Not on a country by country basis, but a town by town or even block by block basis.

That's why real estate is so different from stocks, for both the global investor and even someone working in his own country. With stocks, you can read research done by a number of people from afar and still find a basis for comparison between different industries and nations. With real estate, however, it is almost essential that you be at the place you are considering, or at least that you have a deep understanding of that specific region. When your knowledge of an area is great enough in real estate, bargains can often be found.

EK: Probably nothing can hit the front pages of the financial press faster than a good bulge [rising prices] or break [falling prices] in the gold market. I've never seen the name Templeton associated with gold in any way, shape, or form. Have you purposely avoided the subject over the years? Have you ever invested in gold?

JMT: Gold is a good illustration of the fact that we as an organization aren't always right. There was no reason why we couldn't have bought gold for our clients 16 years ago for $35 per ounce and made a great deal of money for them; we just missed it. We weren't thinking in terms of gold, so we bought our clients some stocks that went up, but not as much as gold went up. With the price held at $35 per ounce since 1941, we should have recognized that there was not much downside risk in buying gold, but great potential for it to go up. And it did go up to $870 an ounce temporarily. We could have made a handsome profit in gold. But there are risks with precious metals. Some of my friends did make money in gold, but none of them got out at the right time and made as much as they could have. They rode the roller coaster up and then back down again. Similarly, the gold funds that did extremely well when gold was soaring are now doing terribly. So, while gold did represent an opportunity, it is by no means a panacea for profit.

EK: Can you bargain hunt when trading gold? Are there some Templeton yardsticks of value that can be used to decide when to buy or sell?

JMT: At the time other people were buying gold, I was buying silver. We didn't put it in our mutual funds. I was buying the commodity personally, following a line of reasoning that seemed to me to be just simple common sense. At that time, you could go into any bank and buy silver dollars. They cost, obviously, $1 each. I looked up the amount of silver contained in each of those coins, then determined how much the price of silver would have to go up for that silver to become worth more than $1. I found that the price of silver would have to go up 29% for the silver in a dollar to be worth more than $1.

I was taking a risk on silver's price rising by almost one-third, but my downside risk was actually quite small. Since the silver dollar is currency, it couldn't go lower than $1 in value, no matter what happened to silver prices. I figured, from the monetary standpoint, my risk was zero. I also figured that the potential for profit was not much, unless silver should go up substantially. But since the risk was so slight, I decided to try the investment.

I bought large quantities of silver dollars and put them in safe deposit boxes. Happily for me, silver did go up from $1 an ounce to as high as $45 an ounce in 1980. Of course I had sold some of my holdings before that point. It proved to be a successful commonsense investment.

I didn't attempt this with gold because, at that time, it was against the law for an American to own gold and there were no gold coins you could just walk into the bank and buy.

NB: What about commodities? Do you think that the [Templeton] organization will ever trade them?

JMT: Commodities are very interesting. We don't have a commodities fund now, but we might at some time. The main reason we don't is the lack of dividends. But there are opportunities around the world that we can see. So it might be possible that we might start to invest in commodities.

[The opportunities that Templeton sees focus on taking advantage of the essential instability of commodity prices.] There are opportunities in the big swings in commodity prices. For instance, you can sometimes buy copper for half of what it costs to produce. Now, you know that if you hold that copper contract long enough, it will increase in value. The price is down because of surplus supply. And when there is a surplus and depressed prices, mine after mine is going to close down. In time, this means that instead of a surplus you'll have a shortage of copper. Then the price will go up, and you will have a potential for profit.

Another example is sugar. Recently (1985), the price of sugar went down to two and a half cents per pound. Nobody in the world can produce sugar for two and a half cents a pound. On the face of it, a commodity selling far below what it costs to produce represents a bargain. Following the swings of commodity prices presents opportunities to make significant amounts of money.

I believe that investing in commodities is a sensible thing to do. If you study the markets and seek bargains diligently, commodity investing can be both satisfying and profitable. It is essential, however, that, as with stocks, commodities be examined for long-term potential, not short-term killings. You can make money in commodities as long as you don't try to determine bargains on a day-to-day basis. The people who lose money in commodities are the ones who think they're smart enough to buy today and sell tomorrow. They aren't.

NB: Do you consider collectibles an investment form?

JMT: Not really. Collectible investment is really only for plea-sure. I think people can do well buying collectibles, but each item is unique, so that you have to spend a large percentage of your time gaining knowledge to be an effective participant in the market.

This must be a labor of love, not bottom line considerations. Take antique clocks, for instance, you must become a real expert in clocks to tell if anything is of value or not of value. In a sense you have to get to know every type of clock in the world and then track down the valuable ones and try to buy them. Because each market is so individualistic, collectibles are too time con-suming for serious investment.

I have a small collection of old atlases, and one of old Bibles, but the amount of money invested in them is tiny, perhaps one thousandth of what I have invested in stocks and bonds.

The true purpose of buying collectibles is pleasure. If you have plenty of free time, then go ahead and collect them and enjoy them. Profit is not the only purpose in life, by any stretch of the imagination.

[*Templeton pauses and thinks for a moment. Then he continues.*] I said that collectibles aren't an investment vehicle. In thinking it over I want to give one caveat. A person who is not a profes-sional investor would have difficulty becoming expert in the en-tire economy of a foreign country, let alone those of many countries. However, through collectibles a person who wants to become more familiar with global investing could become expert in one small corner of a foreign economy—the clock factories in Germany, the furniture markets of England, the artifact busi-ness of Latin America.

An individual would need to follow the same procedures on a small scale that global investors use on a larger one: research, publications, personal contacts and other means of acquiring de-tailed, reliable data; trips to determine local customs, sources, problems; study to find a method of identifying bargains and acquiring assets for favorable terms.

In this way a person can discover just how difficult it is to be expert in German clocks and then can realize how even more difficult it is to understand the whole German economy.

EK: Could you define what you would consider to be the com-ponents of an ideal investment portfolio? Let's suppose that we are talking about a young family, one child, one wage earner.

Let's keep it reasonably general and talk in terms of three broad components; percentage of monetary assets such as term deposits, savings bonds, T-bills, etc; mutual funds, and common shares.

JMT: We are investment counsellors and we are expected to give tailor-made advice. Why do investors need investment counsellors? Well, you wouldn't expect a doctor to give the same medicine to every patient, and by the same token the investment counsellor has to design a program tailor-made for the client, that's what we do with our private accounts.

The optimum portfolio composition would depend on the individual's income, his expectancy to inherit, tax status, number of dependents, etc. We would have to look carefully, make recommendation, and then constantly revise. But here are some guidelines. We generally recommend cash reserves (bonds and other fixed assets) equal to about 25% of annual income. At present, up to two-thirds of your portfolio should be in common stocks and the remainder in real estate and life insurance. You should have no less than 10 stocks, no more than 25% in any one industry, and no more than 80% in any one nation. But this applies only to people with $1,000,000 or more in assets. Otherwise, the two-thirds portfolio component should go not into selected shares but into well-managed equity mutual funds.

EK: A diversified portfolio of mutual funds?

JMT: No. Probably not. Too much diversification is counterproductive. An investment in a well-diversified and properly managed mutual fund provides the degree of diversification necessary.[3] If you hold a large number of different funds, you may earn only the average return earned by the mutual funds industry.

CHANGE AND GROWTH

Templeton often talks about the influence that both Adam Smith's *Wealth of Nations* and the *Declaration of Independence* have had on the social and economic forces at play in the world. He talks about how each has encouraged free enterprise, and how free enterprise has spurred innovative growth—socially beneficial growth—through change.

Building on those thoughts later, Templeton said:

In the 210 years [since Adam Smith] of relative freedom, the yearly output of goods and services has increased more than 100 fold. . . . that's real goods and real services after taking inflation into account. Before Smith's time, there were fewer than a thousand corporations in the world; now new corporations are being created at the rate of 4,000 every business day. In Smith's day, 85% of all the people were needed on farms. Now, fewer than 4% of America's population work on farms and produce a great surplus of food. And our children and grandchildren now being born may enjoy even more progress than we.

Templeton harks back to his own birth year to put growth and change in perspective. In 1912, he says, the highest salaried person in his Tennessee county was paid less than $2,000 a year, and the federal debt was only $1 billion. There were no income tax, no Federal Reserve, no investment counsellors, and no mutual funds. Neither were there transcontinental telephones, radios, vitamins, plastics, or synthetic fibers.

And, says Templeton,

Much later, after the great 1929 boom, Americans still had no Social Security, no unemployment insurance, no Securities and Exchange Commission, no capital-gains tax, no inheritance tax, no airmail, no airlines, no Xerox, no telefax, no antibiotics, no nylon, no frozen foods, no television, no transistors, no lasers, no nuclear energy.

Who could have imagined back then the great variety of new blessings in my lifetime? Who can imagine now the even greater blessings in store for our children and grandchildren?

At the peak of the 1929 boom, the Federal budget was only $3 billion. Now the gross national product is 30 times as high as it was 50 years ago, and in the next 50 years it may grow again 30 fold. If it does, it will rise from $17,000 per person now to more than half a million dollars per year per person 50 years from now.

Never far from the economic effects of change, Templeton allows, in an aside, that pension fund managers will have to set some pretty severe goals for themselves if that projection holds. But he returns to thoughts of change as it might affect the quality of life in general; he "speculates," as he puts it, about the future:

> If we are able to preserve and enhance freedom, the positive trends may continue and accelerate; we may expect more rapid change, and wider fluctuations. Life will be full of adventure and opportunity, never dull or routine. In America alone this year, more than $110 billion will be dedicated to research and development. That is more in one nation in one year than the total of the world's research before I was born.
>
> In America alone, more than $65 billion will be donated this year to churches and charities. Each year the generous and voluntary giving by Americans exceeds the total income of all the world's people in any year before Adam Smith. . . .
>
> The evolution of human knowledge is accelerating, and we are reaping the fruits of generations of scientific thought. More than half the discoveries in the natural sciences have been made in this century. Fifty percent of all that is known by the medical doctors today was unknown just 20 years ago. More than half of the goods produced since the earth was born have been produced in the two centuries since Adam Smith. And over half the books ever written were written in the last half century. More books are published now each month than were written in the entire historical period before the birth of Christopher Columbus.
>
> And it was less than 60 years ago that the great astronomers became convinced that the universe is a hundred billion times larger than any human being ever thought before. Who can imagine what will be discovered if research continues to accelerate? Each discovery reveals new mysteries. The more we learn, the more we realize how much more there is still to discover.

Change. Growth. Progress. They're truisms, inevitables. They're the future.

And they're global.

THE WORLD AFTER "BLACK MONDAY," 1987

Being a long-term investor, John Templeton does not time the market as do technically based traders. Yet his long experience and understanding of economic cycles has served him well over the years. Appearing on "Wall Street Week" on the fifth anniversary of the bull market (August 14, 1987), when the Dow Jones Industrials were in the 2700s, he remarked:

> It would be surprising if we didn't have bear markets. Bear markets normally carry down by about one-third. So that would be about 1,000 points. But it's temporary.[4]

The collapse of stock prices in the U.S. and other markets came just over two months later. Remarkably, the Dow Jones Industrials dropped a total of 984 points.

The week of October 19th, 1987, badly damaged confidence among investors. Recognizing the magnitude of the event, Louis Rukeyser cancelled the food stocks expert he had scheduled for his October 23rd broadcast of "Wall Street Week" and called in three financial heavyweights. Templeton was among them. His comments were reassuring:

> If you never buy investments with borrowed money, you can always be comfortable. Human nature is such that we're always going to have periods of enthusiasm and pessimism. Every 10 years, there'll be bull markets and bear markets, but if you don't have borrowed money, you have nothing to worry about.[5]

Having experienced first hand the aftermath of the 1929 crash, Templeton offered these comments about Black Monday:

> The panic this time was much greater, much larger. But at that time [October 1929] the stock market would have recovered within a year, except that the panic spread into general business conditions. I don't expect that this time. Things are so different. In '29 there was no unemployment insurance, no guarantee on bank accounts, no insurance on brokerage accounts. There was no social security. This time, I think there is simply a bear market in the stock market which will be borne out by little if any decline in general business.
>
> You might say we are being offered a great opportunity. Those who weren't quick enough to get in on the ground floor, when the bull market started in 1982, are now being offered a chance to get in on the ground floor for the next bull market.[6]

His advice to shell-shocked investors? As always, be patient.

> Be a long-term investor. Be prepared financially and psychologically to live through a series of bull markets and bear markets

because in the long run common stocks will pay off enormously. The next bull market is likely to carry prices far higher than this past one.[7]

A FINAL PERSPECTIVE

When John Templeton views the global investor's world, he sees broad potential for profit, but he sees something more. Templeton is a visionary, and he sees global investing not just as a way to make money, but as a force for international social good.

> Global investing has enormous advantages from a standpoint of knowledge of other people. By making us more knowledgeable about other countries it promotes understanding of other people around the world. Worldwide brotherhood is promoted by it. Certainly worldwide prosperity is greatly promoted by global investing, as well.
>
> Just think how different the world would be if the people who work in the Kremlin had their investments in 12 other nations. What an understanding they would have! What different attitudes they would have! How much less likely they would be to bomb New York, and so forth, if they had just investments in 12 nations. There is an old saying that "borders closed to commerce are crossed by armies." We can say the same thing about Americans or anybody else. The more world investing there is, the better off from a spiritual standpoint, peace, brotherhood, and especially prosperity. If you have world trade where each nation produces what it's best in, then the commercial interaction of nations will work for everyone. The growth of prosperity in the world will be greater when we can all invest in each other's progress. That's a very inspiring idea for me.

ENDNOTES

1. Henry Ford, *My Life and Work*.
2. John Templeton, "Looking Ahead: the Future for Investors," Speech, London, Winter 1986.

3. One could probably argue that a single mutual fund portfolio may have at least superficially eliminated the non-systematic risk of individual stocks, but the holder still faces the risk of managerial incompetency.
4. "Wall Street Week," August 14, 1987, Maryland Public Television, Owen Mills, MD 21117.
5. "Wall Street Week," October 23, 1987.
6. Ibid.
7. Ibid

AFTERWORD

AN UPDATE

Success often breeds success. Lead portfolio managers Tom Hansberger and Mark Holowesko, who were mentioned earlier in the book, recently received two LIPPER Awards for their performance. Templeton Global Opportunities Trust and Templeton Smaller Companies Growth Fund, respectively, are under their guidance. Mark Mobius, also mentioned previously, received two LIPPER Awards for his Templeton Emerging Markets performance, a closed-end fund that is on the big board. Since inception (March 1987) to June 30, 1992, the fund has had an annual total return of 25.4% assuming that all capital gains and dividends were reinvested at the net asset value. Mobius probably spends half of his life on a plane searching for bargains anywhere in the world. We were fortunate to catch him on the ground recently in San Francisco to uncover some of the secrets of his success.

NB: What are some of the pitfalls of investing in emerging markets?

MM: A limiting factor in emerging markets is the custodial bank—dealing with large banks who worry about potential liabilities because of their past experience. Take, as an example, the bad loans in Latin America. There were billions in bad loans that, until the past few years, are beginning to be paid down in one form or another.

NB: Why do you need a custodial bank to buy foreign stocks?

Where Few Investors Dare to Tread
Below are the seven diversified emerging markets funds that are now available
to small investors.

Fund	Assets (in millions)	Minimum Investment	Annual Expenses	12-Month Return[1]
Govett International Emerging Markets[2]	$ 1	$ 500	2.50%	N.A.
Lexington Emerging Markets Fund	25	1,000	1.60	19.8%[3]
Merrill Developing Capital Markets[2]	110	5,000	1.77	28.7
Montgomery Emerging Markets Fund	5	5,000	1.90	N.A.
Morgan Stanley Emerging Markets Fund	155	None [4]	2.00	N.A.
Templeton Developing Markets Trust[2]	22	500	2.25	N.A.
Templeton Emerging Markets Fund	199	None[4]	1.91	84.2

[1]Through January 31,1992.
[2]Fund charges upfront sales commission.
[3]Prior to June 1991, fund operated as a U.S. growth fund.
[4]Publicly traded mutual fund.
N.A. = Not available. Fund is too new.
SOURCES: Lipper Analytical Services; Morningstar Inc.; fund groups.

MM: The terms of our contract with shareholders require it.
There is always a three-way relationship with shareholders. We
manage the money, but we don't touch any of it. This is always
handled by the custodial banks.

NB: Isn't this a basic protection for shareholders when they
buy foreign stocks through open-end or closed-end mutual
funds?

MM: Right. These are basic principles that we follow around
the world—which is fine. They are very good safeguards and
double-checks on everything for the investor—but for emerging
markets, they create problems.

NB: In other words, you may find a good company, a good
value, and you can't buy shares in it because you haven't got a
bank that will act as custodian in that country.

MM: That's right. But the irony of the whole situation is that
these countries that need capital the most, who need our invest-

ment the most, are the most restrictive! I think there is a definite direct correlation between economic growth and bureaucracy. This is probably reflected in what's happening in America, you know. The U.S. is suffering on the economic growth side because of bureaucracy and its legal restrictions. These things take so much time and this is very evident in these emerging markets. In some of the poorer countries, the bureaucracy is so great, it's difficult to get anything done.

NB: In March of 1992, *The Wall Street Journal* ran an article about reaping gains on emerging nations' growth. You were quoted as saying, "There is no reason why investors should buy the Templeton Emerging Markets Fund at a premium." (Laughter)

MM: Yes, and I caught hell from Tom Hansberger on that!

NB: How do you feel about it now?

MM: I feel the same way. At that time, I was really at an over 20% premium. Since then, it came down to about a 10% premium, which is OK, but it is still a premium.

NB: Some time back, I talked to John Templeton about closed-end funds, and he pointed out that there were more of them than open-end and that they started back at the turn of the century.

MM: That's true. In fact, they began in Scotland back in the late 1800s, and do you know where they were investing? In the best emerging market in the world at that time—in America. (Laughter). One of these old funds that is still in existence was recently described in their annual report, how they would send a team of people out to check things out. . .

NB: Like you do all the time.

MM: Yes—and they would invest in property, in ranches in the west. They would travel by wagon to the sites, and it would be a six- or seven-month trip!

NB: Isn't that something—and today, people are still fearful about investing in foreign stocks. Look how long it has taken public retirement funds to buy international stocks. For example, in New Mexico, the governor only recently signed a bill allowing their state employees' pension fund to go global.

MM: America is not alone. Even in the U.K. there are certain restrictions about retirement funds. If you go around the world, almost every country has these kinds of restrictions and mainly because the government wants them to buy their treasury bills and bonds. In fact, there have been some very interesting studies done by the World Bank on social security systems around the world, particularly in emerging markets. Some of them are in deep, deep trouble because they invested in their own bonds and they have not performed well—in fact, a lot of them are under water.

NB: How many emerging markets were there when you started the fund?

MM: We were in five countries then. A lot of others were restricted. Again, the custodial bank problem. Now we are in 16 countries.

NB: How many more are you considering?

MM: Potentially, we could add another six.

NB: Several months ago, I heard you were heading toward South Africa to look at some companies in the hopes that apartheid was about to end. Did you buy anything?

MM: No, for two reasons we didn't. The board members of our funds refused to let us buy anything yet, and the custodian banks in America refused to let us do it. Chase Manhattan said, "We've got clients that have banned this. It would hurt us, bad publicity and all the rest." Now if you go to the U.K. there is no problem. They say, "Go ahead—if it makes money, that's fine." But in the U.S. they say, "What is Citibank doing?" And at Citibank they say, "What is State Street Bank doing? If they do it, we'll do it." (Laughter).

NB: It's almost like, "You go first and then we'll follow."

MM: What I do is try to anticipate. Like someday the place to invest will be Egypt. So I begin hounding the custodian banks now. The phone call I got just now [we had been interrupted for the second time by his being called to the telephone] was from Boston Safe Co. I have been asking them about Hungary, Poland, Pakistan, and Bangladesh. The trouble is that you give them a list of these countries and they say, "Give us your priorities," and I say, "These countries are *all* our priorities." Their response is, "Which countries are most important?" Then they send their team into the country to check things out. A good example is Brazil, where it is urgent we resolve problems, and yet it is very complicated to get in.

NB: You own Telebras [the Brazil Telephone Company], don't you?

MM: Yes.

NB: There's talk they are coming out as an ADR.

MM: Yes, and everyone and his brother in the underwriting field would love to get their hands on it.

NB: John Templeton was high on Brazil five years ago but not ready to invest in it because of their many problems like inflation, a military government, high interest rates, etc. One thing he said to me that time, difficult for me to swallow, was that "The Brazil market, in the long run, will grow as fast as Japan's." Why? Because "their natural resources are the greatest in the world."

MM: I have no doubt about that. As a matter of fact, China and India's market will be bigger than Japan and the U.S. in the next two decades, followed by Indonesia and Brazil. Those will be the four biggest markets. This is clearly within the realm of possibility. You see, you have certain pressures that are taking place, which have to be relieved. First, there is population pressure, and secondly, you have the demands of the people. With communications the way they are today—the things people see on T.V.—they want them now. Communism tried to hinder those things and failed. Now they're going to try something else and hopefully it will be the system we have here in the Western world—but it may not be. Population is increasing so rapidly. The life expectancy is increasing dramatically while infant mortality is decreasing dramatically in many of these countries. (You don't have to have an increase in fertility.) Both of these other factors mean an enormous increase in population—and this has a direct effect on politics and the economy. Any government that claims they can meet the requirements of the people will have to start paying off; otherwise, they'll be out! Some will start taking desperate measures to accomplish this. You're seeing this around the world. They tried communism and it didn't work; they tried socialism and it didn't work; now they're

going to try capitalism. The multilateral institutions, namely
the World Bank, the Asia Development Bank, the Africa Development Bank, the Latin America multinational institutions, are
pushing them in this direction because they find that this will
be the most effective, the fastest way of getting the people what
they want.

NB: Of really upgrading these economies? Upgrading the lives
of the people in these countries?

MM: Exactly. Also, this diffuses the unhappiness and discon-
tent of these people—because if they have a personal stake in
something, it's very difficult to blame the government—which
they have been doing in the past. It gives people hope that they
never had before and it works. Where you have this participation, you see tremendous growth. It's really wonderful! Basically, that is what we are tapping in this fund—the aspirations
of these people. We're sort of riding along on their coattails, so
to speak, trying to participate with them in what they are
doing. That's what is so exciting. Of course, there are setbacks
and problems along the way. Bureaucracies often can't handle
these changes. India is a good example of what can go wrong.
The scandal in their market recently was enormous and not just
because of one unscrupulous broker. Everyone was involved, including the government banks. Their market took a big hit
when it was uncovered.

NB: What's the solution?

MM: To have very strict penalties in two areas—for not making full disclosure and for a lack of liquidity in the market.
These are the two things that trap the investor worldwide. In
the process of encouraging liquidity, you have to have proper settlement, trading facilities, computerization, etc. With these
things in place, it's much easier to monitor. Even in America,
the trading systems are much too inefficient and much too
expensive.

NB: Let's talk about the new Templeton Developing Markets
Trust, which you also manage. How is it doing?

MM: Well, it was started in October 1991, and is now up to
$150 million in assets. It is a clone of the Emerging Markets
Fund, and a big advantage is that it gives us more countries in
which to invest.

NB: Well, also when there is a premium on the Emerging Markets Fund, the investor can buy the Developing Markets Trust and pay at most 5¾%.

MM: Right . . . And an investment over $50,000 means a reduced sales charge—you buy at a discount to that.

NB: Where are you investing now?

MM: Indonesia. Its market has come down quite dramatically. We're still nibbling away at Brazil, but it's been very difficult. We're doing more in Malaysia and also Thailand, where the market was driven down because of the coup. We're increasing our position in Korea even though it continues to get hit. Also, we like the Philippines, especially Philippine Long Distance and Philex Mining Corporation. Taiwan is even starting to look interesting, but the problem there is they won't let us go in the way we want to. They are sitting on $70 billion of foreign reserves! That small country has the largest foreign reserve in the world. They could be investing in America or abroad because they don't need that much money in foreign reserves. But they're still thinking in terms of taking over mainland China. They have this fortress mentality that doesn't make sense. They could be investing in their own country, and they're not. They do have a big infrastructure program, but it's too little, too late.

NB: What could they do to improve their situation?

MM: They could do a lot. We'd like to go in and run mutual funds there, but until they have a completely open market, they're fearful of letting us in. Years ago, I started their first domestic funds in Taiwan, so I'm familiar with the territory.

NB: They sound conservative, and yet they aren't that way when they invest in the stock market.

MM: Well, that's different. One of the reasons the stock market in China has gone through the roof, as a matter of fact, is because of the Taiwanese. They are big speculators over there. To follow up on our original point, though, it is unfortunate they won't let us in because we would be educating them about the advantages of international diversification. They got hit on the foreign exchange, having had too much in U.S. dollars.

NB: How about the Latin America market?

MM: Most Latin American stocks have been pushed up too high.

NB: Do you think it's because of the proliferation? It seems like everyone and his uncle are starting an emerging markets fund. (Laughter)

MM: And there are lots of Latin America Funds as well. So you have to be very careful. You know, Latin America has done it before. There is that tendency to go after the easy money and push thing up—all that excitement. You can get burned if you are not careful.

NB: You sound cautious. What's your advice in this climate?

MM: The challenge *now* for emerging market managers is to figure how to hold back and not rush into things—into a country when it opens or where you think you have to be. Lots of constraints will have to be applied. Not that there won't be opportunities. What's happening is good because it's going to expand this whole area. You have more stocks, more underwritings where firms are more interested in bringing out stocks in these markets. With thousands of brokers opening up markets, it's becoming more respectable, you see. The whole level will get better; but we never lose sight of the objective, and that is to find bargains.

NB: That's right. The name of the game is bargains and being a bargain hunter. Right?

MM: The reason we are in emerging markets is that there are more bargains there than in other markets. As soon as that ceases to be true, maybe we shouldn't be there.

NB: At that point, do you change your name?

MM: Right. You change it to the Templeton *Developed* Markets Trust and the Templeton *Emerged* Markets!

What we have indicated by this update is that John Templeton is proving what he has said many times and in many different ways over the past decade. But he is now putting it this way: "I have the best team I've ever had and that is because I made it my business to hire people wiser than I." And when he speaks with his usual optimism and in more prophetic tones, he says, "The next 30 years may be the most peaceful and prosperous of all time. Why, just think what a wonderful thing it will be when the people of Russia are Templeton clients!"

INDEX